Editor, Actor, Ballplayer, Spy

Editor, Actor, Ballplayer, Spy

An Autobiography of Shelbyville, Kentucky's Award-Winning Bill Matthews

William E. Matthews

Acclaim Press
MORLEY, MISSOURI

Acclaim Press
— Your Next Great Book —
P.O. Box 238
Morley, MO 63767
(573) 472-9800
www.acclaimpress.com

Cover Design: M. Frene Melton
Book Layout: James Mulcahy/Wizard Graphics

ISBN-10: 1-938905-57-1
ISBN-13: 978-1-938905-57-5
Library of Congress Control Number: 2014903332

First Printing: 2014
Printed in the United States of America
10 9 8 7 6 5 4 3 2 1

This publication was produced using available information.
The publisher regrets it cannot assume responsibility for errors or omissions.

Table of Contents

Foreword

Story of a change agent in Kentucky journalism

By Al Smith

A pleasure of living beyond the Biblical three score and ten is to delight in reflecting on the career of a contemporary who has also survived to share memories of how it was when our world was young.

In the case of Bill Matthews, it is an even richer experience to praise the accomplishments of a colleague while savoring the memories of a few spats when we were separately publishing weekly newspapers in Kentucky – friends most of the time, but occasionally rivals over business issues that might have been intense but never left any wounds. This was when we each wanted to add the same paper to our individual chains in the go-go years of the '60s and '70s – when the big boys in Kentucky were creating Humana, merging hospitals, auto dealerships, real estate and insurance agencies, and struggling to change restrictive bank laws in an era that became known as "the Wal-Marting of Main Street."

Once in the '70s, a publisher ready to retire in western Kentucky, told me Matthews had made him a better offer than I did, but he was selling to me. "I don't like chains of any kind," he said. "But Bill's business is bigger than yours and I don't think you are smart enough to ever catch up with him. You are still a country lad, so you can have my paper, Al."

William Edmund Matthews, grandson of a farmer who read Greek, descendant of an Indian fighter with a famous name, Bland Williams Ballard, and son of parents who in their own time upheld the honored traditions expected of leaders in one of Kentucky's most interesting small towns, has told a personal story in this book to be treasured for its honest snapshots of life between the two World Wars and after. It is local history at its best – affectionate remembrances of "who was who" in Shelbyville, Kentucky, named for the first governor of the Commonwealth, and recalled as the last hometown of Kentucky's internationally famous fried chicken franchiser, Harland David Sanders, perhaps the best known of all the Commonwealth's honorary Kentucky colonels.

This is also the story of Shelby Countians who were not the local elite, not much of "who" in terms of prominence, but worth a note because the author recalls the role they played when he was growing up – the boring preacher who overstayed his welcome, the tough teacher who graded our boy down for "attitude," and the filling station operator who gave the kid a job after school when he didn't know how to raise the hood on a customer's car.

The youngest of three sons, Bill was the Matthews boy who did not become a lawyer like their father, the town mayor, but did graduate from their father's alma mater, the University of Michigan, and married Else, the beautiful coed who had forgotten his name after a first date but was chased until she remembered and said "yes." Although I introduce Bill's autobiography at the point where we were both newspapermen, because that's when we met, this was a guy who loved a challenge, almost any kind, as Else soon discovered.

A brief stint as a rookie lieutenant ended with a resignation from the Army to try something more exciting – matching wits with the Soviets in behalf of the CIA, a 10-year tour that took the newlyweds to Europe and an encounter between Else and a flirtatious foreigner curious about her husband's job until he learned she knew he was a Russian spy.

News that one of Shelbyville's two weekly papers, *The Shelby Sentinel*, could be bought was the challenge that lured Bill and Else home and initiated Bill's five decades in journalism. That was the adventure that brought us together – not his movie acting or forays into tourism promotions, but I get ahead of Bill's story.

In 1966, I was one of a handful of weekly editors and publishers who eagerly showed up for a series of talks Bill was giving across the state to explain how he and seven other weekly publishers had established Greater Kentucky Publishers, the state's first cooperatively-owned central printing plant. This was a stunning breakthrough in newspaper technology, led by young Matthews who had barely gotten into the business before he began changing it. Not only was he pioneering in the new printing, he also seemed eager to explain his game plan – well, some of it, but it gets clearer the more you read of his intriguing account.

Two years after our first meeting, which was a talk he gave at the local weekly's office in Franklin, Ky., the state's daily papers bannered the news that the founding president of the innovative printing plant, William E. Matthews, had persuaded most of his partners to swap their papers for stock in a new company, Newspapers Inc. Five years later, when Newspapers Inc. was sold to Landmark Community Newspapers in 1973, Bill was CEO and the company owned 23 newspapers and four printing plants and was printing on contract another 25 papers, shoppers and circulars. It was the largest company of its kind in Kentucky.

Bill Matthews was the entrepreneur and change agent who transformed the business model of Kentucky's community journalism in the 1960s. In less than a decade, he was the leading force who inspired acceptance and devised the financing of the central printing process to change from the hot type process of Mark Twain's day to photo offset and a blossoming of vividly clear photography, both black and white and color in the state's weekly papers. Content – stories, pictures and ads – took on a fresh, appealing and more readable appearance in many Kentucky weeklies before most metropolitan dailies modernized their technology.

At this writing, one of the two oldest living past presidents of the Kentucky Press Association (this writer is the other), Matthews, ever the innovator, should also be remembered for campaigning in the early '60s to reform outdated practices in the association, bringing about a more democratic procedure for electing officers and diminishing the influence of an "old guard" clique that was perceived as running things, and that more at a crawl than a run. This was followed by ethical reforms that have made KPA organizationally more independent of outside influences and more in step with best practices in modern journalism.

At age 84, still active in a different kind of publishing – producing historical books and magazines about Kentucky's colorful past, Bill remains committed to community journalism and to the small town where he was born, has lived most of his life, and continues to provide leadership. He is an exemplar of the creed to which some of us still adhere, that there is no boundary on personal growth and potential to serve so long as one does not permit the city limits sign to obscure a vision of better possibilities.

But back to Bill's early years in newspapering: With the exception of improvements made after the Knight brothers bought the lack luster Lexington papers in the 1970s, and certainly conceding greatness to the Bingham family when their *Louisville Courier-Journal* consistently remained on *Time* magazine's annual list of the nation's top 10 daily papers, nothing in the 20th Century impacted the dynamics of publishing in Kentucky like the effect of Newspapers Inc. on community journalism.

My own case is an example. Frustrated over indecision about the future on the part of the majority owners of the little company of which I was a minority stockholder in Russellville, I resigned as editor, organized a new company of local investors to start a rival paper and eventually added six more in other towns, including the state's largest weekly, in London in Laurel County.

We made our own way, but we traveled the path Bill Matthews had blazed – central printing plants, modern computerized technology, staff members who were stockholders, leadership and new initiatives in the press association, local financing, continuing education seminars, local editorial pages that took sides on local issues (not always as much as I would have liked, but certainly with vigor in our larger papers).

Details of Bill's years in Shelby County and beyond are told in this memoir, followed by chapters on other publishing ventures, including a sports weekly focused on the Cincinnati Reds and then the prize-winning decades of historical publications, an enterprise I especially applaud for what they do to stimulate interest in and preserve the stories of how Kentucky became who and what we are.

Twice chosen to attend White House conferences on Rural Journalism, Bill's recognition beyond the state may compensate somewhat for a foot dragging reluctance in Kentucky's media's circles to award special recognition for the achievements I have listed. Not the least of these were the writing, editing, or publishing of five hard cover books, five magazines on the Civil War, the official commemorative edition on the Lewis and Clark Expedition and several more. All of this followed those amazing "firsts" – the central printing plant and the sports weekly with 19,000 paid subscribers who were eager to read about one baseball club.

Yes, our hero left a few unforgiven bruises along the way, but then there were younger protégés who credit him for big assists in their careers, such as education, medicine, and marketing. In conclusion, I raise a final hurrah for a CIA veteran turned First Amendment champion and media pioneer who is critical of drone warfare that kills innocents, of a government that keeps too many secrets, and of a cherished southern hometown that could have done more for its minorities. There are other reasons to enjoy this book. God bless as you find them.

Veteran journalist Al Smith of Lexington created a chain of weekly papers in Kentucky after a 10-year stint on the New Orleans dailies in his 20s. Founding host-producer of KET's Comment on Kentucky, he was Federal Co Chair of the Appalachian Regional Commission 1980-82 and was cofounder of the Institute for Rural Journalism and Community Issues at the University of Kentucky.

Acknowledgments

The Biography Channel declares that every life "has a story to tell" and then begins to spin stories of people we have loved or hated or knew very little or nothing about. Generally, no detail is spared as the channel brings to life someone whose existence, for good or bad, is someone we are most likely interested in. Most, but not all, are celebrities.

Al Smith

I am certainly no celebrity, nor have I ever wished to be, but it has given me much joy to recall moments or periods in my life when I have played a part in some events, some very small and some of enduring significance.

Whatever success I have had in life is directly attributable to many, many individuals. And since this is a memoir of my life stretching back to 1930, there are many people for me to acknowledge and for whose influence I am most appreciative.

First of all, and not chronologically, I have to express my deepest appreciation to **Al Smith**, who wrote a very generous introduction, and **Duanne Puckett**, who did a whale of a good job editing, rewriting, and supplementing my reflections.

Duanne Puckett

Al, who was the Founder, Host-Producer for KET's *Comment on Kentucky* for 30 years, and I go back more than 50 years. He has been not only a solid newspaperman and great moderator, but a superb human being and family man. Duanne's courage in overcoming the severe handicap caused by a drunken driver and her boundless love of the human race are unparalleled. She has been a joy to work with, and her knowledge of Shelby County people and events is unequaled.

Al and Duanne are both members of the Kentucky Journalism Hall of Fame.

Thank you, Duanne and Al for making this happen.

I would be particularly remiss if I did not recognize my business partner **Mae Peniston** for her invaluable support and assistance;

Mae Peniston

This book also wouldn't have happened if it weren't for the influence, comradeship, or leadership of the following during my 84 years:

Former Gov. **Martha Layne Collins**, for her support and participation in several of our publications;

Shelbyville High School teacher **Mrs. B.B. Bailey** who gave me such a strong foundation in the English language that I was able to survive my first two semesters at the University of Michigan, while both of my roommates received letters of dismissal;

Reverends **Tom Giltner** and **Wayne Bell** of the First Christian Church for their theological guidance and close fellowship during my pre-teen and teenage years;

Shelbyville High School coaches **C. Bruce Daniel** and **Richard "Puss" Greenwell,** who set exacting standards for winning and, just as important, fair play;

Jim Cleveland

Greg Biagi

Ernestine Jennings

Byron Crawford

Michigan English Teacher **W.R. Steinhoff** who didn't believe in "grade inflation," and made me proud to get a "B" in all three of his classes;

CIA boss **Fred Brace**, a carryover from the OSS (Office of Strategic Services) days and a real life James Bond without the Hollywood trimmings, who believed that getting the job done was only worth doing if you got it right…from the start;

Matriarch **Miss Mabel Oats**, a veteran of 53 years at the old *Shelby Sentinel*, who "conspired" with **James "Buddy" O'Sullivan** to make it possible for me to buy the *Sentinel* and embark on a 51-year love affair with the printed word;

Louisville philanthropist and visionary **Major General Dillman Rash,** who was a source of much valuable advice during the formative days of Newspapers, Inc.;

Kentucky's official State Historian **James Klotter** who wrote the overview for our Civil War magazine and has been a source of continuing assistance and inspiration;

Jim Holmberg, curator for special collections at the Filson Historical Society, for providing most of the text for our Lewis & Clark Bicentennial Edition (2003-2006);

Jim Cleveland, Shelbyville, for his collaboration with me on *Portrait of the Past, a Pictorial History of Shelby County, Ky. (1865-1980);*

Greg Biagi, for his collaboration with me on *Shelby County Living, a Pictorial History of Shelby County, Ky. 2011*;

Shelbyville **Mayor Tom Hardesty** and **County Judge-Executive Rob Rothenburger** for their continuing support of our several historical publications and projects;

American patriot and World War II veteran **C.L. Love**, who served with great enthusiasm in so many capacities during my newspaper career;

Ernestine Jennings, beloved high school English teacher and model citizen and churchwoman, who was of great assistance on our book, *A Living History, Shelby County Kentucky 2011*;

Byron Crawford, for writing introductions to two of my books and being an all-around strong supporter of all our efforts; and

James Mulcahy whose "wizardry" in formatting this book reflects his great knowledge of the graphic arts industry and newspaper, magazine and book publishing.

James Mulcahy

Preface

Many people, young and old, have asked me why I chose to write this book. The answer is not complex, it's actually very easy. The reasons are:

First, my children asked me to record the many stories they have heard over the years.

Second, it's important for as many of us as possible to account for the time period through which we lived. This enables future generations to look back at a particular era to see what made that generation tick. What were their likes and dislikes? What influenced them to become doctors, farmers, lawyers, journalists, plumbers, sales representatives, business owners, nurses and pursuers of many other occupations? How did they react to the events of their times?

I did not write this as sort of a "feel good" book. As Billy Andriot told me rather emphatically one day, "There better be some 'bad stuff' in there because I know there's going to be a lot of 'good stuff.'" While there is some "bad stuff," I have been careful not to intentionally hurt any living human being. If I have, then I'm genuinely sorry. I have not, perhaps, been as careful with those who have parted this world, but I have, at all times, tried to remain respectful.

Third, my biggest hope is that this book will inspire others to write their own memoirs as a loving tribute to their families and this community which we call home.

Dedication

This book is dedicated to my wonderful wife of 62 years, Else,
and to my brothers Ben and Bob.
I thank each of them for their unconditional love and loyalty
during the Good Times...and the Bad.

Prologue

No Man is an Island

No man is an island,
Entire of itself,
Every man is a piece of the continent,
A part of the main.
If a clod be washed away by the sea,
Europe is the less.
As well as if a promontory were.
As well as if a manor of thy Friend's,
Or of thine own were.
Any man's death diminishes me,
Because I am involved in mankind,
And therefore never send to know for whom the bell tolls,
It tolls for thee.
John Donne (1624)

My beginnings

In 1930, the planet Pluto was discovered, Al Capone was still riding high in Chicago, the Empire State Building in New York was under construction, and "Hoovervilles" were being built in Washington, D.C. as a rebuke to President Herbert Hoover.

According to census figures in 1930, Shelbyville had about 3,500 residents while Shelby County had about 18,000, including William Edmund Matthews who was born at 11:20 p.m. on April 30, 1930, in a stucco house three miles north of Finchville, Kentucky.

I was the third of three sons born to Robert Foster and Zerelda Tribble Baxter Matthews. My older brothers were Robert F. Jr. (September 14, 1923-October 30, 2010) and Ben Gaines (October 19, 1926).

I was 10 when this photo was taken in front of our home at 1122 W. Main in 1940. My brother Bob, 16, stands behind me, while brother Ben, 13, stands in front of my father, Robert F. Sr.

I have no recollection of the Finchville house, which still stands, because my parents moved to 1122 Main Street in Shelbyville in 1932. This Main Street home was built by former Mayor Luther Willis and is now the home of William L. Shannon and his late wife, Virginia Tichenor Shannon.

Before I delve into memories of 1122 Main Street, let's go back to my birth, which followed, by nine months, a trip to Chicago in July 1929 by my parents. They were accompanied by Charles and Josephine Long, and Lindsey and Deanie Logan. While I was the only child directly related to that trip, Robert Dean Logan came along in January 1931 and Judy Long a few months later.

In the spring of 1967 when my wife Else advised me that she had been to see the obstetrician earlier in the day, I grew quite angry. "This is no time for another baby," I said, as if I didn't have anything to do with it. Later, in discussing the situation with my mother, she related how badly my father had reacted in the fall of 1929 when she told him he was to be a father again. "It's just about the only time in our marriage," she said, "when we almost fell out over my pregnancy. And you're the result." I calmed down after realizing that I too was not a particularly welcome sight to my father.

The year 1930 may not have represented the absolute depth of the Depression, but it was close. According to a book, "Passions and Prejudice" by Linda Light, here's what Shelby Countians were paying for goods and services in that year:

Five gallons of gasoline...85 cents
One quart of oil...15 cents

A haircut...25 cents
A roll of toilet paper...25 cents
Telephone bill...$2.25 per month
Three pounds of rice...18 cents
1 gallon of milk...12 cents
One dozen eggs...22 cents
A bakery-type apple pie...10 cents
Two loaves of bread...10 cents
Two pounds of butter...25 cents
Three pounds of brown sugar...21 cents

Ms. Light quoted one person whom she interviewed for her book as saying, "I used kerosene lamps, and the stove was kerosene run. We had no electricity. My average income from 1930 to 1933 was $3.00 per week. Our first child was born at home."

In Shelbyville, there were no stoplights, and the city limits, from a practical if not legal standpoint, ran from the Fairgrounds in the west to the bridge in the east end of town. Most of the land west of the Fairgrounds and east of the bridge was agricultural. The Coca-Cola plant (now Cola Commons apartments) east of the bridge was not built until 1937.

Businesses that were active at the time included J. William Hedden Grocery, A & P Tea Co., Hardesty's Grocery, Strand Movies, John M. Casey (stoves), Abraham's Court Restaurant, Smith-McKenney (pharmacy), Biagi's (tires and appliances), Hall, Poe & Ruff (general goods), Noble Stores, Sanders & Buckner Pool Room and Bowling Alley, Owen & Moore Hardware, Long's Confectionary & Restaurant, Lawson's (department store), Rothchild & Son Men's Store, Piggly-Wiggly (groceries), Kroger, Duncan Brothers Furniture, Owen S. Kenney (jeweler), Cowley & Co. (hardware & groceries), W.P. Deiss (book store & school supplies), Crane Barber Shop, H.T. Ransdell Drug Store, Armstrong Hotel, Blakemore Groceries, M. Ruben Dry Goods, J.J. Newberry (five and dime store), Bon-Ton Theater, M. Lynch Drug Co., Adam's Hotel & Restaurant, and the Armstrong Agency (insurance). All four banks – Farmers & Traders, Citizens, Shelby County Trust, and Bank of Shelbyville – were also in business.

This was my first (and probably only) tricycle.

While we had more than most families, the early '30s were a time of modest living also for our family. After two terms as county attorney, Dad was earning a living as an attorney. He was also president of the Shelby County Trust & Banking Company, served as an elder in the First Christian Church and became the first person to be popularly elected as mayor in 1934. Up to that time, mayors were selected by the City Council. Even at an early age, I was impressed with my father's intelligence, his non-interest in sports, and his devotion to the Upper Room Sunday School Class at First Christian Church that he and six other men started in 1925.

I'm not sure that my father ever owned a sport shirt and, while he had certain shortness with us as children, he had an obvious pride in his family. Dad was much revered by those who knew him, but it was Mother who provided the family glue.

My mother was busy rearing her children, working on a topic for the Chautauqua Club, directing the church choir, singing at funerals at the Shannon Funeral Home (most of the time for people she didn't know), playing lots of bridge, and presiding at PTA meetings.

Unlike today's "helicopter" parents who oversee their children's every move, my two brothers and I learned a sense of independence at an early age. We were usually up early, gone after breakfast and back home just at dark in the summertime.

Inside Our Home

Perhaps my most vivid memory of the early '30s has to do with James and Mattie Beard who served us as combination chauffeur-handyman and cook-housekeeper respectively. They lived not too far away in a very small house alongside other Black neighbors on south 10th Street.

We moved from 1122 Main to our new home at 1108 Main (pictured here) in 1944.

Readers may wonder how families could afford servants in the Depression. However, in fact, nearly all of the families with whom my parents socialized had someone in the kitchen or in the yard or both – the Paul F. Schmidts, Charles B. Longs, William S. Deisses, Lindsey Logans, George L. Willises, Howard Pearces, J.C. Rays and several others.

Pay was about $5.00 per week per person, and some families helped with room and board in some instances.

James was my best friend. He was my constant companion around the house and in the yard; Mattie was a great cook and had a special touch with fried chicken, creamed lima beans, corn pudding, hot rolls and desserts.

Fire at the Homeplace

The spring and winter of 1935 produced perhaps my first real memories of actual events. Our house at 1122 Main Street caught fire in May of that year just as Shelbyville High School was dismissing for the afternoon. The fire caused extensive smoke damage, but most of the furniture was saved because many of the juniors and seniors at the school carried out most of our belongings while the firemen brought the blaze under control. The fire gave my mother, blessed with a good insurance settlement, the opportunity to redecorate which, to my father's chagrin, wound up costing a good deal more than the insurance check.

That fire led to two of my more humorous memories.

Oklahoma Adventure

While the house was being redecorated, my father suggested the entire family go to Muskogee, Oklahoma, to visit my mother's cousin, Hattie Broaddus, and her husband, U.S. Federal Judge Bower Broaddus.

So off we went… Mother, Dad, and three youngsters in a used Ford sedan that, as I recall, required lots of water along the way. It was a long two-day trip to Muskogee and when we arrived about 3 p.m. on the second day, my mother suggested to Cousin Hattie that she get a babysitter for me. But Hattie declined, saying I appeared to be "beautifully behaved."

Just 30 minutes later I fell into the swimming pool and, being unable to swim, had to be rescued by Judge Broaddus. Two hours later I teased the family dog and that led to my being bitten on the leg. So Mother said, "Hattie, I told you so. He needs a sitter." But Hattie, one of my all-time favorites, declined again.

The rest of the night passed peacefully enough as did the following morning. However, as the morning gave way to the afternoon and everyone started getting ready for a cocktail party at the country club, I began thinking about how I might join in the fun. So about 5 p.m. as everyone began leaving the Broaddus home, I hid behind a bush by the front porch and turned the water hose on the partygoers. Needless to say, no one, except Cousin Hattie, thought it was funny. My father was livid and, had it been left up to him, I would surely have been punished…and punished severely.

But Cousin Hattie's even temperament prevailed, and I was spared. But she did, finally, get a babysitter for the rest of our visit.

Texas Adventure

With the house still uninhabitable, the family headed for Amarillo, Texas, on a Southern Railway train for the Christmas holidays. That's where my father's brother, Charles (Ted) Matthews, lived with his wife, Mildred, and their daughter, Doris. The visit was uneventful until Christmas Day when I exposed my creativity again.

A tricycle and rope were among my major gifts so I decided to put them to use while the rest of the family was enjoying what I thought was a boring Christmas dinner. I hooked the rope to the Christmas tree and then to my tricycle and started pedaling. It didn't take long for the inevitable crash as the tree – loaded with ornaments, lights, and icicles – came tumbling down.

I wasn't so lucky this time as there was no Cousin Hattie around. Still, Christmas being Christmas, my punishment was light. But Mother put Brother Ben in charge of watching my every step until we boarded the train for the return to Kentucky.

Back at Home

I loved the house at 1122 Main Street with its many rooms and bathrooms, and a beautifully furnished twin parlor that contained a 15-foot mirror in each room. There were four large bedrooms on the second floor. Ben and I shared one, Bob had one, Mother and Dad had another, and there was a guest room. Prior to and during World War II, we rented the guest room from year to year to buyers from North Carolina who worked the Shelbyville Tobacco Market.

It was a house made for entertaining, which my parents frequently did. They rotated dinner parties throughout the year with three other couples: Lindsey and Deanie Logan, Charles and Josephine Long Sr., and County Judge George L. and Golder Willis Jr. And, yes, it was customary for the men to wear tuxedos and the women floor-length dresses.

After dinner, there were generally two tables of bridge. Bridge, I think, had replaced canasta as the Number 1 card game nationally. As the years passed, a game of bridge became a regular highlight of our lives, with Mother and Dad and Ben and me squaring off. We were frequently joined by my mother's brother, Edmund Baxter, who lived with his wife, Margaret, and their daughter, Bonny, in Washington, D.C. He became a high ranking official with the Department of Health, Education & Welfare.

Whistlers Club

The earlier adventures in Oklahoma and Texas revealed my desire to be creative (some might call it mischievous) as a child, and back home I enjoyed organizing my friends into clubs. When I was about six years old, we formed the Whistlers Club, which included Bob Logan, Charles Ray "Rue" Ferguson, Joe Deiss, Bobby Owen Collins, and Johnny Buckner. Each of us had a "secret" whistle that only members of the club understood.

I got the idea from listening to a popular radio show of that era, "Jack Armstrong, the All-American Boy," who was always getting the best of the bad guys as he bounced from one adventure to another. Other than doing a lot of whistling, however, our spin-off club was rather benign.

Early Education

My first-grade teacher was Miss Irene Shrewsberry in a small white building on north Ninth Street where it eventually stood behind Northside School until a new facility forced demolition of both buildings in 2013-14. Other teachers were Katherine Clark, second grade; Leona Martin, third grade; Sara Belle Waters, fourth grade; Sue Wilson Doyle, fifth grade; and Mary Middelton, sixth grade. Fortunately I missed the two toughest teachers – George Ann Carpenter and Florence Dudley Jesse.

The class was divided into two sections, with A through L getting one set of teachers, and M through Z another set. While I appreciated not having Misses Carpenter and Jesse, my best friends, Bob Logan, Bobby Owen Collins, and Charles Ray Ferguson, were in the other section.

Grade School

I had two strong rivals in grade school, James Swanson and Reed Yount. Both were exceptionally smart, and, to boot, I thought they also studied too hard. I was delighted when, following sixth grade, James moved out of town with his family. This left me to battle it out with Reed for the next six years.

This is my first report card provided by my teacher, Irene Shrewsberry. Notice that grades were given in "Effort" and "Writing."

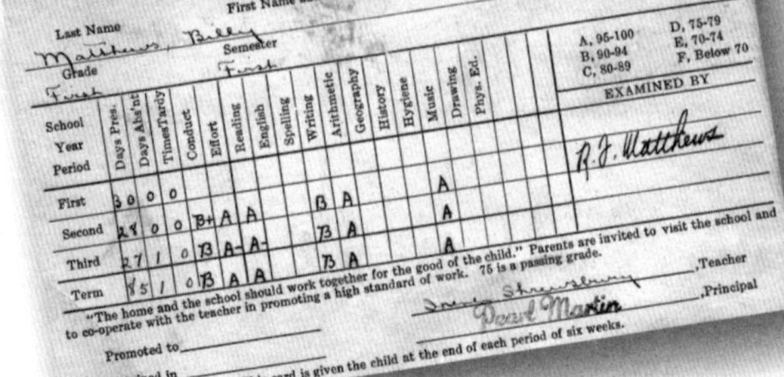

When the "new" Northside Elementary School opened on College Street in 1939, I was there as a student in the fourth grade.

On September 1, 1939, World War II officially began with Germany's invasion of Poland, and I remember paper boys going up and down Main Street in Shelbyville yelling "Extra! Extra! War declared!" as they pushed special editions published by the *Louisville Courier-Journal* for 10 cents.

Two years later, on December 8, 1941, I was a sixth-grader and remember when all grades were marched into the basement to hear President Franklin Delano Roosevelt give his famous "Day of Infamy" speech on the radio following the attack on Pearl Harbor the day before.

Best Buddies

There were five of us who were generally inseparable: Bob Logan, Bobby Owen Collins, Charles Ray Ferguson, Allen Willis, and me. The highlight of any summer was being invited to spend the weekend on the Wallace Collins' farm on the Mount Eden Road. There was plenty of room to roam, watch the cattle, swim in the pond, climb the silos, operate the cream separator and ride the wagons as they brought in the various crops.

We tortured a few chickens, suffered a few dog bites, played a lot of basketball with a hand-made hoop, suffered greatly from poison ivy and delighted in getting up early and going to bed late.

Bobby Owen's mother, Lucille Collins, was a wonderful cook with a particular bent for making salt-rising bread. There was absolutely nothing better than freshly baked salt-rising bread with freshly made butter and Welch's grape jelly.

I've often wondered how much my collection of metal toy soldiers would be worth today if I still had them. Many a battle was waged in the Logan's back yard between my soldiers and tanks and those of Bob Logan, Charles Ray Ferguson, and Allen Willis.

My Friend's Funeral

I experienced death the first time on September 4, 1940, when nine-year-old Allen Sandidge Willis was struck by a car near his home on U.S. 60, about two miles west of town. He lived just a few hours before dying at the local King's Daughters Hospital, located on Henry Clay Street. The driver of the car was exonerated as Allen had darted out into the highway in a losing effort to beat the car.

I had been to visit my grandparents, J.G. and Lottie Baxter, on their farm near Richmond, Kentucky, and had ridden home on the Greyhound bus from Lexington with Allen's brother, George III. When Lindsey Logan Sr., Charles Long Sr. and my father met the bus in Shelbyville, I realized that something was wrong. They took young George home and explained what had happened. The next day I attended my first funeral in which I knew the person involved.

Change in Housekeepers

About 1936 or 1937, Mattie and James left our employ under circumstances that I never understood and we retained Susie Brown as our chief cook and maid. Susie was very slight of build, but, boy, could she cook! She had a radiant smile and became a personal friend.

However, Susie had a penchant for losing husbands. Twice, the men to whom she was married – and they were big men – didn't wake up when morning came. They were found in bed in the little house in Martinsville, which, because Shelbyville was strictly segregated in terms of housing, was neighborhood to most Black families. There was a never-confirmed suspicion that Susie had poisoned her husbands, but my father served as her counsel and adviser and Susie was never charged.

She worked off her legal fee by staying with us until 1940 when she left town and Frances Taylor took charge of our kitchen. Frances was as big as Susie was small. We all loved Frances who was paid $7 for a six-day week plus board.

However, in 1943, Frances got a much better offer – $12 a week plus bus fare and board – to work for a Louisville family and from that day on we didn't have a regular cook, but a succession of day workers who could cook or keep house with varying degrees of efficiency. This is when I learned how to mop floors, make up my bed, close the door to my closet, and shut the drawers in my chest.

Electric Trains

Christmas 1938 was a memorable one not only for me, but also my Mother and Dad. On the eve of the big day, my father put up a Lionel train for my brother Ben. Yet, in the process of putting up an American Flyer train for me, he discovered that the manufacturer had failed to include a transformer necessary for running my train. Since he discovered this at 9 p.m., it looked very much like Ben was going to have the only train running on Christmas morning.

Mother, however, who always seemed to be in the forefront of rescue actions, called Bill Frederick, a personal friend and president of Stewart's department store in Louisville, and asked him what could be done. Rather than call one of his employees, Bill went to the store himself, found an appropriate transformer, drove to the Greyhound bus station and put it on the midnight bus to Lexington. An hour or so later, my father met the bus at the 11th and Main railroad tracks, retrieved the transformer, and, just a few hours later, I was busy playing with my train.

Incidentally, unlike today's parents, mine never tried to make things equal. Bob always got the most on Christmas Day, Ben the second most, and I the third most. I never thought about this being unfair.

Easter Rabbit

This reminds me of an earlier time, when I was about five years old, on Easter morning and found a big velour rabbit in an alcove off the main entrance to our house at 1122 Main. When I ran with glee to my mother, she explained, "Billy, Ben was supposed to find that" and handed him the rabbit. I got a basket of eggs instead. Since I still think about it, maybe it did bother me just a bit as being unfair.

"Tough Love"

In today's society, being whipped by your father is now considered child abuse.

But many years ago, one was supposedly whipped out of a father's love for the child.

I endured three whippings as a youngster. Two were justified; one wasn't.

The first of the two that was justified had to do with my "borrowing" 40 cents from my mother's purse. Now, before my father administered a whipping behind the knees with his belt, there was always a moral to be taught. I understood the moral here.

The second justified whipping was probably the worst I ever suffered. When I was about 13, Patrolman Hubert Black told me to get my bike off the sidewalk and into the street. I smarted off as to how my father was the mayor and I could ride my bike anywhere. When Officer Black reported the incident to my father, Dad actually closed his law office and sent word that I was to come home.

If he had just proceeded with the whipping, that would have been painful but okay. As it was, he had to lecture me for about 10 minutes about taking advantage of someone else's position. That was the maddest I ever saw him.

The one whipping I got that wasn't justified (at least in my mind) had to do with being an early entrepreneur. I bought pencils, paper, rulers, and other school items at Cleveland's Grocery on my way to school, and then had them on hand when one of my fellow students needed something. I doubled and tripled the price I had paid but my classmates didn't seem to mind. If you need a pencil, you need a pencil.

However, the principal, Pearl Martin, told my father by phone that I was taking advantage of the other students… whereupon I got another lacing with the moral being "Don't take advantage of someone else's misfortune."

Incidentally, my father never said, "This hurts me more than you."

The Alphabet Gang

When I was about 12, I came up with an idea for an Alphabet Club. So I wrote a postcard to each of my best friends and gave them a letter in the alphabet and a color. I made myself the White Z.

Our first meeting was under the railroad trestle at south Eighth Street. Bob Logan became the Red S, Charles Ray Ferguson the Blue T, Bobby Owen Collins the Orange U, Joe Deiss the Purple V, Frank Lee the Yellow X, and Bo Moesser the Green Y.

Assignments ranged from knocking out streetlights, tipping over garbage cans, soaping cars at Halloween, letting air out of police cars, and other acts of minor mischief as well as fixing up our headquarters in an abandoned lumber yard located off Magnolia Avenue on what is now Willis Street.

Club members worked in pairs, which meant that I could leave the postcard assignments for everyone at the club site well before we met at 7 o'clock on Friday nights. Because no one else knew what anyone else was doing, the White Z was rarely involved. However, on one occasion when I did venture out, we had a close call with the police who nearly caught us roaming around the Hall & Davis Lumber Yard on north Seventh Street. We escaped by seeking refuge on the roof of the old telephone company building (now The Needle Nest) at the corner of Seventh and Washington Streets.

After two good summers (1943-44), we disbanded when a gang of kids from the east end of town sent word that they intended to take us on in battle and were going to destroy our lumber yard location that we had fortified with large rocks.

A pouch of money, as far as I know, is still buried under the walkway (and one-time wooden trestle) leading to Southside School.

Paperboy

My brothers Bob, Ben and I all delivered daily newspapers. There was good money in carrying papers, particularly a morning route since it didn't interfere with school as much as an afternoon route. I started carrying papers for Brother Ben when I was in the seventh grade, and, upon his graduation from high school in 1944, I had my own route. I started at 18 cents a morning and, later, 25 cents when I was carrying for Ben. Eventually I was making $8 to $10 weekly with my own route.

It was a lot more fun carrying papers in the summer months when the weather was nice. I can remember my mother thawing me out in a tub of lukewarm water after a brutally cold morning when I arrived home, almost in tears, and couldn't feel my fingers or toes.

In those days, carriers were responsible for their own collections and remittance to the

Courier-Journal, so if someone didn't pay, it was the carrier's loss not the *CJ*'s. Today, of course, with direct-billing, carriers have no liability if someone doesn't pay.

"Hop a Freight"

When I was 14, close friend Bo Moesser and I decided to "hop a freight." I don't recall that we were particularly mad about anything or at anybody, but we just decided that it might be more fun to live elsewhere.

So around 4 o'clock one summer afternoon, we climbed into a box car on a siding at the Eighth Street L & N station and waited for an engine to pick us up and carry us away on a new adventure. We waited, and waited, and waited, and nothing happened. As night began to fall and the shadows began to envelop the box car, we began to wonder if becoming hoboes was really a good idea.

"You know," Bo said, "our mothers are probably really worried. Let's do this some other time." I agreed, and we headed home.

When I got home and slipped up the back stairs to my room on the second floor, no one was there. In fact, no one was even in the house. We hadn't been missed at all.

Adair Little Potatoes

Back in the 1930s and 1940s there were few, if any, organized sports other than those involving junior high and high school athletics. There was no Little League, no mini-leagues for elementary and junior high school teams. So, if you wanted to play football in the fall, basketball in the winter, or baseball in the summer, youngsters had to organize their own teams and find appropriate facilities for their activities.

I began developing an interest in baseball at an early age. The house in the background was the home for many years of my grandparents, Benjamin Franklin and Margaret Matthews, who had an apartment on the second floor.

For several years, Joe Deiss, Charlie Ray Ferguson, Bob Logan, Bobby Owen Collins and I were part of a baseball team called the Adair Little Potatoes.

Our principal adversary was the Magnolia Red Hots that included boys a good deal older such as Quintin Biagi, Howard Logan, Cal Schmidt, and my brother Ben. I don't think we ever won a single game because of the age difference, but it didn't seem to matter.

The baseball games were played in what was then a vacant lot on Magnolia and is now filled with homes with street numbers ranging from 519 to 615, then the home of Mr. and Mrs. Clyde Hall.

The game invariably ended when a foul ball or an errant throw broke a window in the basement of the Hall home.

The game resumed when we had raised enough money to replace the window.

Camp Piomingo

Several of us started attending YMCA-sponsored Camp Piomingo in 1938. It cost $1.00 per day or $14 for two weeks room and board. All campers belonged to a particular Indian tribe, and beginners all started as Shawnees. Other tribes included Cherokee, Ojibwa, and Choctaw.

I developed bad cases of poison ivy along with mosquito and chigger bites each year.

I was only eight years of age when I first started going to camp along with Bob Logan, Charles Ray Ferguson, and Joe Deiss.

When one reached the age of 10, campers qualified for a large embroidered P that could be affixed to a sweater. I was the only one of our group who didn't get a P that first year so my mother, who was picking up the group at the end of the session, went off to find out. I knew that was "bad news!"

Camp Director James Brown told her that I confused being a camper with being a counselor and that I seemed to think I was a "Chief" instead of an "Indian."

He told her that I had "great organizational skill" that was misused.

Naturally, we had a very serious talk when we got home, and thereafter I always qualified for a P.

Touch Football

When I was about 10 we began what became a family and almost community tradition… touch football.

It started with my Brother Bob and me taking on Brother Ben and Uncle Ed (Baxter), my mother's one and only beloved brother who had grown up with her in Richmond.

I don't believe that Bob and I ever won during those few years. But the tradition grew, and, in time, the annual game and the number of participants grew by leaps and bounds. We generally played during the Thanksgiving or Christmas holidays.

Over the years, many of Ben's and my friends participated, including George Willis III, Lucien Kinsolving, Billy Chenault, Howard Logan, "Simp" Greenwell, and, of course, our children.

The final game in 1971, played on Christmas Day with several inches of snow on the ground, included my nephews Alan Matthews and older brother Charlie, who had just been mustered out of service following a tour in Vietnam. Again, Ben captained the winning team and Bob the losers. Whatever the score and who won or lost, it was great fun not only for us, but the many folks who stopped by to watch.

Junior High Misadventure

In the fall of 1942 I left the elementary school on College Street and entered junior high consisting of grades seven, eight and nine at Shelbyville High School on Main Street. As far as I can remember I did well but the end of the year was marred by what my mother called a "major failure."

It was a custom at the time for members of the senior class to "tap" junior high-school students who had exemplary grades and conduct. My two brothers had been "tapped" during their previous school years and it never occurred to me that I wouldn't be tapped. But that didn't happen, so my mother was furious when I told her that I had no explanation for what I was sure was an "oversight."

She charged over to the school, and I must admit recalling that I didn't think that was a good idea.

When she returned, she had an explanation. Two of the teachers said that I had an "officious attitude," that I frequently offered advice to both teachers and students when none was needed. The word "conceited" also came up.

This was in an era when parents supported the school system over their own children, a process that has been unfortunately reversed in recent years.

Mother and I had a "serious" talk (fortunately she didn't involve my father), and she said that she fully expected me to be "tapped" at the end of my eighth grade. This did happen, and I learned a valuable lesson.

Created Our Own Fun

When my grandson Henrik was a teenager, he asked me one day what we did for fun as teenagers during the "olden" days: "Did you have anything like a 'Gameboy,' … could you send and receive text messages, … did you 'tweet' or 'twitter,' … how did you communicate?"

When I explained that we didn't have "Gameboys," and couldn't 'tweet' or 'twitter' or send e-mails, he responded, "Sure glad I didn't live in the olden times."

As I look back on our teenage years, however, I can't help but think of the fun we had pitching a tent on the Collins' farm for the weekend, and playing all sorts of games, or going down the railroad tracks with, first, our bb guns, and, later, our .22 rifles. We enjoyed shooting tin cans in Clear Creek, climbing trees, roaming the woods, spooking animals, and running races. In short, we created our own fun, our own entertainment. In the summertime we were gone from sun-up to sun-down, and the last thing on our minds was a pedophile or someone else out to do us harm.

Piano Playing

I started taking piano lessons from Mrs. Harry Lockridge when I was in the fifth grade. She came to the house on Main Street twice a week and gave me a one-hour lesson for 50 cents.

My proficiency on the piano was sufficient enough that I began playing for the 15-minute daily assembly at school each morning when I began the seventh grade. There were four of us, including Kathleen Cleveland and Alice Mae Poe, who rotated playing an opening hymn. This was followed by one of the teachers, or, occasionally a student, giving a brief talk and a short Morning Prayer. Superintendent (Mrs.) Willie C. Ray usually brought the assembly to order and later dismissed it. I assume these assemblies came to an end with a Supreme Court decision in the early 1960s that had the effect of outlawing prayer in school.

Beginning with the ninth grade, I started taking piano lessons from Frederick Cowles in Louisville. A noted organ master, churches from all over Kentucky called Mr. Cowles whenever they wished to have an organ dedicated.

He and I clicked from the beginning, although he questioned why I would want to play football and basketball rather than pursue what he called "a natural talent" for the piano.

My most memorable moment came during my senior year when I was performing at the Memorial Auditorium in Louisville. Each of his students played in the order of his or her ability, and, after four years, I was the final student to perform. It was also the one and only time that my father ever came to hear me play.

I had a tendency on some occasions to get carried away with how well I was playing and this can be very dangerous if your mind drifts too much. Well, that's what happened that night and, as I was concluding the 19-page Grieg Sonata Opus 40, I suddenly found myself back on page 2 instead of the last page.

Unfortunately my mother leaned over to my father and said, "I think Bill is going to play it again."

Because Dad was always a perfectionist, he broke out into a cold sweat, wiped his brow several times and began to squirm in his seat.

Near panic, I looked off stage where Mr. Cowles had a big grin on his face and mimed, "Now get yourself out of this one."

For the first and only time in my life, I ad libbed, got back to the last page swiftly, and finished the piece. I don't know who was sweating more at the finish – my father or me.

Class of 1948

As of this writing, only 10 individuals remain from the 44 students who graduated from Shelbyville High School in May 1948. Interestingly enough, there were an equal number of boys and girls in the class.

Officers were Bill Acree, president; Helen Shelton, vice president; Cora Scobee, secretary; and Bobby Owen Collins, treasurer. Other members were Elnora Bowles, Gene Bramlett, Robert C. Brummett, Ada Cinnamond, Tommy Cinnamond, Ray Conn, Betty Craig, George Devine, Josephine Ellis, Charles Ray Ferguson, Walter Lee Gaines, Bill Green, Sammy Harrod, Edith Helm, Carl C. Hurn, Katherine Jennings, Betty Jane Johnson, Dorothy Kays, Junior Kingsolver, Evelyn Landers, Anne LeCompte, Barbara Lee, Bob Logan, Nancye Long, Wanda Lyons, Peggy McClain, Betty McClaskey, John Lyle Miller, Wanda Newby, Juanita Powell, Marjorie Puckett, Dorothy Purvis, Lillis Roberts Jr., Georgeann Rutledge, Leslie Shuck, Nellie Swigert, Elise Wallace, Reed Yount and Lawson Zaring.

Excellent Teachers

I had some highly-learned and influential teachers throughout my four high school years. Most fondly remembered are Sarah Lewis (math), Virginia Lewis (Latin and French), Mrs. B.B. Bailey (English), Mrs. T.M. "Blondie" Beard (commerce), Roy Barlow (manual arts), and Joe Beach (music).

Others on the staff were Agnes Sleadd (math), Richard "Puss" Greenwell (history) Mrs. E.J. Paxton (history), Elmo Head (physical education), Josephine Lapsley (social science), Carolyn Goodson (English), Evan Settle (mathematics), and Loretta Jones (home economics).

Sadly, Miss Jones was killed in a two-vehicle crash near Versailles in the fall of 1948, along with community favorite and two-time state tennis champion Jackie Byrd.

Outcome of Rivalry

My biggest rival, as mentioned previously, was Reed Yount who always produced a higher grade point average than I. My father never failed to ask me, "What did Reed Yount get?" I never had a good answer. Only in my senior year did I summon the courage to answer my father's usual question by responding, "Dad, I believe Reed is just plain smarter." I should have said so years earlier.

Reed's parents had little, if any, money, but Superintendent Ray prevailed upon Purdue

University to grant him a "full ride" four-year scholarship. He responded by excelling at the university and then having an outstanding career as a chemist and then executive with Colgate-Palmolive in Cincinnati. I didn't see him again until shortly before his death in 1998. He came to Shelbyville in 1996 to attend the funeral of his uncle, longtime postal carrier Robert Yount.

Debate Disaster

In addition to three high school sports – football, basketball, and baseball – I participated in numerous activities, including debate. I was trying to follow in the footsteps of my brother Ben who, along with Paul Swanson, had won the Kentucky State High School Debate Championship in 1944.

Patsy Hays, daughter of Chevrolet dealer C. Joe Hays, and I represented Shelbyville High School in statewide debate competition in my sophomore and junior years (Patsy was one year older). We won some, lost some, and the only debate that sticks out in my mind occurred at Georgetown High School my junior year.

Reflecting my usual confidence, I was convinced we had won the debate only to have the judge declare Georgetown the winner. I was so incensed that I refused to shake hands with the winners. I actually told Patsy that I thought the judge was someone who had been dragged in off the street.

Some months later, I attended a dance at Georgetown College and began "sweet talking" a beautiful young lady. Before I could continue, she said, "You don't remember me, do you?" When I said, "No," she responded, "I'm the person you refused to shake hands with after we beat you in debate." That dance ended abruptly. Later I learned she was Janey Hill, daughter of Georgetown College President Samuel Smythe Hill.

State Music Mishap

What one might call another mishap occurred in my junior year at the state high school music competition. I was in a quartet with Ted Igleheart, Bill Acree, and Reed Yount. Our leader was Joe Beach, one of Kentucky's all-time best high school band and vocal instructors.

We had gained a "superior" rating in the regional contest and, consequently, approached "state" with plenty of confidence and enthusiasm. On the way to Lexington, Mr. Beach suggested I begin our selection with no help from his pitch pipe. I was singing bass and had the first few measures all by myself. We had not done that before, but I assured him that I could hit the note on key when I began singing.

Unfortunately I started about a half note "off-key" so that when the others joined in we sang the entire selection off-key.

The judge could have given us a "poor" (the lowest ranking), but, instead, he gave us a "fair" for "having the courage to sing the entire song off-key."

On the long ride home, no one spoke a word. We all knew that Mr. Beach was mad, particularly at me so we just let him simmer.

Many years later, at our 50th class reunion, Joe Beach was nice enough to attend (he was then playing First Violin in the Lexington Symphony). I inquired as to whether he remembered the debacle 51 years previously. He laughed and said, "Of course, I had never been so mad in my life, but, then, the next day, I realized that it was my fault that I hadn't 'pitched' the opening note for you."

Agony of Miss Agnes

If I had some teachers who liked my work and effort a great deal (Mrs. B.B. Bailey, and Misses Sarah and Virginia Lewis), I had one who not only didn't like me but the Matthews family in general.

Her name was Miss Agnes Sleadd and she taught most of the high school math and science courses. When I was a freshman, she confronted me one day and noted my deficiencies in one of her courses and said, "You will never be the Valedictorian."

She then went on to tell me that my oldest brother Bob, in his senior year, had skipped out on the senior class party that had consisted of a picnic at one of the senior's home. She noted Bob and his best friend, Bill "Petey" Deiss, had "picked up a couple of town girls," and disappeared. Miss Sleadd, it turned out, was the class sponsor and was deeply offended by the incident. So seven years later, I learned that I was to be the "fall guy."

Miss Sleadd was true to her word, and due to my less than stellar grades in her classes, I finished a distant second to Valedictorian Reed Yount. This was long before grade inflation and bonus points for taking certain college prep classes, so I finished my four years with a 93.8 average to Reed's 95.8. Reflecting the tough grading system at that time, only nine members of our senior class of 44 finished with a grade point average above 90.

Stage Debut

My mother, who was always my biggest supporter until her death in 1984, said she had never known anyone who could turn a drama into a comedy until I made my stage debut in the spring of 1948.

The play was called "Midnight" and since it was shortly after the end of World War II, playwrights were still writing plays about Nazis and their evil ways. This play dealt with an attempt by a German spy to break into a house in a Midwestern industrial town and steal a secret formula. I was the spy!

Midway in the first act, I knocked on the door of the house and told the occupants that my aide (played by Cora Scobee) was sick and needed help. While I was explaining the problem to the residents and playing for time, Cora "fainted" and I helped her to the couch.

After determining that the chemist who owns the formula is actually in the house, I excused myself and made plans to leave and return again under the cover of night to complete my assignment, which was to steal the formula. But, naturally, I had to take Cora with me.

She had decided the night of the play to wear her mother's big, heavy fur coat. So when I tried to pick her up, she represented about 150 pounds of dead, very dead weight. So I tried and I tried again, each time saying "lift up, lift up," so I could get my arms under her waist. She was playing the scene for all it was worth and wouldn't raise up one inch.

The audience, which included my very embarrassed father, howled until I finally got my arms under her, lifted her, and zigzagged off the stage.

For some reason the play's director, Virginia Lewis, had decided that I needed to wear a mustache. Unfortunately it fell off in the middle of the second act.

The real denouement came in the final act when I emerged from a "secret" door in one of the bookcases and cried out to everyone, "Hands up!" Unfortunately again, my hand hit the side of a chair, and the gun went flying the length of the stage. So while 10 people held their hands up high, I walked about 50 feet and retrieved the weapon. Again, the audience roared with laughter.

Needless to say we weren't asked to reprise the play the following night, which had been the custom for some of the plays performed previously.

My father's only comment when I got home was, "William, I don't think the stage brings out the best in you." But my always supportive mother said, "You made a very memorable debut."

This staged scene from our senior play "Midnight" reveals me standing on the landing (far left). Others in the play were Barbara Lee, Betty Craig, Bob Logan, Bill Acree, Josephine Ellis, Bill Green, Bobby Owen Collins, Reed Yount, Cora Scobee, Helen Shelton, Peggy McClain and Charles Ray Ferguson.

Football 'Fame'

The 1948 class of Shelbyville High accomplished something in sports that the school had never accomplished before. The 1947 football team went undefeated in winning the Central Kentucky Conference football title, and the 1948 basketball squad took the school to its first high school state tournament appearance.

Before recounting those stories, I would like to begin with my football debut in the fall of 1945. Whether it was a coincidence or not, the '45 season proved to be the final year of Coach C. Bruce Daniel's fabled coaching career.

Possibly the only five-star athlete ever to come out of Georgetown College, where he also excelled academically, Daniel came to Shelbyville High School in 1928. In his first year, he coached all sports, taught five classes and was paid $1,700 for his services. He became high school principal in 1934. He served as principal for 20 years, was a pioneer in Christian leadership in athletics, and was a pivotal figure in the development of the Kentucky High School Athletic Association. He and his wife, Hildreth, were among the founders of the Kentucky Retired Teachers Association.

All told, Daniel's football teams won 82, lost 43, and tied 5. Six of those losses came in 1945 and I always blamed myself for one of them.

After losing the season opener to Georgetown by one point, Shelbyville traveled to Versailles to play the Yellow Jackets. We were up comfortably, 20-7, with about four minutes to play when Daniel inserted me and several other reserves into the game to "get some experience."

On the very first play after I entered the game, Versailles intercepted an errant pass and raced 60 yards to score. On the extra-point attempt, the runner circled around my end to make it 20-14. I probably should have been yanked out of the game at this point, but, surprisingly, I was left in.

Versailles kicked off, straight to me. I fumbled the ball, the enemy recovered, and with less than a minute to play, the runner again circled around my end to tie the game 20-20. The extra point was good, and Versailles prevailed 21-20. It was a very inauspicious debut, but my father, who could always be counted on when things looked or were going bad, consoled me by saying, "I think you will be the best football player in the family." I knew he was kidding, but events eventually proved him correct.

I played little in my junior year as the Red Devils won six, lost one and tied one, the only loss, a bad one, coming against Lexington Henry Clay, 46-0. New coach, Richard "Puss" Greenwell, accused the team of "quitting." He was probably right.

Bruce Daniel

As for my senior year, Sports Editor Bob Logan, who passed away in 2012, recalled our deeds in our senior class annual called The Reflector. Here are his words:

As we look back on this year's football season, we see the most successful one that has ever been enjoyed by Shelbyville High School.

At the opening whistle who would have dreamed that this year's team, with only 13 returning lettermen, and without the services of last year's quarterback, Bill Green, who was out with a hip injury, would accomplish a feat that has never been done before in the history of the school, completing the season 8-0, and winning the CKC title. This makes the third time that SHS has won the championship, but the only time that they have been both undefeated and untied.

The season's opener was with the Winchester Shawnees who made an unsuccessful invasion of Daniel Field, and were turned back by a 13-7 score. The first blood of the season was drawn by John Lyle Miller, who plunged over from the one-yard line, and by Bob Logan, who raced 75 yards to pay dirt.

The following week an improved Devil 11 humiliated Anchorage, 26-0. The touchdowns were credited to Logan, freshman Jake Brummett, Collins, and Humston.

The following week the Devils added Georgetown's Buffaloes to our list of victims by a score of 34-7. Bobby Owen Collins flipped to Matthews who sprinted the remaining 50 yards for the first tally. Others to score were Collins, who plunged over from the one, and Logan, who scored twice, from 32 and 15 yards respectively. Johnny Buckner gathered in Billy Humston's end zone pass for the final marker.

After the successful home stand, Shelbyville made their first invasion of enemy sod. "Jarrin" John Miller, who filled in for Collins, who was sick, and for Logan who was out for the season with an old back injury, roared into the "Promised Land" three times as the Devils goose-egged the Versailles Yellow Jackets 20-0. Ben Pollard was credited with a safety.

The ancient rivalry with the Frankfort Panthers was renewed again on Daniel Field before a capacity crowd. Shelbyville edged the visitors 18-6 in a particularly hard-fought game. The first marker was attained by a pass from Collins to Matthews, who waltzed nimbly down the sidelines for 40 yards. Miller followed by bulling his way into the end zone for two more touchdowns.

Probably the first time in the history of the school that local fans had ever seen a football game turned into a track meet was when the Red and White squad pushed over 13 touchdowns (and had five called back) to swamp Lawrenceburg, 81-0. The regulars played only the first quarter as Coach Greenwell gave the reserves, including Bo Moesser, Charles Ray Ferguson and others, a chance to play the game.

The next threat to Shelbyville's unmarred record came at Harrodburg where the Devils whipped the previously unbeaten Pioneers, 25-0. Miller broke loose for two touchdowns, and Matthews and his replacement Sammy Harrod also crossed the goal line.

Finally, the last obstacle blocking the way to an undefeated season was the highly-rated and once-beaten Paris Greyhounds. Devil supporters were stunned when Paris capitalized on a Shelbyville fumble and scored a few plays later. Some feared that the Devils, behind for the first time during the season and playing without the ineligible Miller (who had turned 20 before the game), might collapse. But Shelbyville did just the opposite as the sensational passing combination of Collins to Matthews exploded for three touchdowns to pull the game out of the fire and provided a 21-6 triumph.

Miller was elected to the third team, All-State, and the following five received Honorable Mention – Collins, backfield; R.C. Brummitt, tackle; Mac Catlett, guard; Martin Deim, guard; and Matthews, end. Collins and Miller served as the team's co-captains.

The great success of this year's team can be attributed to three things. First, to the dynamic leadership of our mentor, Coach Richard "Puss" Greenwell and the watchful eye of former football coach Bruce Daniel. Second, a joint tribute goes to our powerful line and our hard-driving backfield. Prominent members of the line were Acree, Brummitt, Krieger,

Catlett, Sherrard, Harrod, Buckner and Matthews. The backfield was composed of Miller, Collins, Brummitt, Logan, Leslie Shuck, and Martin Deim who, through his agility, was able to play both line and backfield. Third, the drive, fight, and spirit of this year's team which will long be remembered in the hearts and minds of all the townspeople.

(Editor's Note: This ends Logan's account.)

With all due respect to the 1947 team, it is difficult to predict how we would have fared if we had played traditional opponents Lexington Henry Clay and the Danville Admirals. Both had been dropped from the schedule after the 1946 season.

It's also debatable that we could have held our own against Coach Daniel's powerhouse teams of the mid-1930s, which won 30 games and lost only 3. Still, I do not wish to denigrate anything that our 1947 team accomplished because in the final analysis we must have been quite good, as evidenced by the 238 points we scored to our opponents' 26.

It is important to note that of those mentioned previously:

-Ben Pollard graduated from Purdue University, became a jet fighter pilot, and was shot down over North Vietnam. He was held prisoner for five years before being released as part of a peace settlement;

-John Lyle Miller starred as a freshman at Murray State University and played in the Tangerine Bowl;

-Martin Deim lettered in baseball, football, and basketball at Centre College in Danville and was signed to a minor league contract by the St. Louis Cardinals. He captained the football and baseball teams.

8th Region Champs

Due to its length Bob Logan's account of the 1947-1948 basketball season will not be repeated here but his account of the 8th Region final is worth telling:

The team entered district play with a record of 15 wins and only 6 losses. After winning three straight district games, the Red Devils were upset by Waddy in the district finals, 55-49.

But since both district finalists qualify for the regional, both Waddy and Shelbyville advanced. Shelbyville squeaked by Eminence, 38-37, in the regional opener, got revenge against Waddy, 53-45, in the semi-finals, and, in another squeaker, upset the Valley Vikings and its star "Corky" Cox, in the finals.

The Valley game became the last obstacle to hurdle before our dreams of a glass backboard could be fulfilled – that was a big order. Shelbyville had never beaten Valley.

From the opening whistle the fans could tell that the Devils had the determination to win, and they knew that they had the ability to back it up. Shelbyville led by a few points most of the game, but with 30 seconds to go, Valley rallied to take the lead by one point. At this point many of the fans thought that Shelbyville would crack under the strain, but we didn't. With just a few seconds remaining, in a beautifully executed play Buckner took a feed from Logan under the local basket and laid in a crip shot to win the game 48-47 as time expired. Deim led Shelbyville with 14 points. For the first time in the history of the school, Shelbyville had won the 8th Region tournament and had advanced to the state tournament at the old Armory building in Louisville.

The tournament ten included Deim, Mac Catlett, Buckner, Logan, Jimmie Mac Ratcliffe, Bill Green, Moesser, Humston, Martin, and Matthews. These boys edged out Pollard and Arthur Landers who were highly regarded by Coach Evan Settle.

Finally, out of this slow but sure elimination process, 16 teams survived out of more than 500 schools that began the tournament.

Our first game was played against a favored Garrett squad, but we played a good game and led all the way to win, 58-50. Buckner tallied 18, Logan 11, Deim 10 and Ratcliffe 10.

Then, unluckily, we had to face an unbeaten Brewers team that went on to win the state tournament. All you can say is that they had too much class for us and we were defeated 57-34. Deim and Catlett each scored 9.

(Editor's Note: This ends Logan's account.)

"Too much class" is a real understatement. Brewers ran over, around, and under us in taking command at the outset. The forwards had to help out the guards just to get the ball over the center line. We shot poorly, fouled too often, and found ourselves on the embarrassing short end of a 37-12 score at halftime.

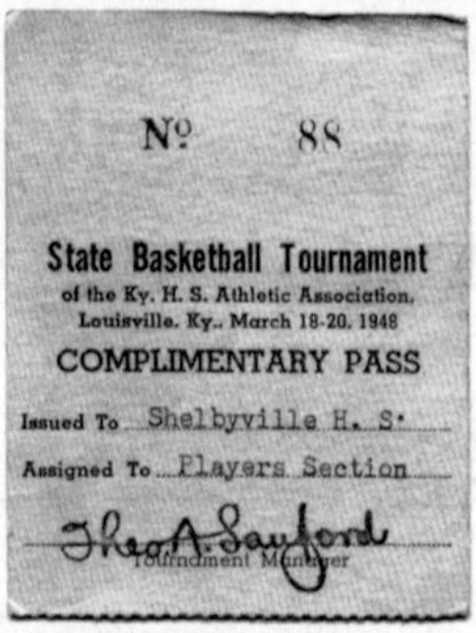
Nº 88

State Basketball Tournament
of the Ky. H. S. Athletic Association, Louisville, Ky., March 18-20, 1948

COMPLIMENTARY PASS

Issued To Shelbyville H. S.

Assigned To Players Section

Theo A. Sanford
Tournament Manager

BASKETBALL CHAMPIONS OF REGION 8

*(11) Johnny Buckner, *Forward*
*(10) Bill Matthews, *Center*
*(12) Bill Humston, *Guard*
*(2) James Martin, *Forward*
*(9) Bob Logan, *Forward*
Evan Settle, *Coach*
*(4) Mac Catlett, *Center*
*(8) Martin Deim, *Guard*
*(5) Jimmy Ratcliffe, *Guard*
*(3) Bill Green, *Guard*
*(6) Bo Moesser, *Forward*

*Asterisk before figures in parentheses denotes number on Jersey.

Coach Settle was fuming, putting it mildly, when we entered the dressing room at halftime. In unmistakable language, he inquired what we planned to do in the next half. I whispered to Bob Logan, "Let's freeze the ball." This would be a good way to hold down the final score, I thought.

Settle overheard me and was so furious that he aimed the basketball squarely at my head. At the last possible half-second, though, I realized what was coming so I ducked to the left fast. The ball hit the concrete wall and caromed right back, hitting the coach squarely in the gut. He was rendered speechless.

Getting together for one of Charles "Skippy" Connell's quarterly gatherings were several of Coach Settle's ex-basketball players, including, left to right, Martin Deim, Jimmy Lee, the "Skipper," Settle and me.

No one dared even smile, much less laugh. Yet, the incident seemed to relax the team and we went out and played a respectable half, losing 57-34, to a team that finished the season 36-0, and remains the last undefeated team in Kentucky High School basketball history. Of course, it helped that Brewers played mostly reserves against our first team in the second half. I had fouled out early.

I never played up to my potential (whatever that was), according to Settle. He started me at forward as a junior, but I couldn't seem to score, despite my brother Ben's loudly yelled admonitions to "shoot" whenever he came to a game.

My biggest embarrassment came my senior year when I first sampled champagne at the Lexington Country Club on a Friday night before a game in Shelbyville against Anchorage the following evening. I drank too much, and then, at Howard Logan's suggestion, I ate a hamburger in a local diner as we headed home.

I got violently ill during the night and all the next day as my mother gave me only dry toast and consommé.

This was during the busy holiday season and I was scheduled to attend a dance for a debutante in Louisville between 5 and 7 p.m. and return to Shelbyville in time for the Anchorage game. My mother, as usual, told me to "Drive carefully but don't be late."

If I had felt bad during the day, I felt even worse when I walked out (the other players ran) on the hardwood court.

Settle started me at center and I literally couldn't jump and, in fact, could barely get up on my toes. Needless to say I didn't last too long and I'll never forget Settle yelling "What the devil is wrong with you?" I could hardly tell him that I was "hung over."

I didn't start again until the Regional final against Valley. Settle gave me the unenviable job of guarding Valley's high scoring guard "Corky" Cox (who subsequently found national fame at the University of Louisville). I picked up three fouls in the first half and was a non-factor in our team's historic win that sent us to the school's first-ever state tournament.

Baseball Successes

Our baseball team had a successful spring 1948 season, winning 13 and losing 9 against a tough schedule including two-game series against St. X, Frankfort, Lexington Henry Clay, and Versailles high schools.

Our class Sports Editor Bob Logan sized up the players in the following terms: Sammy "Speedballer" Harrod on the mound; Bill "Trapper" Matthews, first base; "Smooth-fielding" Bo Moesser, second base; Bob "Slats" Morrison, shortstop; Martin "Slugger" Deim, third base; and "Dependable" Charles Ferguson, "Clever" Leslie Shuck, and "Versatile" Walter Gaines in the outfield.

While I may have been a "trapper" on defense, I wasn't much of a hitter, batting only .293 for the season.

Later that summer, I was named to the American Legion District All-Star team. We won the district when Martin Deim, in relief of Sammy Harrod, got the one batter he faced to line into a game-ending double play.

Try-out Camps

I went to three different baseball try-out camps – in Louisville, Lexington, and Owensboro. On all three occasions I survived the first day based on my fielding and speed, but couldn't survive the second day because of inadequate hitting. Of all the camps I attended, two sponsored by the Reds and one by the Cardinals, only one person was ever signed to a professional contract.

First Love

The "love bug," as they say, struck me in the summer of 1948. One of the highlights of the Shelby County Fair & Horse Show was the annual Hop Club Dance. The local Hop Club had been organized one year before the Civil War. It was the preeminent dance each year not only in Shelby County but in the entire Bluegrass Region. There were other Hop Clubs in Harrodsburg, Frankfort, Lexington, Louisville and Eminence, and members of those clubs always enjoyed blanket invitations to attend the Shelbyville affair. There were usually three dances a year, at Christmas time, in June, and another one at Fair time.

When the Hop Club started way-back-when, tails were the required dress for the men; then came tuxedos, and in the summertime, white dinner jackets. Later, Bermuda shorts, black or blue socks with madras jacket and matching cummerbund were allowed. For many years, Ben Staples stood guard at the door to make sure that the gentlemen were appropriately attired and didn't have any flasks in their back pockets.

As for the dances, there were six on a card, and each gentleman had the first and last dance with his date, and traded with another couple for the other dances. During Fair Week, the dance started at 11 p.m., and ended at 5 a.m.

The day before the Fair dance I was introduced to a young lady from Georgetown, Kentucky, who was staying with Judy Long, daughter of Mr. and Mrs. Charles B. Long. Her name was Martha Nell Blackburn. We took one look at each other while we were with mutual friends at Tucker's Lake near Middletown, and she accepted my invitation to attend the dance.

I had to arrange for a corsage quickly and the next night we were off to the dance at what is now called Settle Gym (formerly Shelbyville High School Gym).

The Fair was in July so we had barely enough time to get to know each other when she headed off to the University of Kentucky and me to University of Michigan. However, in those few weeks in July and August we became extremely close. It also helped that she had a pre-World War II white Lincoln Continental convertible.

We corresponded daily from September until I came home in December. Her efforts to teach me how to smoke fizzled, and in a few days we each realized that the flame had gone out.

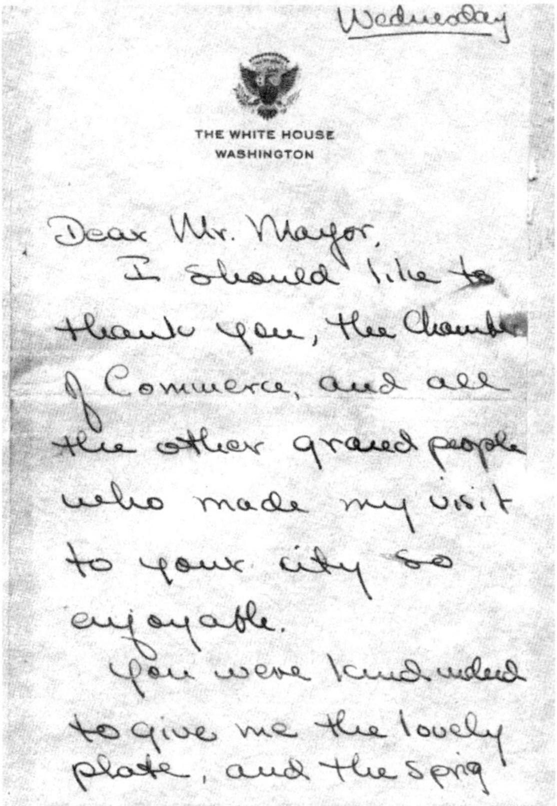

Wednesday

THE WHITE HOUSE
WASHINGTON

Dear Mr. Mayor,

I should like to thank you, the Chamber of Commerce, and all the other grand people who made my visit to your city so enjoyable.

You were kind indeed to give me the lovely plate, and the sprig

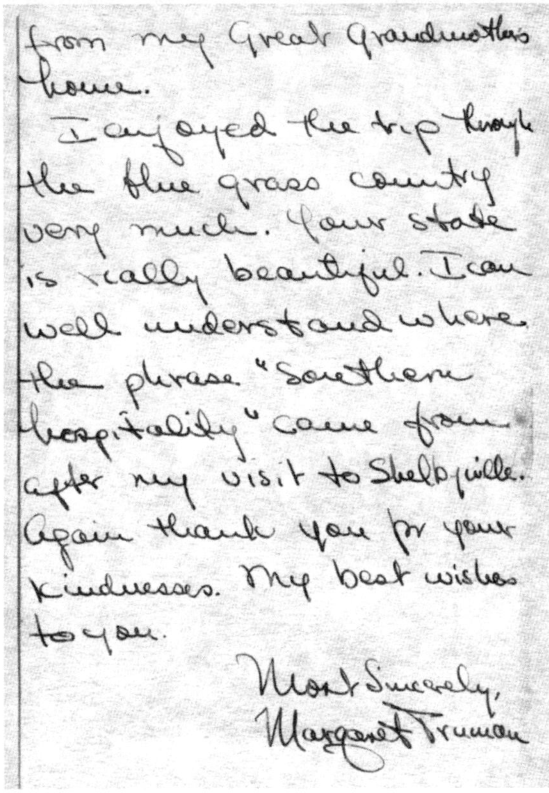

from my Great Grandmother's home.

I enjoyed the trip through the blue grass country very much. Your state is really beautiful. I can well understand where the phrase "Southern hospitality" came from after my visit to Shelbyville. Again thank you for your kindnesses. My best wishes to you.

Most Sincerely,
Margaret Truman

THE WHITE HOUSE
WASHINGTON

WASHINGTON
MAY 8
7-PM
1946

The Honorable Robert F. Matthews
Mayor of Shelbyville
Shelbyville
Kentucky

While I was in high school, in the spring of 1946, Margaret Truman, daughter of President Harry S. and Bess Truman, visited Shelbyville and traveled to Christiansburg to view the homes of both sets of her great-grandparents, who were married and lived here. This is a copy of a letter which she addressed to my father, then Shelbyville's mayor, upon her return to Washington, D.C.

Summertime jobs

Summertime and the working began

Although I had been carrying papers since I was 12, I knew it was time to get a real job when I turned 14 years old. I applied at Smith-McKenney in downtown Shelbyville for a job as a combination soda jerk-delivery boy and was hired. The pay was 50 cents an hour, which wasn't bad at the time. The highlight of each day was when we closed the store at 6 p.m., and I was given a free milk shake and tuna salad sandwich. A Mr. Hogg owned the store at that time, but he sold out to Charles Bradbury shortly thereafter.

Texaco Serviceman

When I turned 15, I accepted employment as a service station attendant at the Texaco station on U.S. 60, adjacent to the Fairgrounds. It was owned by Lewis Mathis Sr., and the manager was James "Perk" Perkins from Simpsonville.

My first day was memorable. "Perk" left me in charge while he went to lunch and almost immediately a motorist arrived and wanted a quart of oil. Since I didn't know where to put it, I told him that we had just run out. He said he had never heard of a service station without oil and I agreed. He drove on.

The next customer was a man who had a host of children in his run-down old car. He announced that he thought his engine was "missing" and would I please check it. After the oil incident, I no longer wanted to act dumb and told him I would check it out. So I grabbed a monkey wrench and a pair of pliers and lifted up the hood. Not realizing that the engine was still running, I grabbed hold of one of the sparkplugs. You might guess the rest. I got the shock of my life as I was lifted about a half-inch off the ground! Almost speechless, I cried out in a very shaky voice, "Everything's fine."

I quickly learned where to put the oil and by the end of the summer I had become the station's specialist at repairing tires. This was way before tubeless tires, so I learned how to patch the inner tubes that fit within each tire.

Funeral Home Attendant

The following year Johnny Buckner and I, now 16, started an odd jobs business, advertising in the two local papers that "no job was too big or too small." The problem was, of course, that we were ill-trained to fix either a big or small job. However, one thing we had plenty of was confidence. We worked either independently or together, but we pooled our income.

One of my jobs consisted of helping at the A.B. Weaver Funeral Home directly across the street from our house at 1108 West Main Street. The assignment I recall most vividly was helping Mrs. Weaver dress a five-year-old youngster who had been killed in a car crash. She gave me a $5 bill and asked me to purchase a sun suit for the little lad at the local J.J. Newberry Store. She and I worked together to prepare him for the services.

I drove a very old hearse and, following Mr. Weaver's directions, we eventually reached a modest little home somewhere in the hills around Hatton, which is about five miles from Bagdad. Because of the circumstances surrounding the youngster's passing, it was a particularly mournful service with a great deal of weeping. Following the service, I helped Mr. Weaver lower the small casket into a freshly-dug grave into the family cemetery.

Landscaping Disaster

Perhaps the most memorable job for the Buckner-Matthews business was an assignment to trim the approximately 60-foot long hedge that separated the Howard Pearce home on Magnolia Avenue from the next door neighbor. Johnny started at one end, and I the other end, but when we came together near the center an hour or so later, Johnny's portion was about two inches lower than mine. So we reversed course and started clipping away. One hour later, the hedge was still very uneven. Finally, we started working together and eventually got it aligned.

We were still admiring our work when Mrs. Pearce returned from Louisville. Upon getting out of her car, she took one look and exclaimed, "What happened to my hedge? I'm going to call your mothers!"

It turned out that our efforts had reduced her five-foot hedge to a three-foot hedge. But at least it was level. We did no more landscaping after that.

Driver Education

One of the more challenging jobs that I handled alone was driving a social welfare worker from the courthouse in Shelbyville to LaGrange three days a week. She was a rather nervous, timid soul who had never learned to drive. She did have a car at her disposal with a siren on it, however. Frequently I would turn the siren on when we were out in the countryside. Where the siren came from or how it came to be attached to the car was never made clear to me.

We struck up a nice relationship and the pay, $15.00 per day, was better than most of the jobs that Johnny and I had. We generally left the courthouse at 9 a.m. and took about 35 minutes to get to the courthouse in LaGrange where I generally had lunch with a distant relative of my father.

As my assignment drew toward the end, she asked me to teach her to drive. She had been watching me closely during the weeks in which we drove back and forth to LaGrange, and said she was ready to put her observations into practice.

So on my next-to-last day, we drove toward "Cozy Corner" on the Eminence Road and switched positions. I had explained to her that she had to let the clutch out very slowly as she put her foot down on the accelerator. She replied, "I've got it." But she didn't have it.

She let out the clutch much too fast, hit the accelerator and off we went. We easily cleared a ditch on the side of the road, and plowed into and through a farmer's fence before I could wrest control of the car. She collapsed.

The farmer whose fence we mangled had watched the entire action and quickly drove his tractor down to the scene. When I explained what happened, he laughed, and said he would fix the fence without cost to my errant driver or me. I recall his saying, "It was well worth watching."

Farm Equipment Guard

One of our more lucrative jobs consisted of "guarding" the farm equipment overnight during the Shelby County Fair. At that time, reflecting our county's strength as an agricultural leader in the state, each of the farm machinery dealers brought his equipment to the Fairgrounds where fair-goers could inspect it during the day and also during the show at night. Johnny and I were paid $15.00 per night to keep an eye on things. Our only visitors during the overnight hours were some carnival workers who kept us on edge with some hair-raising stories of mischief and murder. In retrospect, most were probably made-up yarns designed to frighten a couple of naïve teenagers.

Young Entrepreneurs

Probably our most creative effort at employment had to do with providing chairs to those who stood in the center of the amphitheater ring at the horse show during the fair. At that time, seating wasn't provided so we borrowed about 30 to 40 chairs from Shannon Funeral Home and charged 50 cents per night per chair.

The next year, however, the fair board decided we had too much of a good thing so the board took charge of the chairs and cut us out of the deal.

Poison Ivy

My biggest personal disaster came with our employment to harvest bluegrass seed. Not being much of a farm boy, I didn't bother to check what else was in the field beside bluegrass. It turned out the field was also covered with poison ivy so that within a few hours my body was covered from head to toe with an extremely virulent rash. The real pain and discomfort that followed sent me to bed with all sorts of antidotes. I learned my lesson, though, and have studiously avoided a repeat nightmare. I can spot a poison ivy leaf from a mile away.

First Newspaper Job

In the spring of 1949, while finishing my freshman year at Michigan, I wrote to Daniel and James (Buddy) O'Sullivan about working at *The Shelby Sentinel*. The longtime office manager, Miss Mabel Oats, responded in writing that no help was needed. However, I persisted and eventually landed a job at $5.00 per day to write some news, service the newsstands, and run the folding machine in the back shop.

By the end of the summer I was writing virtually all the news, started a sports section, collected the money from the newsstands, ran the folder, and became the paper's first-ever photographer.

This was long before what became known as the "offset" method of printing. The "letterpress" method of printing had been the standard since the invention of the linotype machine in 1884. Prior to that, printers "picked" type out of a type case. That meant picking up letters one by one to create words. It was hot, dirty, and smelly. Also, publishers were at the mercy of their well-trained employees in the back shop.

When the offset or cold type revolution came in the mid-to late-1950s, publishers were suddenly freed from the demands by their back shop because, suddenly, women were just as effective, if not more so, than the almost solidly corps of men who worked in the back shop. Whereas letterpress employees had to undergo substantial training, women could be employed with very little know-how. And women were a whole lot cheaper!

My first photographic assignment that summer was capturing the dedication of the new dam on Lake Shelby. Lake Shelby was Shelbyville's principal water source and did not give up this title for many years to come. I had to send my film to Lexington via Greyhound bus. It came back in the form of a metal engraving on a block of wood. I'm still proud of that first photo, although, later, I realized that it could have been better.

That summer of 1949 also found me writing my first printable story.

As my first assignment, Dan O'Sullivan decided on a series of articles about the various county communities, starting with Finchville. When I arrived in Finchville, I stopped first at the post office where Bill Robertson (later to find fame with country hams) was in charge. He chuckled when I apprised him of my assignment, noting that local folks were very leery of reporters and did not wish to see local happenings in print.

Bill was certainly right. I knocked on a lot of doors up and down the main (and only) street in the southwest community. A few residents opened their doors, however, being a working community, many doors remained closed. My best information came from chatting with shoppers and loafers at Riester's Store, probably the best known country store in Shelby County.

When my story appeared, not one word was heard from Finchville that indicated to me that either no one read the story or, if they did, they didn't want to lower themselves by commenting on it.

Writing stories on Bagdad, Waddy, Mount Eden, Simpsonville, Cropper, and Harrisonville was much easier. The people were far more accessible and far more talkative.

Page 36 photo: This is what the rundown *Shelby Sentinel* building at 418 Main Street looked like when I bought it in the spring of 1962.

Michigan college and courtships

Michigan Wins

Even though my father had attended the University of Michigan, my older brothers did not follow in his footsteps. They headed south: Robert F. Jr. (William & Mary undergraduate and University of Virginia for his law degree) and Ben G. (University of Virginia for two semesters, and the University of Louisville for his undergraduate and law degree).

My ID card from my sophomore year at the University of Michigan.

I wanted to follow in their footsteps. However, since my father indicated he would be sending his check to Ann Arbor, I decided that I should go where the check was going. So in September 1948, I began a four-year long adventure at the University of Michigan.

Unknown Illness

About a week before I was due to leave, in late August, I became ill with a serious rash. Mother and local doctor Harmon Nash treated me for impetigo. When I began to blister badly on my forehead and the headaches grew more intense, Mother decided I needed to see a specialist.

That specialist was a Dr. Mapother, one of Louisville's best-known dermatologists. He gave me an injection and a prescription, then sent me home. He prescribed rest and said he would see me back in one week.

I never saw Dr. Mapother again. My mother, not realizing the seriousness of my disease, decided against further treatment and joined my father in putting me on the B & O for Detroit on Saturday night.

From Detroit, I caught a local train to Ann Arbor and arrived there on September 1, ready for school.

However, upon checking into my room in the West Quadrangle, the counselor noticed my very inflamed forehead and sent me to the hospital. It was there that my mother found me three days later and asked, "What's wrong with you?"

I had contracted a case of the shingles, which is rare for a teenager and an ailment about which my mother was not familiar when I first became ill. Several years previously, though, it caused the loss of an eye to a Mrs. Lawrence, wife of one of Shelbyville's leading physicians. In time, my shingles abated, although, to this day, I still have tiny pock marks on my forehead as a reminder of that awful attack in 1948.

Hitting the Books

I shared a room at Michigan with two other lads, Chuck Stanulus from Detroit, Mich., and Doug Mikolasek from Menominee Falls, Mich. Both were in engineering school. At that time the main campus in Ann Arbor was home to nearly 35,000 students; today it accommodates 45,000. Chuck and Doug were gone by the end of the first semester, having flunked out because of their inability to master freshman English.

I well remember my first class at Michigan, an English class taught by W.R. Steinhoff. At 8 a.m. on opening day he arrived, may have said "Hello," and wrote out five topics on the blackboard. All were obscure including, "What was the principal outcome of the Peloponnesian War?" Another was "How is war beneficial?" Still another was "What were two significant advances in physics in the past five years?" The other two were equally difficult for me after hearing our assignment to write an essay on one of the five and return it to Mr. Steinhoff at the end of the one-hour class.

Not only was I stumped at which one to choose, but, thankfully, everyone else in the class was stumped as well. Finally, I selected "How is war beneficial?" and wrote about 300 to 400 words on the many medical advances that World War II had witnessed, including the use of the sulfa drugs and the first use of penicillin. I also touched on several of the technological changes that had come about along with the role women had played on the home front.

A few days later Mr. Steinhoff asked for a "Mr. Matthews" to join him in his office at the end of his class day.

That afternoon, full of trepidation, I walked into Mr. Steinhoff's office. He first asked, "Did you take English in high school?" After I had answered "Yes," he continued, "Where did you go to high school?" When I said "Shelbyville, Kentucky," he smiled and said, "That doesn't surprise me."

My paper that he returned was so full of marks that I was barely able to read what I had originally written. There were red marks, question marks, and other sorts of marks.

After mildly berating me for various grammatical missteps, he eventually said, "Actually, your paper was better than most. At least you wrote about something which you had either read about or learned. Many of the students picked a subject on which they were either poorly informed or just ignorant."

"I do think there's some hope for you," he continued, "but be aware of too many commas and please cut down on the hyperbole."

I wound up getting a B in English 31, and another B in a second English course the following semester that Mr. Steinhoff also taught.

I didn't see Mr. Steinhoff again until my senior year when I took a course in creative writing that he taught. There were only 12 in the class which, for U of M, was a remarkably small class considering the thousands of students enrolled on the main campus at that time.

In writing an original story I recall describing one of the characters as "red-headed." When I got my paper back, it had this notation, "I've never seen a 'red-headed' boy. I assume you meant 'red-haired'." Of course, he was right.

All things considered, especially since I had had a severe case of shingles at the outset, my first semester went well with 2 As, 2 Bs, and 1 C (political science).

Historical Blind Date

It was during that first semester that I met the girl who was to eventually become my wife.

Else Jorgensen had been in the same class at Redford High School as my roommate, Chuck Stanulus. Her photo in his senior class yearbook was certainly attractive and so I asked about her. "Better stay away," he said, "We called her 'grandmother'." When I asked why, he retorted, "Too cold. You can't get anywhere with her."

Naturally, his remark presented a challenge, so he arranged a "blind date" with his onetime schoolmate.

It was on October 14 that we met at Drake's, a local coffee shop and short-order restaurant. I was recovering from shingles so I wasn't a pretty sight, but I was so impressed with my date that I asked her out again.

The day before we were scheduled to go out, she telephoned Chuck and told him that she was too busy to go out with "Bill Marshall."

That made the challenge even greater since she hadn't even remembered my name. Now, all these years later, I apparently met the challenge. We were married Friday, June 13, 1952, in Martha-Mary Chapel in Greenfield Village, Dearborn, Mich.

However, our relationship during our Michigan years was anything but harmonious. After dating constantly during our freshman year, we decided early on during our sophomore years to date others. In fact, Else fixed me up with one of her dormitory acquaintances and we were getting along quite well when Else called to tell me that I should drop the girl because she was "too fast." Naturally that suited me just fine, but, in time, I realized that we didn't have too much in common, so I returned to Else.

Athletics, Academics, Artillery

I went out for baseball in the spring of 1949 and, to my great surprise, I made the freshman baseball team and have a sweater to prove it. I realized early on that my ability to play baseball at the Big 10 level was lacking. After a brief fling in the batting cage in the spring of 1950, I realized that I would never be able to hit a Big League curveball and promptly retired.

Academically, my sophomore year went well enough, and little did I realize how much my decision to join ROTC was going to affect my years at Michigan. Actually I had joined in my freshman year, but that was more of an orientation program and we didn't get serious about training until my sophomore year.

On June 30, 1950, North Korea attacked South Korea and succeeded in almost overrunning the peninsula before the United Nations, spearheaded by the United States, stopped the invasion and began a counterattack.

Brother Ben's Marriage

That same weekend in 1950 my middle brother Ben married Jean Blair Lee of Richmond, Va., and I was fortunate enough to serve as Best Man. Following the wedding in St. Stephens' Church, the reception was held at the home of Jean's aunt, Lelia Northrup, at her estate called Norcroft. Aunt Lelia had been widowed early in her marriage in the early 1900s when a new car that Mr. Northrup had purchased ran over him in a tragic accident.

Jean's brother, Blair, had put a big black snake in Ben's Studebaker that we thought he would be taking on his honeymoon. Sometime during the afternoon, Ben persuaded my mother to let him take her car and leave the Studebaker for me to drive back to Shelbyville.

Needless to say the trip home was nerve-wracking for me because I never knew when the snake might appear. What caused me even more concern was the fact that I was transporting three of my mother's best friends – Josephine Long, Natalie Nash, and Mary Pearce – along the way.

Fortunately, the snake kept to itself and upon our return I took the Studebaker to Pearce Motor where my good friend Jack Pearce dislodged the reptile from his hiding place.

Where the Girls Are

My junior year at Michigan was uneventful except for the number of girls I dated as Else and I drifted apart and she actually encouraged me to see others. That Christmas, I brought three of my fraternity brothers – Tom Sawyer, Bob Isaacson, and Dick Lee – home to Kentucky for the holidays. They had never been exposed to such a vigorous social scene as we travelled from Shelbyville to the Lexington Country Club and then to the Louisville Country Club along with the Pendennis Club.

I courted a young lady named Mary McDowell Van Meter during the holidays and, later, in early February, accompanied her on the train from Lexington to Ann Arbor for the big dance of the year called the J-Hop. The orchestra for the occasion was Les Brown's "Band of Renown."

The reason we were forced to take the train was a big snowfall brought more than a foot of snow to the Bluegrass State and made driving very hazardous.

Lessons in Diversity

When we boarded the train in Lexington, we got into a car with some Negroes. This prompted Mary McDowell to comment that "we are in the wrong car." So I had to explain that the train was not segregated and that we had to sit with any and all who boarded it. She was adamant that we find a "whites only" car, which we did, and off we went to Ann Arbor.

Mary McDowell later married and divorced prominent Lexingtonian Hilary Boone.

In thinking about that incident, I am reminded at how bewildered, if not shocked, I was by my first real experience with diversity in Michigan. On weekend nights particularly, boys and girls gathered near the dorm entrances before they closed at 10:30 (midnight on the weekends) and did a lot of hugging and kissing. That was fine with me except I noticed that white boys were snuggling black girls, and black boys were kissing white girls. No one seemed to care or even notice.

The president of the senior class at Michigan in my freshman year, 1948-1949, was a black man, Val Johnson, who lived in my dormitory. He realized that I also couldn't believe a black man was president of the senior class. In time, we became great friends, and I began to realize just how different the world was outside Shelbyville.

Drinking Dilemma

On April 30, 1951, I turned 21, which in Michigan made me legally able to drink alcohol. I was contemplating how I was going to celebrate the occasion when my parents walked into the Delta Tau Delta house at 1928 Geddes Avenue. This was the first and only time they visited me in Ann Arbor and we made quite a day of it with lunch at the Delt house and dinner later at a local restaurant. Even later we adjourned to Rice's, a local hole-in-the-wall, where the three of us, with several of the "brothers" in tow, enjoyed several rounds of beer.

What made the day particularly noteworthy is that my mother asked me what had become of "that cute Else Jorgensen?" She said it would be nice to say hello to her. She remembered Else from the spring of 1949 when she had accompanied me to Shelbyville during spring break.

That get-together with Else signaled what eventually turned out to be a turning point in my life because it led to my asking her to be my date for the spring formal at the Delt house. At the time I was dating a girl by the name of Nancy Hilton rather seriously, but, as it turned out, not that seriously.

The spring formal came and I, as well as the other "brothers," had a good deal to drink so in the course of some rather torrid dancing I asked Else if she would be interested in my fraternity pin. When she said "Yes," I was faced with a dilemma because I had already given it to Nancy.

When I told Else I thought my pin had gone to the laundry, she gave me an ultimatum: Either she received the pin by dormitory closing time of 10 o'clock on Monday night (the dance was two days earlier) or I could quit calling her … forever. Her exact words were (to the best of my recollection): "I have fooled around with you for almost three years and you can either pin me or forget it. And I mean it."

This put me into quite a situation because I knew it would be difficult to get my pin back from Nancy and, yet, I knew Else was dead serious. So all day Sunday and Monday I debated whether she really meant it and, if so, what did I do about it.

Finally, I asked my roommate Dick Lee if I could borrow his pin "for a few days," and I made it to the dormitory with just a few minutes to spare. So I was now pinned to two girls.

Trying to explain the situation to Nancy proved rather difficult and, in fact, several of her sorority members appeared surreptitiously at the Theta house where I serenaded Else, with the traditional Delt love song.

Nancy ultimately forgave me (I think) and married the captain of the U of M wrestling team. He was later killed in a commercial plane crash.

So ended my spring of 1951 at the University of Michigan.

ROTC was 'Arresting'

That summer I headed to Fort Lee, Va., near Richmond, for ROTC training. The Korean War was in full swing and many of us who were in the Quartermaster Corps were switched involuntarily over to the infantry side. Infantry 2nd Lieutenants were in much greater demand in Korea than Quartermaster officers.

I drove from Shelbyville to Fort Lee in a 1937 Plymouth that a fraternity brother of mine, John Purvis, and I had bought for $200 during our junior year. I drove the car from Ann Arbor to Shelbyville and, after a few days with my parents, continued on to Fort Lee.

The trip was a nightmare as the engine kept heating up and the radiator kept boiling over. I nursed the car through the mountains, finally easing into Lexington, Va., where, miraculously enough, I found a radiator repair shop open on a Saturday afternoon. The owner flushed out the radiator, put in a new hose and sent me on my way.

The training at Fort Lee was intensive. I learned to shoot handguns, the M-1 rifle, and the Thompson sub-machine gun. It was up at 5 in the morning and to bed by 10 that night.

However, it wasn't all work and no play, and, in fact, one of my escapades led to my arrest, the first and only such incident in my life.

My brother Ben's wife, Jean, had a lovely group of friends whom she had left behind when she married Ben in the summer of 1950, and it was my good fortune to date one of them, Margaret Will. Working all day at Fort Lee and whipping into Richmond at night left little room for sleep, though.

Incidentally, Margaret's mother was a Sauer, as in the C.F. Sauer Company, which got its start in 1887 and is still operating today at 1911 West Broad Street in Richmond.

Margaret was a beautiful red-haired young lady, full of life, and interested in marriage. In addition to her parents' beautiful home in Richmond, they had a home on the Rehoboth

River. It was there that Margaret one night told me that, if I married her, I would never have to lift anything heavier than a teacup. The only problem, I told Margaret, was that I didn't love her. She retorted, "That's no problem." I have to confess that I was halfway tempted at the time to accept her offer but, technically, I was pinned to Else, and I had better let things cool.

One night while returning home from a date with Margaret, I was stopped just outside Petersburg, Va., by a deputy sheriff who accused me of speeding. He only issued a warning and said not to come back to that locale.

When I got back to the base and reported the incident, I was informed that I was "lucky," because, as everyone but me seemed to know, Petersburg operated a speed trap.

The very next night I was off to Richmond and, in the course of the evening, had an extra drink and got a late start for the base. Now there was a route around Petersburg that many of the troops took to avoid the speed trap but it took an extra 20 minutes.

Checking my watch I realized that I was way past curfew and the only option was to take the Petersburg route. Bad decision!

Just before I got to Petersburg, all hell broke loose with a couple of sheriffs' cars and a City of Petersburg police car. There were all sorts of lights and sirens as I was forced over to the side of the road.

Three officers jumped out, guns in hand, and told me to get out of the car. One of them said that a Greyhound bus driver had stopped to tell them a dirty, brown, old Plymouth was weaving all over the road.

I complied with the officer's directions but then made a bad mistake. Even before the officer spoke I said something to the effect that "you fellows are operating a speed trap."

Whereupon the officer said, "You're drunk and under arrest."

He put me in the back of his car and drove us away until we turned down a dark street and pulled up before a small frame house in a suburb of Petersburg. We went in through the basement of the house whereupon a local judge of some sort greeted me and put me in a room and locked the door.

About three hours later, well after midnight, the judge opened the door and asked me how much money I had on me. I had little money but I did have a Shelby County Trust & Banking Company check. He directed me to write a check for $125.00 that he considered my bail and directed me to appear in his court about 10 days hence. He also counseled me that, except for my court appearance, to "never come into Petersburg again, drunk or sober," or I would pay a stiff price. He said he was only letting me go because of the uniform that I had on and the fact that the nation was at war and might need my services.

Repentant at last, I got into the Plymouth and got back to Fort Lee as the sun was rising.

Marriage - Yes or Later

Two longtime fraternity brothers, Tom Sawyer and Barry Dunne, rented a basement apartment with me just off campus when I started my final year at Michigan in September 1951. We called it "Pine Manor" because the principal room was paneled in pine. Otherwise it was barely livable. Our single beds were in a combination kitchen-bedroom and we had to walk down a short unheated corridor to reach the shower. Tom had started medical school.

To earn money to buy a wedding ring for Else, I took a job working in the main university library. I was later promoted to the natural history library where three days a week I was the only person on duty in the reference library. Over the course of the year I earned about $800.

Academically, my senior year was more of a negative than a positive. Because of my job, and my attention to Else, I slipped somewhat in my grades. Living in Pine Manor also offered a daily temptation to skip classes.

That Christmas Day of 1951, Else and I became officially engaged. She took the B & O from Detroit to Cincinnati and I picked her up there and brought her to Shelbyville. I gave her a diamond ring as we sat on the couch and opened Christmas presents. The ring, slightly more than one carat, had cost about $900 and had been purchased through a diamond dealer friend of a family member.

We had scheduled an engagement party on New Year's Eve but, only hours before the party was to begin, Granddad Matthews was found dead in his apartment that was located across the street from our home. The discovery was made by George Lane who lived with my grandfather and was later to enjoy a very successful banking career. At the time he was employed by the Shelby County Trust & Banking Company.

Else and I returned to Ann Arbor by train to finish our senior years.

Spring 1952 ran by swiftly, and I became depressed over the idea of marriage and giving up my freedom. I was also depressed over the idea of going into the U.S. Army and undoubtedly heading for Korea where war was now raging. In April, I suggested postponing the ceremony but Else maintained that "The invitations have gone out and you will have to deal with my mother."

Else's mother, Ellen Jorgensen, and I had never hit it off, and she favored her daughter's marrying someone with a supposedly brighter future and definitely more conventional behavior.

Saying 'I Do'

The day of the wedding – Friday, June 13, 1952 – is still very vivid in my mind. One reason has to do with my spending most of the day drinking with various sea captains and crew members whose ships were docked in the Detroit harbor. When I told them of my plans to marry, I was rewarded with many stories about awful things that happened on Friday, the 13th. The more they talked, the more I drank, so that when I finally got back to our hotel, The Dearborn Inn, to prepare for the ceremony I was slightly inebriated and red-faced. My mother's first words were, "Where have you been? It's 6:40 and the ceremony is 50 minutes away." Needless to say she was upset. No… angry would be a better word. It was the first and only time that I can recall my mother being downright mad at me.

We got to the church on time and I chatted with my best man, Brother Ben, about the upcoming event. After telling him that I was depressed, he responded, "William, don't worry about it. You may be depressed now, but you'll get over it in six months."

The ceremony began in the Martha-Mary Chapel at the Henry Ford Museum in Dearborn and after a brief organ number, Else came out of a room at the back of the church and, just at the top of the center aisle, I vividly remember she came to a complete stop. When I asked her later why she stopped, she said, "I looked down the aisle where you and Ben were standing and you were so red-faced I knew what you had been doing. But I realized the ceremony had to go on so I started up again."

So we were pronounced man and wife on Friday, June 13, and left the next morning for our honeymoon at Sea Island Resort, Ga.

The ocean was great, the food even greater, but we both became very ill. So instead of a seven-day stay, we cut it to five days and, still under the weather, we headed back to Shelbyville.

Serving Uncle Sam

I reported to Fort Lee, Va. on August 1, 1952 as a freshly-commissioned 2nd Lieutenant in the U.S. Army. The news from Korea for 2nd Lieutenants was not good. The casualty rate was inordinately high and, according to rumors, several had been shot in the back by their own men (this would occur even more frequently during the Vietnam War). I had been commissioned in the quartermaster corps. Apparently, the army needed infantry lieutenants more than they needed quartermaster lieutenants, so I was immediately transferred to the infantry.

Providence appeared during the second week at Fort Lee, when a recruiter for the Central Intelligence Agency appeared one day and inquired, while we were in formation, whether anyone there was interested in joining the CIA. It took me only a few seconds to decide that the agency had to be a better bet than Korea. My commanding officers, Captain Conte and Major Fragala, took a dim view of my decision to leave the army after just a few days of active service. Both had already served one term of service in Korea and both were headed back.

So, after only 19 days of active service, I received an honorable discharge and headed back to Shelbyville.

Working While Waiting

Because I was advised that a security clearance could take up to six months, I decided to look for a job and found one, almost immediately, with the State of Kentucky Health Department, the publications division located on Third Street in Louisville.

Sara Stice, director of publications for the health department, named me an editorial assistant and put me in charge of producing a quarterly booklet telling all the good things that were happening in health departments across the state.

She was a great boss, an even better editor, and the months between July and December rolled by quickly.

Duty Calls

About the first of December, I received a letter from the agency giving me a start date of the first Monday in January 1953. So it was that we spent the Christmas of 1952 at home prior to leaving for Washington, D.C. on New Year's Day 1953. I knew little about the CIA, which was in its infancy. But, at least, I was employed.

Central Intelligence Agency

Inside the CIA

We arrived in Washington in early 1953 to start my role with the Central Intelligence Agency and immediately took up residency in the basement of my Uncle Edmund Baxter's home in Silver Springs, Maryland. We stayed there for about three months until we found a suitable apartment at Barcroft Apartments in northern Virginia.

The agency at that time had its headquarters at 2430 E Street and it was there that I reported for duty. The first order of business was to be fingerprinted and take a lie detector test. I was then assigned to the Foreign Broadcast Information Service (FBIS), an ouvert part of the agency.

The National Security Act of 1947 established the CIA, a successor to World War II's Office of Strategic Services (OSS). The act declared that the CIA (hereafter referred to as agency or company) was to have "No police or law enforcement functions, either at home or abroad."

The agency is now located in the George Bush Center for Intelligence at Langley, Virginia. While it has an estimated 20,000 employees and a budget of around $14.7 billion, the actual numbers are classified.

Monitoring Stations

FBIS has as its primary function the monitoring of foreign radio broadcasts and the analysis of foreign language publications. At the time I joined the agency, the primary target for our monitoring and press scrutiny operations was the Soviet Bloc that included the USSR, Poland, Bulgaria, Czechoslovakia, Romania, and Albania. Monitoring stations were located all around the world and included Reseda (California), London, Vienna, Saigon, Cyprus, and Okinawa. After I left the agency more than 10 years later, additional monitoring stations had been established in West Africa, the east coast, and other locations.

The purpose of the monitoring was to establish what kind of intelligence could be gleaned from this information, but, more important, to determine what kind of propaganda was being fed to the people who lived in communist nations all around the world. The agency had highly trained foreign nationals, as well as Americans, who translated the broadcasts into English and transmitted them back to the U.S. We did not monitor the radio broadcasts of those countries, large and small, which were deemed pro-Western.

When I joined the agency, anti-communist hysteria was at its height, and, one year later, the Joseph McCarthy hearings in Washington would keep virtually everyone in the D.C. area tuned to their TVs.

The Korean War was winding down, but a truce had not yet been signed. Dwight Eisenhower took office for the first of his two presidential terms at the same time I took my oath to the agency. I worked in several sections – Far East, Middle East, and Latin America – during the next three years.

At the same time, in our need for extra money to help meet our expenses, I took a part-time job at the National Education Association and the Senior Citizens of America. So, from the spring of 1953 to the late fall of 1955, I worked for both the agency and SCA. My starting salary as a GS-5 was $2,840 and after six months I was promoted to GS-7 at a salary of $3,400.

The spring of 1953 saw the winding down of the Korean War, with a truce being signed on July 27. Also in 1953 the United States developed and tested a hydrogen bomb, and Soviet dictator Josef Stalin died. And, years later, the CIA acknowledged its role, along with that of the British Intelligence Service (MI6), in deposing the democratically-elected premier of Iraq, Mossadeque, and installing the Shah on the throne.

1954 was significant because school segregation was deemed unconstitutional by the U.S. Supreme Court, the first kidney transplant was made, and Mao Tso-Tung was elected to lead the People's Republic of China.

In 1955 Germany became a full member of NATO, the first McDonald's restaurant opened in California, and Disneyland became the first major theme park to begin operating.

The years from 1953 to 1955 were marked by increasing anti-communist hysteria, headlined by the McCarthy-U.S. Army hearings in early 1954.

Our first child, Lisa Gaines Matthews, was born on October 18, 1954 as Hurricane Hazel was winding down from 13 days of devastation beginning in Haiti and ending in Toronto, Canada. Else began having severe contractions in early afternoon and I was summoned home from the office to escort her to the New Woman's Hospital in the District of Columbia. Before we could leave our apartment, I had to vacuum both upstairs and down because, as Else put it, "My mother is coming to help and I don't want a dirty house to greet her."

I dropped her off at the hospital and headed to the CIA office, located on the waterfront of the Potomac River. Two hours later I received a call from the hospital saying that I was a new father. Blue-eyed Lisa was already straining to get a look at the world when I reached the hospital. Still slightly drugged, Else told me, "Bill they have given me the wrong baby. It's a girl and I wanted a boy." A few days later she didn't remember what she had said and Lisa gave every indication that she was just right for us.

Hard at Work

I worked seven days a week, five days at the agency (off Saturday and Sunday) and five days at SCA (off Tuesday and Wednesday).

My final stint before going overseas was working on what was known as the B-Wire, where reports from all our monitoring stations all over the world were transmitting breaking news to us. The B-Wire editor's job was to place the teletypes in the right slots according to geographic location. This was well before the Vietnam War, but I recall working on the B-Wire when the report came in that those French soldiers who were left had surrendered at Dien Bien Phu in May 1954. According to the Geneva Accord, the communists-nationalists, the Viet Minh, territory north of the 17th parallel, and anti-communist forces were given the southern half of the country which still had an emperor, Bao Dai.

During this period I turned down an opportunity to go to Cyprus where FBIS maintained a particularly strong monitoring station. I knew that Vienna, Austria, would be coming up in early 1956 and I politicked for what everyone knew was a choice assignment. Fortunately I had the eye of Alan Warfield, chief of FBIS.

In late 1955 I had surgery to correct a medical condition, a pilonidal cyst, which I had lived with for a number of years.

I got word, in January 1956, that I was being posted to Vienna, making Else and my dream come true. Our operation there consisted of only three people, since it was one of the smallest FBIS stations.

We traveled to Vienna via London on a four-engine, piston-driven Trans World Airline flight that had great food and beds in which to sleep. The flight to London took 15 hours compared to the 7 hours that it takes to make the same flight today.

We were housed in the Red Lion Inn in Henley-on-the-Thames and during the day I visited with and worked at our FBIS station in London, one of our biggest and busiest stations. Our operation was housed in the same building as the BBC.

The Crabbe Affair

It was in April 1956, shortly after we had arrived in England, that what became known as the "Buster Crabbe Affair" occurred. Popular accounts indicate MI6, the British intelligence service, recruited World War II naval hero and decorated diver Crabbe to attach a listening device to the Soviet battle cruiser *Ordzhonikidze*. It had brought Soviet leaders Nikita Khrushchev and Nikolai Bulganin to London for a major diplomatic conference. Apparently the mission failed because Crabbe disappeared during the night of April 19, and the Soviet government announced that a British diver had been caught snooping around the Soviet ship.

Commander Crabbe's body was never found, a greatly embarrassed British government denied that he had been retained for such work, and the diplomatic mission failed. Years later, a Soviet diver said that he had intercepted Crabbe and stabbed him to death.

Off to Vienna

We spent two weeks in England and then flew to Vienna aboard British European Airways (BEA). After several weeks in the Regina Hotel, we were situated in a very nice two-bedroom apartment at 18 Wallreissgasse which, by Viennese standards, was huge.

I replaced a man by the name of Jack Vanderpol. Our station was located at the end of the streetcar line in a mansion-like building at 19 Poetzlinedorf. The location had been picked because of its relatively high elevation, which made radio monitoring somewhat easier than if we had been located on lower ground.

The station chief was 67-year-old Fred Brace who would make James Bond look like a sissy. A real life hero, Fred had lied about his age and saw his First World War I action as an ambulance driver on the Albanian front. He traveled the world between the two big wars, and then served in the OSS during World War II. He was about 6' 4", balding with mustache, still handsome and statuesque in appearance, and an ever charming ladies' man. Most weekends he slipped off to Salzburg to romance some young lady (by young I mean 40 years younger). Girls of all ages were attracted to Fred because he was a smooth dancer, a gentleman at all times, and one who could upstage anyone with an account of some daring action during either of the great wars.

Else and I, plus Lisa, our first born, settled into a comfortable routine in Vienna that included a full-time cook-maid, lots of embassy parties, and plenty of tennis. One of our regularly scheduled weekly matches involved the U.S. Ambassador to Austria, Harold

Mathews (no relation). The highest ranking ambassador in the U.S. Foreign Service, this was to be his last post prior to retirement.

I had been there only a few weeks when on a late Friday afternoon (Fred had already slipped away for the weekend), Russ Langelle called me from the embassy security office to tell me that we would have to fire three of our modest total of 10 employees. The reason: all three had falsified their applications for employment. Richard Jelinek and Herwig Schuler were, or had been, Nazis, and Helmut Scheffler was a Luftwaffe pilot, having participated in the invasion of Crete, Norway, and the Soviet Union.

"Hell no!" exclaimed Fred. "We're not firing anybody. The Nazis are on our side now, and Scheffler is our best radio maintenance man."

Because State Department security had no jurisdiction over CIA employees, no one got fired, and as far as I know, all retired with generous pensions from the U.S. Government.

Richard Jelinek, left, and Helmut Scheffler, right, joined Else and me on Thanksgiving Day in 1957 at our apartment at 72 Wallriessgasse.

Several of our FBIS staff gathered outside our operation a 19 Poetzleindorf in Vienna. In the front row are Fritz Niederhoffer, Vlado Korbanoff, and unidentified; second row; Bureau Chief Jerrold Brown, Herwig Schuler, Otto Gutmensch, Ferdi Klassman, Herbert Galton, and Deputy Bureau Chief Bill Matthews.

Our much diversified staff included:

Fritz Niederhoffer, Romanian, who was chief of the foreign language section, responsible for the output of all of our foreign nationals. His wife, Coco, was the daughter of the physician who tended to Romania's last king prior to the start of World War II. She and Fritz, both Jewish, had gotten out of Bucharest just hours to spare before the Nazis took over in 1940. They fled the new dictatorship for Cyprus with only the clothes on their backs and what they could carry in a Persian rug. He translated Romanian into English.

Vlado Korbanoff, Bulgarian, wanted by both the Nazis and the Communists at the end of the war. Vlado had earned his living during the war as a "double agent." He translated Bulgarian and Russian into English

Herbert Galton, Polish, whose immediate family and his wife's family had all been "gassed" at Auschwitz concentration camp. Herbert, himself, had had his life saved by a family relative who paid to have him released. He translated both Russian and Polish into English.

Otto Gutmensch, Czech, who had fled Czechoslovakia shortly before the Nazis crossed the border in 1938. He translated Czech into English.

Herwig Schuler, Austrian, who translated German into English.

Helmut Scheffler, Austrian, who maintained the equipment.

Ferdi Klassman, Austrian, who translated German into English.

Richard Jelinek, Austrian, who translated German and Czech into English.

Helen Counts, Austrian, who translated Romanian into English.

Tomas Mezei, Hungarian, who had served in the last Democratically-elected legislature prior to Hungary's alliance with Nazi German. He translated Hungarian into English.

We also had an office manager and three female operators who teletyped the translated material back to Washington.

This Russian tank was destroyed during the Hungarian Revolution.

Hungarian Revolution

All seemed too quiet, if not perfect, until one afternoon in October 1956 when all hell broke loose in Budapest, Hungary, one of the seemingly staunchest communist capitals in Eastern Europe.

Joseph Stalin died on March 5, 1953, and almost immediately cries were heard throughout the Soviet bloc for a more liberalized treatment of people in Poland, Hungary, Romania, Bulgaria, and Czechoslovakia, and even in the Soviet Union itself. In Hungary in March 1955, Imre Nagy, a more independent communist leader in the vein of Marshal Tito of

Yugoslavia, became Prime Minister and soon distanced himself from the hard-line policies of his predecessor Matyas Rakosi. But Nagy's reforms went too far for the Moscow-dominated puppet state and in February 1956, Rakosi returned to power, ousting Nagy.

The reformers grew even bolder in March 1956 when Soviet leader Nikita Khrushchev gave a "secret speech" (to party insiders only) denouncing Stalin's short-sighted politics during his murderous reign of more than 30 years. This provided a signal that Eastern European governments could experiment with modest social reforms. The Poles and the Hungarians were suddenly in the forefront of demonstrations seeking more freedom for their people.

In June of that year, 50,000 Polish citizens demonstrated against the communists. Their efforts were squelched by the Soviet and Polish armies. Many died, hundreds were wounded.

In Hungary, students began demonstrating at the various universities, criticizing the Rakosi government for its restrictive policies. They wanted Nagy returned to power and among their demands were: (1) Formation of a multi-party system; (2) Free elections; (3) Dissolution of Hungary's AVO State Security Agents; (4) The withdrawal of Soviet troops; and (5) Hungary's withdrawal from the Warsaw Pact (an alliance of Moscow and Eastern European countries).

So the stage was set for the violence that shattered the world on October 23, 1956. On that date, students at Budapest Technical University started a peaceful march to show their support for the Poles, to demonstrate that Hungary wanted to be politically and economically independent, and to end the Soviet occupation.

In the afternoon, the students – joined by workers, writers groups, and plain citizens – tore down the massive Stalin statue. They planted the Hungarian flag in what remained of Stalin's boots, and the head fell to the ground.

Meanwhile, in Vienna, our Hungarian-to-English translator picked up the first broadcasts by a group calling itself the "Hungarian Freedom Fighters." Word was flashed to Washington and the next few days turned into an around-the-clock monitoring ordeal for our small staff.

All sorts of "free Hungary" radio stations began transmitting messages, advising listeners of progress and problems in dealing with Soviet troops and sympathizers.

AVO secret police fired at the freedom fighters and a riot followed with many killed and wounded on both sides. The Hungarian Communist Government asked for the Soviet army, which was stationed in Budapest under the Warsaw Pact, to help restore order. Khrushchev was hesitant to use military force, but, eventually, he sent Russian tanks into the capital.

The Hungarian people were more defiant than ever, and began to destroy Soviet tanks with their home-made "Molotov cocktails" (hand grenades).

All over Hungary, Revolutionary Workers Councils were formed and there was a call for a general strike. Soviet war memorials and other manifestations of communism were turned into rubble. Communist symbols, books and files were burned.

Revenge was exacted on AVO agents and Soviet-aligned sympathizers. Many were tortured to death. A particularly chilling form of torture was to insert a piece of glass in the victim's penis, and then crush it with a hammer. Many simply bled to death.

On October 27, Nagy formed a new government. He abolished the AVO and told an anxious nation that negotiations had begun for the complete withdrawal of Soviet troops. He also abolished the one-party communist system and the ceasefire became effective.

Three days later, on October 30, Hungarian Cardinal Mindszenty, the Catholic prelate, who had been imprisoned by the Rakosi regime, was rescued by freedom fighters and gave a warmly-received speech praising the bravery of those fighting for the nation's liberation.

On that same day, the Soviet troops pulled out of Budapest to the countryside. The Hungarian people thought they had won, and virtually everyone was congratulating their family, friends, and neighbors. Success was at hand!

However, world excitement over the events of October 30 soon turned sour because, on the previous day, war broke out in the Middle East. Egypt had nationalized the Suez Canal prompting the British and French troops to parachute into the canal, begin bombing Egyptian targets, and send the Israelis to invade the Sinai Peninsula.

For years, through CIA's Radio Free Europe, the United States had promised East Europeans that it would come to their rescue in the event they rose up against their oppressors. Suddenly the U.S. went silent on the subject. It found itself in a real dilemma, opposing the aggression by its friends – England, France, and Israel – and taking no position on the Soviet aggression in Hungary.

Both Egypt and Hungary asked for help. As it turned out, we helped the Egyptians and sacrificed the Hungarians.

Premier Nagy pleaded for help when on November 1 Soviet troops began their assault on the Hungarian people. His exact words were, "This is Prime Minister Imre Nagy speaking. At dawn, Soviet troops attacked our country in order to overthrow the legitimate Hungarian democratic government."

Even though America heard Nagy's words, President Dwight D. Eisenhower and the American government weren't interested in helping.

Hungarian Defense Minister Pal Maleter was lured into a "peace conference" on November 3 with the Russians who promptly arrested him and, two years later, executed him.

On November 4, Soviet tanks and troops plowed into Budapest with overwhelming force and crushed the revolution. Freedom fighters fought for another week valiantly throughout the country, but they were no match for the Soviets. Thousands died, 26,000 were put on trial and of those, 13,000 were imprisoned and 300 executed.

The revolution was over.

Meanwhile during the few days in which Hungary was literally free, 200,000 refugees escaped into Austria or Yugoslavia and began new lives in England, France, Germany, Switzerland, Canada and the United States. From late October through January 1957, 40,000 Hungarians came to the United States to start new lives. Among those who escaped was Ferenc X. Vegh Sr., whose son, Ferenc Jr., is a veteran employee of Shelby County Farm Bureau Insurance. The senior Vegh was in a Hungarian army unit that took up arms against the Russians. He defected in early November, and escaped to Vienna, and eventually to Salzburg in Austria. He now lives in Smithfield, Kentucky.

As for Nagy, after being promised safe passage from the Yugoslav Embassy, which had granted him temporary asylum, he was arrested. In June 1958 he was executed after a "show trial" where he was found guilty of two crimes: abandoning the Communist Party and directly threatening the unity of the Soviet Bloc by withdrawing from the Warsaw Pact. Following the fall of the Soviet Union, in 1989 the bodies of Maleter and Nagy were exhumed and given state funerals. Those funerals were considered the symbolic burial of Hungarian Communist.

Changed Locations

During those hectic days of late October and early November, our FBIS unit was unusually busy. In fact, Else reminded me as I was writing about this time in our lives, I was "never home." She kept our bags packed and our passports ready in the event the Soviets crossed the border into Austria. Our first child, Lisa, was two years old, and she was three months pregnant with Beau when the hostilities erupted.

At my suggestion, we moved our operation to the Vienna Woods where the higher elevation would enable us to better monitor what was happening in Hungary. The Vienna Woods, at its highest point, is 2,930 feet above sea level. It represents a transition from the Eastern Alpines to the Carpathian Mountains. During the approximately six days when Hungary was legally, if not actually, free, radio transmitters sprung up all over the country, and we had difficulty monitoring so many of them at one time. Their broadcasts constantly asked for "Help, help, help" in both Hungarian and English. No help came.

When the Soviets cracked down, it was "lights out" for those stations. In the last hours of the revolution, we could literally hear the Russians battering down the doors of the stations and the defenders being shot at their posts.

Dr. Mezei had tears in his eyes as he looked at us; we Americans who had promised so much over the years and did absolutely nothing when the chips were down.

The CIA reportedly recommended to Eisenhower that he issue a statement promising U.S. intervention if the Soviets intervened. In the final analysis, the U.S. State Department position, advocating caution, was adopted. The State Department reasoned that intervention on our part could mean World War III. Those of us there on the scene believed that the "red carpet" of communism in Eastern Europe, which was eventually rolled up entirely during the Reagan administration, could have been hastened by 30 years if the U.S. had shown some guts in 1956.

There was only one organization, the International Red Cross, and Marshal Tito's Yugoslavian communists who helped their neighbors. Tito had been a thorn in Russia's side since the end of World War II when his independent communists seized power. The Yugoslavs parachuted food, clothing, and weapons into the embattled nation.

The "cold war" became even colder after the Hungarian Revolution and Russia's successful launch of Sputnik, the first artificial earth satellite. The surprise success of Sputnik triggered the space age and the race between the United States and the Soviet Union for space superiority. Twelve years later, in an even more startling success, the United States fulfilled late President John F. Kennedy's challenge for our nation to put a man on the moon.

Our second child, William E. (Beau) Matthews II, was born on April 18, 1957. He was delivered by a medically licensed obstetrician while most babies born in Austria at that time were delivered by midwives.

Else and The Spy

One of the more amusing incidents occurred at the annual U.S. Armed Forces Day celebration in May 1958. The celebration brings out a large number of both diplomats and military officers of many countries who drink champagne and wine, and feast on many types of hors d'euveres. It's one of the "can't miss" events during the year-long number of social events hosted by virtually every embassy or legation in Vienna. These events attracted not only diplomats but the "spooks" (spies) who were always seeking out useful information.

Else was looking particularly beautiful on this occasion but I wasn't paying much attention to her. I was roving about, socializing myself. Shortly after we had arrived, my boss, Fred Brace, asked if I was aware of the person with whom Else was talking. When I responded "No," he said, "that's Alexi Kundrochev (spelled phonetically), the Soviet Union's top spy in Europe. "I suggest you break it up," he continued.

When I approached Else and attempted to break in, she said, "We're talking. I'll see you later." When I persisted in breaking into the conversation, she said, "Don't be rude, can't you see I'm talking?" It was at this point that I physically led her away and in a quiet voice asked her if she knew who the man was. Very agitatedly she explained, "He's a businessman from New York. He speaks such beautiful English."

When I explained to her exactly who Alexi was, she responded, "Couldn't be, he's a perfect gentleman." Finally, she acknowledged that Alexi had asked her what her husband did and where he was located. Fortunately, Else knew so little about our operation that Alexi could have talked to her all day and night and learned little, if anything, about our operation.

Later in the evening, Austrian Foreign Minister Leopold Figl kissed Else's hand as he made his entrance into the gathering.

Change in Chiefs

Fred Brace retired as bureau chief late in 1957 and was replaced by Jerrold Brown who had begun his Agency career in 1950. He was especially proud of his Combat Infantryman Badge that he had earned during the World War II Italian campaign in 1944. He won the Bronze Star twice.

Brown was still suffering recurring nightmares about a dreadful incident in which he had been a very unwilling participant as the war wound down. He and two other soldiers had been charged with guarding 12 or 13 German prisoners, so two would sleep and the other would guard. After working his shift, he and another private turned the job over to a corporal who commanded the three-man unit. Jerrold and the other private had just gotten to sleep when they heard multiple shots being fired. Grabbing his gun, Jerrold quickly confronted the corporal and asked him about the shots.

The corporal responded, "I was desperate for sleep, so I 'eliminated' the prisoners." Jerrold, who died on October 21, 2013, said he had never gotten the image of the piled up corpses out of his mind.

As for the corporal's report, it read, "Prisoners shot while trying to escape." There was no investigation.

'Heavenly' Encounter

It was in 1958, during a vacation to Italy, that Else and I had the thrill of a lifetime. We just happened to be in St. Peter's Square in Rome and were situated in the principal room where the Pope normally greets and blesses visitors. Suddenly, there was a large commotion and Pope John XXIII, in a throne chair borne by six men, started down a long aisle. He came within four feet of the two of us and, although I am not given to swearing, I swear that he looked directly at me and gave me the most magnificent smile I have ever known. I was so transformed that I thought "This may be the closest I ever get to heaven."

Confessions on the Homefront

After a two-year stint, we came back to the United States in the summer of 1958. It was then that I had my last lie detector test, more professionally known as a polygraph test. All agency employees returning from overseas after a sizeable time abroad are required to take the test to insure that his or her actions didn't or wouldn't compromise the agency.

I anticipated taking the test with no consequences. Wrong. After I was wired up and the questions began, most of them rather innocuous, I was asked, "Did you sleep with anyone you shouldn't have?" The next question was "Did you have any contact with a Soviet Bloc agent?" And then, "Did you borrow anything from the Embassy that you shouldn't have." There were additional tough questions to which I always answered "No."

After about 45 minutes of questions, I was told that I had "failed" and would have to come back in two weeks.

Those were two of the most anxious weeks of my life. My wife Else suggested I confess to something minor to get them "off my back." I'd long since heard that "confessing anything would be disastrous." While the interviewer maintained that if I confessed that I had done something wrong, the admission would be noted, the file would be closed, and no further action would be taken.

That certainly sounded good, but I was dubious about the consequences of confessing to something I hadn't done.

So I took the test again in two weeks and, once more, I failed.

By now I was ready to confess just to get the ordeal over with. Once again, when the tough, highly sensitive questions were asked I maintained my "No" position. Suddenly, with no explanation, the interviewer said, "You're clear to return to work."

It was then that I realized that, as the questions got tougher, many employees probably broke, and volunteered important information that compromised them or the agency. Their careers were over.

Homosexuals "Weeded Out"

When we got to Vienna in 1956 the McCarthy era was coming to an end, but not without tragic consequences for homosexual men and women in the U.S. State Department at home and abroad. The person I most recall as losing his job and simply disappearing from the State Department was the Department's Chief Financial Officer for the Embassy.

No one seemed to know why Francis Dejmal didn't return from home leave in 1958. It was later we learned he had been "weeded out" because he was believed to be homosexual. Francis and I had a mutual friend, Joe Fernandez, who was the Embassy's treasurer and also a friend of Francis. Not only did Francis not come back from leave, but no one, not even his friend Joe or his other friends in the embassy, ever heard from him again.

Major Moments

During our four years in Vienna, these major additional events occupied the world's attention:

1957 – The United States and Soviet Union launched Intercontinental Ballistic Missiles; Federal troops integrated Little Rock, Arkansas, schools;

1958 – The United States launched its first rocket-propelled satellite named Explorer I;

1959 – Alaska and Hawaii were admitted to the Union, becoming the 49th and 50th states; and

1960 – The U-2 spy plane piloted by Gary Powers was shot down over the Soviet Union.

Back in the U.S.

We left Vienna for home on June 26, 1960, boarding the U.S. Constitution in Naples for the 10-day trip to New York.

Our last train trip as a family followed our arrival in New York. We traveled via the B & O to Louisville where we were met by both my parents.

We returned to Washington and a new apartment in mid-August 1960. At the suggestion of his Shelbyville doctor, A.D. Doak, Dad was examined for possible prostate cancer by Dr. Robert Lich, chairman of the Department of Urology at the University of Louisville, and two of his associates. Only one of the urologists was suspicious of the tissue, and Dr. Lich said he viewed the biopsy "favorably" and that my father had "many years ahead of him."

Unfortunately Dr. Lich was dead wrong. Dad died on April 14, 1961. His funeral was presided over by Dr. Wayne Bell, whom my father had mentored when he came to Shelbyville in 1942 to begin his ministry at First Christian Church. It was the biggest funeral I had ever attended, and Governor Bert Combs was among the mourners. Dad had been state finance chairman for the Democratic Party during the 1950s, and my brother Robert was state finance commissioner in the Combs administration at that time.

I gave some serious thought to going to law school since my father had developed a huge practice, and my brother Ben said he would not be opposed if that's what I would like to do.

However, a growing family and a major investment which I had already made in the CIA persuaded me that my future lay in Washington, not Shelbyville.

International Broadcasting

We moved into an apartment in Alexandria in mid-August and I became the FBIS liaison officer to the State Department. I was also what we called the B Wire Editor on the 4 o'clock to midnight shift, responsible for briefing senior division officials on what had transpired throughout the world overnight based on our monitoring of international radio broadcasts. Our offices were then located in some left-over World War II prefabs along the Potomac River.

This was no easy assignment because of the wealth of material involved and my analysis of that material that had to be reduced and produced on an 8 ½ x 11-inch sheet of paper.

So it was on the morning of April 17, 1961, that our east coast bureau intercepted a Spanish-language broadcast by a clandestine transmitter proclaiming,

"Alert, Alert: Look well at the rainbow. Look well at the rainbow. The fish will rise very soon. The fish will rise very soon, 'Chico' is in the house; visit him. The sky is blue; place notice in the tree. The tree is green and brown. The letters arrived well. The letters are white.

Prisoners at the Bay of Pigs.

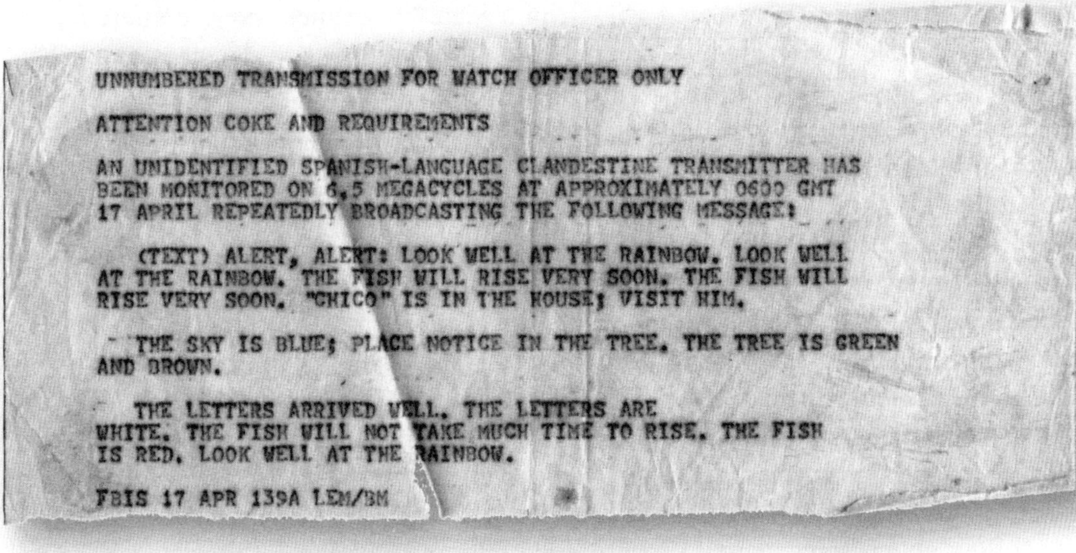

UNNUMBERED TRANSMISSION FOR WATCH OFFICER ONLY

ATTENTION COKE AND REQUIREMENTS

AN UNIDENTIFIED SPANISH-LANGUAGE CLANDESTINE TRANSMITTER HAS BEEN MONITORED ON 6.5 MEGACYCLES AT APPROXIMATELY 0600 GMT 17 APRIL REPEATEDLY BROADCASTING THE FOLLOWING MESSAGE:

(TEXT) ALERT, ALERT: LOOK WELL AT THE RAINBOW. LOOK WELL AT THE RAINBOW. THE FISH WILL RISE VERY SOON. THE FISH WILL RISE VERY SOON. "CHICO" IS IN THE HOUSE; VISIT HIM.

THE SKY IS BLUE; PLACE NOTICE IN THE TREE. THE TREE IS GREEN AND BROWN.

THE LETTERS ARRIVED WELL. THE LETTERS ARE WHITE. THE FISH WILL NOT TAKE MUCH TIME TO RISE. THE FISH IS RED. LOOK WELL AT THE RAINBOW.

FBIS 17 APR 139A LEM/BM

The fish will not take much time to rise. The fish is red, look at the rainbow."

The message was being broadcast on 6.5 megacycles repeatedly at approximately 0600 GMT and was directed to the "watch officer only."

Not having a clue what it meant, I advised the duty officer to alert all of the senior FBIS officials and, through them, senior CIA and State Department officials. Later in the day, as events unfolded, I realized that I was among the first to know that what was under way would become known as the Bay of Pigs invasion.

CIA Director Allen Dulles was forced to resign after the Bay of Pigs disaster. He had been a super spy during World War II as a member of the Office of Strategic Services.

Bay of Pigs

The Bay of Pigs Invasion was a "Perfect Disaster" by a CIA-trained force of Cuban exiles to invade southern Cuba, with material and financial support from the U.S. Government. Launched less than four months after John F. Kennedy took office as President, the invasion was a total victory for the Cuban armed forces, armed and trained by the Soviet bloc nations, who humiliated and humbled the U.S.-backed invaders in just three days.

Prior to exiting the presidency, Eisenhower had briefed Kennedy on plans to overthrow Fidel Castro. Kennedy gave his blessing to the proposed invasion, or Operation Zapata, on April 4. One month earlier, the CIA had helped exiles in Miami create the Cuban Revolutionary Council (CRC), chaired by Jose Miro Cardona, former Cuban Prime Minister.

The Bay of Pigs disaster embarrassed

the Kennedy administration and on April 21, in a State Department press conference, he said, “There’s an old saying that victory has a hundred fathers and defeat is an orphan. What matters is only one fact: I am the responsible officer of the government.”

Of the approximately 2,600 Cuban exiles and American officers and pilots who took part in the invasion, only about 1,200 eventually came home to the United States. Cuban losses included 176 killed in action and an undetermined number wounded or missing.

CIA Director Allen Dulles, who was forced to resign because of the disaster, later said that agency planners believed that once the troops were on the ground, any action required for success would be authorized to prevent failure. That is what Eisenhower had done in Guatemala in 1954 after the CIA-sponsored invasion there had begun to sputter.

It has never been confirmed, though it is still widely believed, that the United States had positioned several battalions of either U.S. Army troops or Marines in international waters off Cuba to invade Cuba in the event things went badly. Some analysts at the time said that it was our ambassador to the United Nations, Adlai Stevenson, who persuaded Kennedy that no follow-up assistance should be provided. No one had apparently bothered to tell Stevenson about the pending invasion, and he professed dismay when he was approached by reporters shortly after the invasion was announced.

CIA reference photograph of Soviet R-12 intermediate-range nuclear ballistic missile (NATO designation SS-4) in Red Square, Moscow.

Cuban Missile Crisis

In May of 1962, I received a call from my brother Ben that *The Shelby Sentinel* was going up for sale. Within a few weeks, I had bought the paper, and our family was established in Shelbyville.

I had been back in Shelbyville only a few short months, from May until October 1962, when the Cuban Missile Crisis unfolded.

This crisis represented, almost certainly, the closest time in world history in which nuclear warfare became a near reality. With the clock ticking, Russian Premier Nikita Khrushchev "blinked" and a possible catastrophe was averted.

The crisis began on October 15 when a U.S. U2 flight revealed that the Soviet Union had installed SS-4 nuclear weapons in Cuba, just 90 miles off the coast of the United States. This caused President John F. Kennedy to bring our armed forces up to their highest level of readiness, and Soviet Field Commanders were authorized to utilize tactical nuclear weapons if U.S. troops began an invasion.

For their part, the Soviets were concerned that the United States had more missiles, particularly those which were stationed in Turkey just 150 miles from the USSR.

At the time U.S.-Cuban relations were at an all-time low, partly because of the failed Bay of Pigs invasion the previous year, partly because we had stopped buying Cuban sugar and supplying oil to the island nation, and partly because Cuban leader Fidel Castro and Khrushchev had developed such a "buddy buddy" relationship.

Although many of those close to Kennedy favored an air strike, he decided, because of the likely high number of casualties, to establish a blockade around Cuba. He hoped that a blockade would help cut off the supply of any additional missiles and also bring the Soviets to the negotiating table.

On October 21, another U-2 flight revealed that Russian bombers were being rapidly assembled and cruise missile sites being established on Cuba's northern shore.

On October 22, Kennedy brought the nation up to date on the crisis, noting that U.S. ships were preparing for the quarantine, the Marines at our Guantanamo Bay base were reinforced and instructions were given to field commanders to be ready to launch missiles within minutes of the president's speech.

The Organization of American States unanimously approved the U.S. decision to quarantine Cuba.

By the end of the day on Tuesday, October 23, 1962, U.S. Navy ships at the quarantine line were prepared to destroy any Soviet ship that dared to cross it.

On October 24, as the world waited and watched, Russian ships stopped at the quarantine line and the world breathed more deeply.

However, the crisis was far from over as the two nations bargained, with mankind's future hinging on the outcome.

On Thursday, October 25 military alert was raised to DEFCON 2, the highest ever in our military's history. We were prepared, with little notice, to launch an attack on either Cuba or the Soviet Union or both. On Saturday, October 27, the worst day of the crisis, one U-2 flew off course into Russia and another was shot down.

Khrushchev raised the stakes for removing the missiles that day. He wanted U.S. missiles out of Turkey as well as a commitment that we would never invade Cuba if the Soviets removed their missiles.

The crisis was finally resolved on Sunday, October 28 when Khrushchev announced to the world that the Soviets would dismantle their nuclear weapons in Cuba if we pledged not to invade Cuba. He dropped the demand that we remove our missiles from Turkey.

Nine months after the crisis was resolved, Kennedy and Khrushchev signed an agreement to ban nuclear testing in the atmosphere. However, only a few months later, Kennedy was assassinated and 11 months later, Khrushchev was removed from office.

Kennedy Assassination

On November 22, 1963, Kennedy was assassinated by Lee Harvey Oswald. Many in the media and some Americans theorized that the CIA was the culprit, selecting Oswald to do their dirty work in revenge for Kennedy's failure to bring the invasion to a successful conclusion. Kennedy is quoted as saying that, after the Bay of Pigs failure, he would like to disband the CIA.

The failure represented the Kennedy administration's biggest failure and one might speculate that his later willingness to stand up to the Russians during the Cuban Missile Crisis was prompted by his "caving in" when the Bay of Pigs invasion started and finished badly.

Perhaps the American public will never know who the conspirators were that acted in concert to end President Kennedy's life. Certainly it wasn't Oswald acting alone. What possible motive could he have had?

While the CIA is a major suspect, the Mafia and Vice President Lyndon Johnson are also strong possibilities. The Mafia was mad as hell that U.S. Attorney General Bobby Kennedy was putting the heat on all their operations, and Johnson, expected to be indicted within a few days of voter fraud, was worried that Kennedy would replace him on the 1964 Democratic ticket.

I've always found it intriguing that Oswald knew the exact route that the Kennedy motorcade would be taking on November 22. Who told him and who placed him in just about the one place where he could have a perfect angle on the president's car?

Whoever the conspirators were, they certainly couldn't allow Oswald to live. Hence, he was very publicly exposed when Jack Ruby conveniently entered a Dallas jail and shot him from virtual point zero range.

Personal Impact

And how did all of this affect me and my family? The answer is "rather substantially."

About 10 o'clock on the night of the President's speech at the outset of the Cuban Missile Crisis, I got a call from my old boss in the Agency, Roger Seely, inquiring as to my availability to come back to Washington and "help out" during the crisis.

I replied rather quickly that I had just started my newspaper career, our competition (*The Shelby News*) was well ahead of us and that my wife was eight months pregnant.

But Roger laid that old "patriotic" message on me and I agreed to "help out." So I kissed Else goodbye and, reminiscent of the Hungarian Revolution five years previously, I disappeared from public view in Shelbyville.

Editing World Reaction

For the next few days, or until October 29, I became the editor of the Agency's World Reaction Report, as determined by our monitoring of radio broadcasts from nations all over the world. We focused primarily on broadcasts being beamed from the western world, as well as those being intercepted from the Eastern Bloc and South America.

My final report, as indicated by the attached letter, was hand carried to The White House.

Joseph Larocque, Jr. CIA deputy director, "I think you would like to know that the reaction report which you worked on during your last eight hours with us was extremely highly thought of, and was taken to the White House on Saturday morning by the boss."

FBIS Chief Seely wrote, in part, "You are to be especially complimented on the Latin

America roundup this morning. Had further work been needed in connection with this planning project you so ably developed a few months ago, we would also have turned the project over to you, but actually nothing needed to be done on it at this time.

"Best regards to you and Else, and thank you again for the sacrifice you made in coming to Washington at such a critical time."

I got back to Shelbyville late on a Friday night and was at the office at 412 Main Street very early on Saturday morning. The phone rang well before 9 a.m., and one of my better advertisers, Smith-McKenney owner Charles Bradbury, was on the phone. He was obviously upset, which puzzled me because Mr. Bradbury had always been rather quiet spoken in my presence. He said, "I want to see you right away."

If I had thought he was upset when he called on the phone, that proved to be an understatement when he reached my office. Without hardly pausing to say, "Hello," or something similar, he asked me very directly, "Where were you last Friday night?" I responded, "Mr. Bradbury I was out of town." That wasn't good enough for him, so he said, "I'd like to know where you were." When I responded, "I can't tell you," he asked me if I knew the significance of a particular date. The date and time he mentioned is about the time that we were literally about 13 hours away from what possibly could be World War III.

When I still wouldn't amplify my answer, he continued, "On that night Shelbyville beat Danville, 6-0, to win the Central Kentucky Conference in football."

When I still refused to tell him my whereabouts on that fateful night, he added, "I have run my last ad in your newspaper."

True to his word, Smith-McKenney never did run another ad. The incident just goes to show how different our perspectives can be. I was worried about World War III, and he was worried about the Shelbyville-Danville football game.

Final Agency Thoughts

That was almost, but not quite, my last involvement with the CIA.

In the spring of 1964, a representative of one of the agency's covert divisions, "Contacts," visited me in Shelbyville. I was offered a position in the St. Louis office which, at that time, primarily dealt with briefing and debriefing individuals headed to and from a Soviet Bloc company. I passed on the opportunity.

Another event during this time, important to Else and me, but hardly on the scale of nuclear war, was the birth of our third child and second daughter, Ellen Baxter, on November 29, 1962.

Looking back on those nearly 10 years in the CIA, I can very much appreciate how living abroad and being involved, directly or indirectly, in three crises that shook the world, can change your outlook on how the world works. The development of nuclear energy with all its possibilities for peaceful and wartime use is a reality that previous generations up until World War II didn't have to contend with or be fearful of.

Thus, the need for useful intelligence to help protect our nation has never been more urgent. While the CIA has suffered many acknowledged failures, as set forth in the book, "Legacy of Ashes" by Timothy Weiner, it has also scored many successes which cannot be detailed because they were just that… successes.

The assassination of terrorist Osama bin Laden by a team of Navy Seals in 2011 was set up by a "hush-hush" CIA operation that located him and actually directed the operation.

The assassination of many other alleged terrorists by CIA-operated drones also redounds to the agency's credit. The tragedy, of course, is the deaths of wives and children of those terrorists when the drone-directed missile incinerates the car in which the terrorist and his family are riding, or the building in which the family is hiding.

Almost from the beginning of the agency in the 1950s, the assassination of leaders and/or influential military figures has been an Agency solution to a perceived major problem. Over the years, beginning with Fidel Castro in the 1960s, according to Weiner's book, congressional hearings, and Internet sources, CIA-supported foreign nationals have assassinated or failed to assassinate the following (many of them were on or had been on the Agency payroll):

Fidel Castro of Cuba (Miss)
Michael Manley, Prime Minister of Jamaica (Miss)
Ahmed Dlimi, Morocco (Hit)
Mohammed Mossadegh of Iran (Miss)
Jacobo Arbenz of Guatemala (Miss)
Sukarno of Indonesia (Miss)
Patrice Lumumba of the Congo (Hit)
Gen. Abdel Karim Qasim of Iraq (Miss)
Che Guevara of Cuba (Hit)
Premier Charles de Gaulle of France (Miss)
Jose Figueres of Costa Rica (Miss)
Rafael Trujillo of the Dominican Republic (Hit) (Personally approved by John F. Kennedy)
Prince Norodom Sihanouk (Hit)
Rene Schneider of Chile (Hit)
Salvador Allende of Chile (Hit)
Orlando Letelier of Chile (Hit)
Manuel Noriega of Panama (Miss)
Omar Torrijos of Panama (Hit)
Muammar Qaddafi (Miss) (Personally approved by President Reagan)
Sheik Mohammed Hussein Fadallah of Lebanon (Miss) and
Osama Bin Laden of Afghanistan (Hit) (Personally approved by President Obama)

It is particularly ironic that Osama Bin Laden was a longtime trained CIA operative who helped the Afghans rid themselves of the Russians. He then turned on the United States and became this country's No. 1 enemy.

According to NSA "turncoat" Edward Snowden, all of the U.S. agencies, which comprise the National Intelligence Program, have a total budget of $52.6 billion and employ 107,035 people. (Snowden gained asylum in Russia after revealing many details of National Security Agency's spying on friend and foe alike.)

I remain a strong CIA advocate but it's obvious, in my judgment, that we cannot and should not try to reverse the election of Democratically-elected governments, as we did or tried to do in Cuba, Chile, Nicaragua and several other countries. I am also opposed to the use of drones when, unfortunately, we also kill the wife and children of the target. It is not too far-fetched to believe that someday, drones will hover over the United States, monitoring the whereabouts and activities of the perceived "bad guys."

I am very much opposed to the National Security Agency's listening in on the innocent conversations of millions of Americans or intercepting thousands of e-mails of no value. However, with Congress sympathetic to its mass monitoring program, that will continue to happen, perhaps with formal Congressional approval.

As for the familiar phrase, "Land of the free, home of the brave," we are still a "brave" people, but "free" we're certainly not.

CENTRAL INTELLIGENCE AGENCY

WASHINGTON 25, D. C.

November 5, 1962

Mr. William Matthews
1108 W. Main Street
Shelbyville, Kentucky

Dear Bill:

Just a note to tell you how grateful I am that you came back to help us during the past week. I have heard of no one else who voluntarily gave up his time to come back and help in this emergency.

I am afraid that your various assignments while here were not what you expected, and the various night shifts may have been a bit exhausting and frustrating. However, I think you would like to know that the reaction report which you worked on during your last eight hours with us was extremely highly thought of and was taken to the White House on Saturday afternoon by the boss.

I hope to see you back again soon.

Sincerely and gratefully,

Joseph Larocque, Jr.

CIA Headquarters in Langley, Va.

FOREIGN BROADCAST INFORMATION SERVICE
P.O. Box 2604
Washington 13, D. C.

3 November 1962

Mr. William E. Matthews
c/o The Shelby Sentinel
Shelbyville, Kentucky

Dear Bill:

I had hoped to see you again before you left to thank you for coming to Washington. The situation here necessitated assignment of people to whatever duties would best meet the heavy demands on FBIS, and your work was invaluable. You are to be especially complimented on the Latin American roundup this morning. Had further work been needed in connection with the planning project you so ably developed a few months ago, we would also have turned that project over to you, but actually nothing needed to be done on it at this time.

Best regards to you and Elsa, and thank you again for the sacrifice you made in coming to Washington at such a critical time.

Sincerely,

Roger G. Seely
Roger G. Seely
Chief, FBIS

CENTRAL INTELLIGENCE AGENCY
WASHINGTON 25, D. C.

15 NOV 1963

Mr. William E. Matthews
c/o The Shelby Sentinel
418 Main Street
Shelbyville, Kentucky

Dear Mr. Matthews:

In accordance with your letter of 27 October 1963, we are processing your resignation from this Agency to be effective 30 October 1963.

We have enclosed self-explanatory forms which may be of interest to you. Please let us know if we may be of further service to you.

Very truly yours,

B. DeFelice
B. DeFelice
Chief, Benefits and Services Division

Enclosures:
Form 8
Form 56
Form 2802

Memories in black & white

My brothers Ben, left, and Bob, right, joined me in celebrating our mother Zerelda's 80th birthday on March 3, 1982.

I went to Washington in both 1977 and 1978 to represent the Commonwealth of Kentucky in two White House Conferences on Rural Journalism. President Carter was an enthusiastic host and would answer questions very forcefully and accurately.

The Cumberland Rotary Club presented me with a plaque in 1976 on the occasion of my purchase of the *Tri-City News,* which encompasses the three communities of Cumberland, Lynch, and Benham in southeast Kentucky.

The Shelby Sentinel Minor League Champs in the 1967 Little League competition were, front row, left to right, Keith West, Al Poulter, Scott Chappell, Johnny Spalding, Ricky Hardesty, Steve Hayden, Paul Willard and Tim Renfro; standing are Orie Mullen, Dennis Coulter, Mark Smith, Beau Matthews, Terry Hawkins, Herbert Tinsley, and George White. In the rear are Coaches Keith Coulter and Bill Matthews.

Landmark Community Newspapers

Landmark's newest division is Landmark Community Newspapers, a group of 25 weekly and semi-weekly newspapers in Kentucky, Indiana, Virginia, and Maryland.

The newspapers have a combined paid circulation of about 126,950. Its publications include six controlled-circulation "shoppers," including two in the Louisville suburban area, which are distributed to an additional 50,050 households.

In addition to its own papers, Landmark Community Newspapers prints 51 weekly and daily newspapers on contract for publishers in Kentucky, Indiana, Ohio and Virginia. It also handles commercial printing.

Landmark Community Newspapers is based in Shelbyville, Kentucky, a city about 25 miles east of Louisville. The Division maintains six computerized typesetting centers and seven printing plants, which encompass 37 web offset printing units.

Printing plants are located in Shelbyville, Elizabethtown and Cynthiana in Kentucky; Tell City, Indiana; Cincinnati, Ohio; Galax, Virginia; and Westminster, Maryland.

Landmark Community Newspapers began in 1968 when its predecessor, Newspapers, Inc., was formed through the merger of eight county-seat weekly newspapers in Kentucky. The firm was acquired by Landmark in 1973.

Each newspaper continues to pursue an independent editorial operation in line with Landmark Communications' philosophy that the only first-rate newspapers are those independently operated by people who live in the community and who are responsive to community needs.

Jan Gilstrap

Russ Metz

Newspapers Inc. plant

Officers of the Kentucky Weekly Newspaper Association were Andrew Norfleet, *Russell Springs Times*; Carlos Embry, Embry Newspapers, Beaver Dam; Lucinda Caywood Miller, *Clay City Times*; standing are Carlos Embry Jr., Beaver Dam; William Matthews, *Shelby Sentinel*; Jack Thomas, *Flemingsburg Times-Democrat*; and Russ Metz, *Bath County News-Outlook*.

The Shelbyville Swimming Pool opened in 1949 and was fully integrated in 1964. The football field and concrete stadium in the background was home to the Shelbyville High School Red Devils. It was named Daniel Field in honor of longtime coach and high school Principal Bruce Daniel.

Officers and Directors of the Kentucky Press Association

President
WILLIAM E. MATTHEWS
PressCo, Inc.

District 4 & Vice President
CARROLL KNICELY
Glasgow Daily Times

District 1 & 2nd Vice President
PAUL E. MICK
The Crittenden Press
Marion, Ky.

District 2
NILES DILLINGHAM
Dawson Springs Progress

District 3
ELIZABETH SPALDING
Kentucky Standard
Bardstown

District 5
JAMES EDELEN
Sentinel-News
Shelbyville

District 6
THOMAS BUCKNER
Lexington Herald-Leader

District 7
WARREN FISHER
Carlisle Mercury

District 8
JAMES CRAVENS
C. Ky. News-Journal
Campbellsville

District 9
R. A. McCULLOUGH, JR.
Ashland Daily Independent

District 10
LOUISE HATMAKER
Jackson Times

State-at-Large
RON BEANE
Leader-News
Greenville

State-at Large
RUSS METZ
Bath Co. News-Outlook
Owingsville

State-at-Large
JOHN FELDMANN
Kentucky Post
Covington

State-at-Large
DONALD B. TOWLES
Courier-Journal &
Louisville Times

I served as president of the Kentucky Press Association in 1977. Of all the KPA officers and directors pictured here, only Jim Edelen, James Cravens, Ron Beane, and R.A. McCullough Jr. and I are still alive in 2014. Edelen and I are the only two shareholders still alive of the original 14 individuals who founded Newspapers Inc.

Edward (Ned) Breathitt, right, governor of Kentucky from 1963 to 1967, presented me with a certificate in 1966 designating Newspapers Inc. as an important new Kentucky industry. Also pictured are Commerce Secretary Katherine Peden and Lewis Conn, chairman of the board of Newspapers Inc.

The pavilion at the Fairgrounds has served as the primary gathering for patrons of the Shelbyville Horse Show. The pavilion has also served as an important backdrop for weddings, receptions, and other social events.

OFFICE OF THE GOVERNOR
FRANKFORT, KENTUCKY

EDWARD T. BREATHITT
GOVERNOR

October 25, 1965

Dear Mr. Matthews:

It is a pleasure to learn that "Kentucky's oldest established newspaper" is celebrating the 125th anniversary of its founding.

The history of The Shelby Sentinel from 1840 to the present is most remarkable. You have every right to be proud of your association with a paper which has become an institution in the Shelby County area. Let me congratulate you and your forebears on many past successes.

May your 125th anniversary edition be marked by the progress which has distinguished your newspaper during the past century and a quarter. On behalf of the Commonwealth, I extend best wishes to the staff and readers of The Shelby Sentinel as you continue to provide an outstanding example of the kind of service it takes to build a greater Kentucky.

Sincerely,

Mr. William E. Matthews
Editor and Publisher
The Shelby Sentinel
Shelbyville, Kentucky

Above: At the dedication luncheon for the NCAA College Football Hall of Fame in Cincinnati, Ohio, in 1978, I exchanged greetings with former Ohio State Coach "Woodie" Hayes. He enjoyed writing "Yea Ohio!" since I was a University of Michigan graduate, his school's chief rival.

On Aviation Day in Huntingburg, Indiana, in 1990, I was selected to ride in a World War II trainer that had been flown in for the day in which many vintage and modern aircraft were available for inspection. My flight went fine until the pilot put the plane in a power dive from 5,000 feet and leveled out just before I thought we were going to crash.

Famed Football Coach and ESPN Sports Announcer Lou Holtz and I exchanged greetings before his keynote talk at a meeting of the Scripps-Howard newspaper editors and business managers in Memphis in 1977.

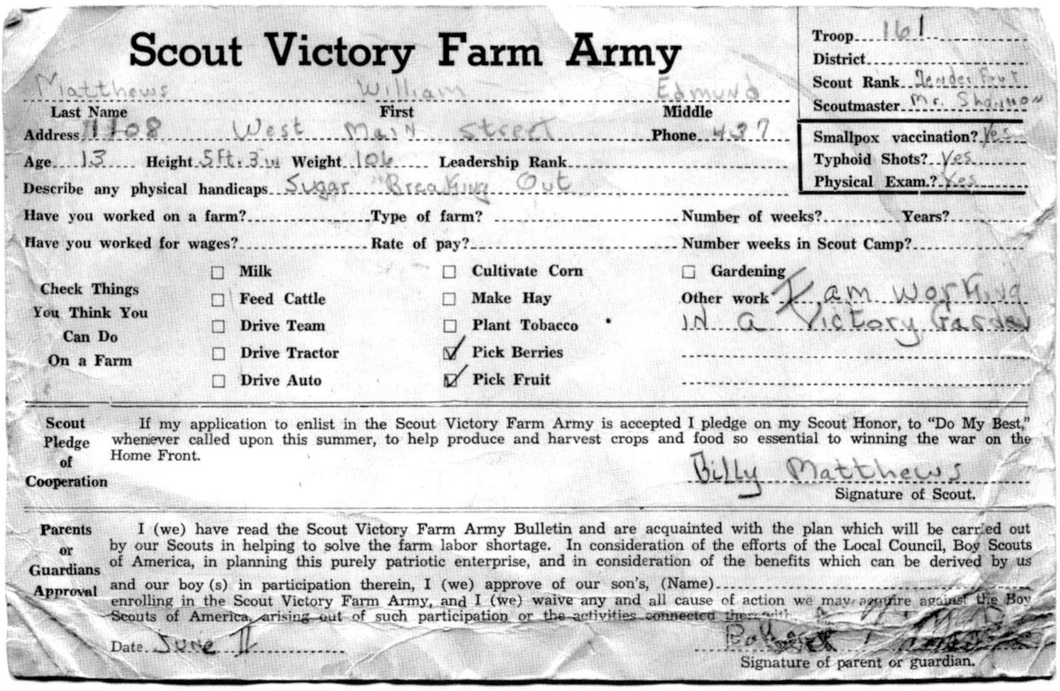

Scout Victory Farm Army

Troop 161
District
Scout Rank Tenderfoot
Scoutmaster Mr. Shannon

Last Name	First	Middle
Matthews	William	Edmund

Address 1108 West Main street Phone 437

Age 13 Height 5 ft. 3 in Weight 106 Leadership Rank

Describe any physical handicaps Sugar Breaking Out

Smallpox vaccination? Yes
Typhoid Shots? Yes
Physical Exam.? Yes

Have you worked on a farm? Type of farm? Number of weeks? Years?

Have you worked for wages? Rate of pay? Number weeks in Scout Camp?

Check Things You Think You Can Do On a Farm

- ☐ Milk
- ☐ Feed Cattle
- ☐ Drive Team
- ☐ Drive Tractor
- ☐ Drive Auto
- ☐ Cultivate Corn
- ☐ Make Hay
- ☐ Plant Tobacco
- ☑ Pick Berries
- ☑ Pick Fruit
- ☐ Gardening

Other work I am working in a Victory Garden

Scout Pledge of Cooperation If my application to enlist in the Scout Victory Farm Army is accepted I pledge on my Scout Honor, to "Do My Best," whenever called upon this summer, to help produce and harvest crops and food so essential to winning the war on the Home Front.

Billy Matthews
Signature of Scout.

Parents or Guardians Approval I (we) have read the Scout Victory Farm Army Bulletin and are acquainted with the plan which will be carried out by our Scouts in helping to solve the farm labor shortage. In consideration of the efforts of the Local Council, Boy Scouts of America, in planning this purely patriotic enterprise, and in consideration of the benefits which can be derived by us and our boy (s) in participation therein, I (we) approve of our son's, (Name) enrolling in the Scout Victory Farm Army, and I (we) waive any and all cause of action we may acquire against the Boy Scouts of America, arising out of such participation or the activities connected therewith.

Date June 11

[illegible]
Signature of parent or guardian.

I was 13 years old when I submitted my Cub Scout Victory Farm Army registration card to my scout leader Bill Shannon. Note our home telephone number was 437.

Shortly after Newspapers Inc. acquisition by Norfolk-based Landmark Communications in 1973, the senior staff of the acquiring company toured many of our newspapers across the state. Here, from left to right, are Art Gormley, Bill Diederick, the two pilots, myself, *Clay City Times* editor Jerlene Rose, and my new boss Bill Armistead.

Five of the U.S. Presidents who have served during my lifetime include George Bush (1988-1992), Ronald Reagan (1980-1988), Jimmy Carter (1976-1980), Gerald Ford (1974-1975), and Richard Nixon (1968-1974).

Lewis Conn owned and operated Kentucky's award-winning suburban weekly, *The Jefferson Reporter*, until Landmark Communications shut down the paper in the spring of 1975. It was my unenviable assignment to fire all the employees, including Lewis. One of the original shareholders in Newspapers Inc., and chairman of the board, Lewis had been one of those instrumental in building the company into the prominent position it occupied in Kentucky's journalistic landscape in the late 1960s and early 1970s.

I was four years old when this photo was made in 1934. My first cousin Doris Matthews is standing alongside me and my brothers Ben, left, and Bob flank our mother, Zerelda.

Shelby News Merges With Sentinel

The paper you are now holding will become a collector's item, for this is the last issue of The Shelby News. The News, founded in 1886 and in continuous operation since that date, will merge next week with The Shelby Sentinel.

The new publication will be named The Sentinel-News, and will be published twice each week, arriving in subscribers' homes each Tuesday and Friday. Present Shelby News subscribers will receive the new paper at no additional cost.

The new newspaper's home will be in the building at the corner of Sixth and Main Streets in Shelbyville, where The News office is presently located. The publication will be printed at the Newspapers, Inc. plant on Hwy. 55, and will reach some 8,000 subscribers.

Heading up the staff of The Sentinel-News will be Editor-in-Chief, Mrs. Sally R. Fay. Managing Editor will be Miss Mabel Oats. Mrs. Bonnie Burks Gossage is Associate Editor, and Gerald Johnson is Advertising Manager.

Believed to have the largest circulation of any newspaper publication in rural Kentucky, the Sentinel-News will also have one of the most experienced newspaper staffs in the state. The total number of years of the staff members' experience is more than 200 years. Both The Shelby News and The Shelby Sentinel have long been recognized for excellence throughout the state, and the new Sentinel-News inherits the reputations of both.

The merger of these two established newspapers is indicative of both solidity and growth in Shelby County. The Sentinel has been in continuous publication since 1840, the The News since 1886. Before the two papers, there were many starts and many failures. No one paper lasted very long.

Now, because of the continuing growth of Shelby County, both in prosperity and population, the publishers have recognized the need for, a twice-weekly newspaper. The merger of two of Kentucky's oldest weeklies was the obvious answer. And because of the seniority of The Shelby Sentinel, its name was chosen to appear first on the new masthead.

Both Shelby News and Shelby Sentinel subscribers will receive the new paper twice each week, with no increase in their bill.

Subscription rates will remain unchanged during the month of February. After that, new subscribers will pay $8.40 anywhere in Kentucky, and $10.00 out-of-state. The new rates include tax.

The Shelby News was founded in 1886 by John C. Cozine on November 10. He died in the early 1900's, and his son, Ben, became publisher. In 1941, half of The Shelby News was purchased by Bennett Roach from Ben Cozine's widow. Robert A. Fay, Roach's son-in-law, purchased the other half upon Mrs. Cozine's death. Mrs. Fay bought out her father's half shortly thereafter and her husband's half in late 1971, as he was attending law school and she was acting as editor.

The Shelby Sentinel was founded in 1840 by Henri Middleton and Morgan Torr, but at that time the paper was called The Shelby News. A few years after the founding, the young Torr died of pneumonia. Middleton continued the paper alone and with great distinction until the troubled days of the Civil War.

A staunch supporter of the Union, Middleton's views made him some bitter enemies. At one time, Morgan's Raiders boasted that they would ride into Shelbyville and hang Middleton from the Court House porch.

But Middleton was quite his own man, and continued his strong views. One example of his courage is shown in The Shelby News flag that appears on this paper's masthead . . . it was Middleton's expression of his Union sympathies.

Some time during the Civil War, Middleton sold the paper, and the name was changed then to The Shelby Sentinel, possibly because of the controversy and bitterness attached to the old name of The Shelby News.

Another Sentinel publisher of distinction was Michael O'Sullivan, who bought the paper in 1904. He was a colorful editor, with decisive views. His sons, James and Daniel O'Sullivan succeeded him as publishers upon his death in 1932, and in 1962 the brothers sold the paper to William E. Matthews, whose loyalty to The Sentinel began as a part-time reporter and errand-boy while in high school.

A lengthier history of The Shelby News was written by former publisher, Robert A. Fay, for the 175th centennial issue of the city of Shelbyville, and appears in this paper. The centennial edition, prophetically, was a combination effort of the staffs of The Shelby News and The Shelby Sentinel.

THE SHELBY NEWS 15¢

SHELBYVILLE, KENTUCKY — FOUNDED IN 1886. . . FINAL ISSUE — THURSDAY, FEBRUARY 3, 1972

THE WHITE HOUSE
WASHINGTON

November 10, 1965

Dear Mr. Matthews:

True to its name, the <u>Shelby Sentinel</u> has been a faithful watchman and observer of the eventful 125 years which span its life.

You, your staff and the readers of your paper have every right to be proud of its enviable reputation for service.

In its efforts to act as a sentinel of the progress of the Shelbyville area, your newspaper has acted, too, as the sentinel of our cherished freedom of the press.

It has successfully advanced this freedom, and, in so doing, it has made a lasting contribution to our American way of life.

I know that you will perpetuate this time-honored tradition in the years ahead.

Sincerely,

Mr. William E. Matthews
Editor and Publisher
<u>The Shelby Sentinel</u>
Shelbyville, Kentucky

HARRY S TRUMAN
INDEPENDENCE, MISSOURI 64050

October 4, 1965

Dear Mr. Matthews:

I am pleased to send you congratulations on the 125th birthday of The Shelby Sentinel.

Much has happened in those 125 years, and more is yet to be. Keep on informing your readers so that they may always respond to the issues intelligently.

Sincerely yours,

Mr. William E. Matthews
Editor and Publisher
The Shelby Sentinel
Shelbyville, Kentucky

Alice Richardson (left) of Shelbyville was the best salesperson I ever had. She worked with *The Shelby Sentinel* and other publications of mine for almost 35 years. She was killed tragically in a car crash in 1993 near Richmond, Ky., on her way to making a sales call.

"Miss Mabel" Oats kept the *Sentinel* afloat for more than 53 years. She started at the paper one day out of high school. Here she is working with intern Libby Duffy (Fraas).

The Shelby Theater on the south side of Main Street between 6th and 7th street was the place to be any night of the week during the 1930s through the 1950s. Note the two gentlemen standing by the parking meter on the right.

President Harry S. Truman stopped at the L & N Station at North 8th Street in September 1948 as part of his "whistle-stop tour" across America in support of his presidential campaign against Republican Thomas E. Dewey.

In 1959, Else and I had the thrill of a lifetime when Pope John XXIII was carried in his throne chair down the aisle in the Vatican to greet well-wishers and receive his blessing. John XXIII was perhaps the most influential Pope of the 20th Century because he was the one who called Vatican Council II which greatly changed the direction of the Catholic Church.

Shelbyville Mayor Tom Hardesty, lower left, and County Judge Executive Robert Rothenburger were on hand on Oct. 1, 2006, for the dedication of the historic marker revealing Shelby County's involvement in the famous Lewis & Clark Expedition of 1803-1806. On the front row, left to right, were Brig. Gen. (Ret.) Ronald Van Stockum, Betty Matthews, Rothenburger, and Hardesty.

KentuckyHistoricalSociety
Highway Marker Program

Dedication of Historical Marker for

LEWIS AND CLARK IN KENTUCKY

1806 RETURN OF EXPEDITION

DEATH OF MERIWETHER LEWIS

Sunday, October 1, 2006, 2:00 P.M.

Kentucky
UNBRIDLED SPIRIT

Kentucky Historical Highway Marker #2214

LEWIS AND CLARK IN KENTUCKY

1806 RETURN OF EXPEDITION

Meriwether Lewis & William Clark, leaders of the 1803-06 journey to the Pacific, visited Shelbyville several times. In Nov. 1806, on the Expedition's return, Lewis arrived with Expedition veterans, Mandan & Osage Indian delegations bound for Washington, DC. Over.

DEATH OF MERIWETHER LEWIS

In Shelbyville on Oct. 28, 1809, Clark learned of the death of his Expedition partner, Meriwether Lewis. Clark stopped in town when traveling eastward and read a newspaper report that Lewis had killed himself in Tennessee.
Presented by the Ohio River Chapter-Lewis & Clark Trail Heritage Foundation, National Park Service, Ky. Lewis & Clark Bicentennial Commission, Shelby County Historical Society.

Location: Shelbyville, 5th & Main Streets, Shelby Co., Ky.

Program

Welcome	*William E. Matthews,* President Shelby County Historical Society
Acknowledgments	*William E. Matthews*
Brief Remarks	*Jim Holmberg,* Curator of Special Collections Filson Historical Society
	Jim Mallory, Board of Directors Lewis and Clark Trail Heritage Foundation, Inc. and member of Kentucky Lewis and Clark Bicentennial Commission.
	Nelson L. Dawson Kentucky Historical Society
	John E. Callihan, P.E., Branch Manager Planning and Preconstruction District 5, Louisville Kentucky Transportation Cabinet
Unveiling of Marker	*Jim Holmberg and Jim Mallory*
Closing Remarks	*William E. Matthews*

Freight and mixed passenger-freight trains on the Shelbyville-Bloomfield line rolled by our home at 1108 West Main St. for many years. The train pictured here was the final train to make the run on October 10, 1952.

Interurban Car 107 is pictured here in 1934 as it started its final run from the turntable at 2nd Street in Shelbyville to Louisville. The Interurban reached the Fairgrounds in 1911, and began operating through the downtown area two years later.

Writing pathways

Within a few months of establishing ourselves in Washington, D.C. in 1953, it became apparent that we needed more money to survive in a relative affluent economy. My starting pay was $3,440 per annum and about $1,000 of that was going to pay the rent.

So while I was checking the "help wanted" ads one day in the Washington *Evening Star* I saw a notice about needing someone with editorial experience to work 20 to 30 hours a week for the National Education Association (NEA).

I responded and was hired the first week of July at what amounted to $30 per day or $90 per week. My job, working for Editor Mildred Fenner of the *Journal of the National Education Association*, was to proofread and provide short stories about teachers and the good work they were doing across the country

Dr. Joy Elmer Morgan, the Journal's longtime editor, had recently retired and had started an organization named Senior Citizens of America (SCA). He still had an office in the NEA building and occasionally I helped him prepare promotional materials as he sought to begin a national organization aimed at helping senior citizens prepare for retirement.

My work for Mrs. Fenner caught Morgan's eye and shortly thereafter, in September, he set up an office on 16th Street and I left NEA to work for him.

Dr. Morgan was the author of the American Citizens Handbook and was the founder of the Future Teachers of America (FTA).

He started a magazine called *Senior Citizen* and within a few months we had more than 5,000 subscribers who paid $8 for their subscription plus other booklets that he had prepared.

In time I began working two full-time jobs: Wednesday through Sunday from 4 p.m. to midnight at the Central Intelligence Agency, and Monday through Friday from 8 a.m. to 4 p.m. at the SCA offices. Despite the hard, long hours, Else (who had a part-time teaching job in Maryland) and I were suddenly making $10,000 per annum, which wasn't too bad in Washington in the mid-1950s.

Perhaps the highlight of my tenure with SCA was the opportunity to join Dr. Morgan in having tea with Edith Galt Bolling Wilson, the second wife of President Woodrow Wilson. Mrs. Wilson had married the President in 1915, only 16 months after the first Mrs. Wilson died in August 1914.

The second Mrs. Wilson was, and still is, the first and only woman to actually run the United States government. Following her husband's severe stroke in 1919, Mrs. Wilson began directing the affairs of the Executive Branch, deciding who would and who wouldn't see the President, and setting the agenda for both domestic and foreign policy. She was criticized by legislators on both sides of the aisle for her aggressive, dictatorial style of ruling. It is believed that she possibly forged some of the documents that bore President Wilson's signature.

When Dr. Morgan and I had tea with her in 1954, she was then 82 years of age and still beautiful by anyone's standards.

I recall little of our conversation in her suite at the Mayflower Hotel, but she did challenge me to "live the best life possible." She died in 1961 at the age of 89.

I left Senior Citizens of America in the fall of 1955 to have some minor surgery and prepare for our CIA assignment to Vienna in the spring of 1956.

I saw Dr. Morgan again in 1958 when I came back home on leave, and again in 1961 just prior to our return to Shelbyville. He had remarried following the death of his first wife, but was saddened that SCA had never really gotten off the ground.

Despite my pleas, Dr. Morgan never accepted advertising for his *Senior Citizen*, and that proved the magazine's undoing. Had he accepted advertising, Senior Citizens of America might have become what AARP is today.

Following his first wife's death in 1914, President Wilson married Edith Galt Bolling Wilson in late 1915. The second Mrs. Wilson is the first and only woman who actually ran the U.S. government following the president's severe stroke in 1919.

‘Emergency’ teacher

In early August 1962, Shelbyville City Schools Superintendent Bill McKay called me at *The Shelby Sentinel* office to inquire if I would “help out” by teaching two English courses and one speech course during the coming year. I believe he called me after talking with former longtime Superintendent Willie C. Ray. Mrs. Ray was a longtime friend of our family, and was apparently familiar with my English skills. I still have the little medals in English I was awarded at the conclusion of my fifth grade and sophomore years.

He said that a newly-recruited teacher had reneged on her contract, accepting a higher paying position at Lexington Henry Clay High School. McKay said the school board would issue me an “emergency” certificate that would enable me to be in the classroom.

I had never taught before and starting at the junior class level caused me to pause for a considerable time before agreeing to his request. The pay would be $207 per month.

That year in the classroom is particularly memorable because it was also my first year as a weekly newspaper publisher. It is also memorable because the other two senior level English teachers were Rhodes Scholar Allen Barnett and Gayle Royce (who later married renowned sculptor from Shelbyville, Barney Bright).

My English class met daily and the speech class three times a week.

The two English classes were as different as night and day. The 8 o’clock class consisted almost entirely of vocationally-minded pupils, many of whom were barely literate in terms of speaking or understanding the English language. The 1 o’clock class was just the opposite with almost all of the students with above average intelligence and several of exceptional intellect.

The 8 o’clock class was a relatively easy one to teach because so many of the pupils were just putting in time. I still tried to do my best to make up for the many years in which they had been passed along and in which not enough interest had been paid to them. However, a kid who should have been held back in the first or second grade is almost beyond helping if he or she reaches the junior year in high school barely able to put 10 words together in a coherent sentence.

While I didn’t neglect the 8 o’clockers, I was challenged mightily by the 1 o’clockers, who I considered sharp, studious, and highly receptive to instruction. Among them were John Cleveland, Carolyn McKee, Carolyn Jackson, Cece Scearce, Tommy Riner, Nancie Mason, Sue Carole Streable, Tish Moffett, Connie Shouse (killed in a car accident in her prime), and Tommy Thompson (killed in Vietnam).

One of the techniques that I had learned at Michigan was how to write a short story on one side of a single sheet of paper. Many of these Shelbyville High students grasped the concept almost immediately and I was amazed at how well they expressed themselves. Later, we began writing longer stories with equally good results.

One of the more humorous moments (of course, it wasn’t humorous to the student) came when I gave an F on one of her papers to one of the brighter students. The exercise consisted of writing a detective story and she turned in a beautifully written paper. However, purely by coincidence I had read virtually the same plot in an Agatha Christie novel a few months before.

In tears, she approached my desk and questioned my wisdom in giving her an F. My response was, "It seems to me that Agatha Christie wrote something very similar." She turned around quickly and knew that she had been caught plagiarizing.

Ironically, our family and her family had been neighbors for years. Several years after the F episode, our youngest daughter Ellen was the flower girl at this person's wedding. The subject was never mentioned again. But I did see her years later when she was the marketing director for a Lexington hospital.

The 1 o'clock class and I also read a great deal of literature, some to improve our knowledge and the other more for entertainment. In the latter category was the novel that made Agatha Christie famous, *The Murder of Roger Ackroyd.* When I asked each student who he or she thought the murderer would turn out to be, all guessed incorrectly. It was one of the first, if not the first example, of a detective story where the narrator turns out to be the killer.

Not only did we learn something about English, but we also learned about history, geography, world politics, and more. Years later, one of my students remembered my talking in 1962 about a little known country at that time, Laos.

I don't recall many of those in the speech class, but that, too, was a challenging experience since the only training, if you might call it that, I had were the two classes in Speech at the University of Michigan.

Despite my lack of experience, several of those speech students became rather eloquent in their delivery before the school year ended. Perhaps my biggest contribution was ringing a bell whenever a student said, "And, uh." I explained that rather than saying "And, uh" just pause for a moment and continue. By the end of the year, the bell had ceased to ring.

Academic Award Input

While my recollections of teaching in 1962 are either brief or fragmentary, I have a distinct memory that revolves around the Rotary Cup. The highest honor presented on Graduation Night, the Rotary Cup is an award given by the local Rotary Club to the most outstanding senior boy. It is awarded on the basis of scholarship, activities, and attitude. It, as well as many other awards, is based on a vote by the faculty.

When the teachers gathered just prior to graduation, one of the athletic coaches asked me about my vote. When I said, "That's an easy one. Mike Saunders is my choice."

He immediately took issue with me, saying that Mike had an attitude problem. While I had never had Mike in class, I understood that he had excelled in every phase of student endeavors, both in the classroom and in athletics.

When the teachers gathered, I nominated Mike. The coach nominated someone else and the debate began. One teacher said she liked Mike, but she thought he plagiarized his book reports. When I asked her for the evidence, she responded, "They're just too good."

A secret vote was taken and Mike didn't win. I certainly had nothing against the winner who seemed like a nice young man.

The day after graduation when the selection had been announced, Mike's father Harold roared into *The Sentinel* newspaper office and asked me who voted for whom. Naturally I couldn't or wouldn't tell him, but he said he thought he knew. That was the last I heard about the matter. Harold later became Circuit Judge from 1972 to 1992. As for Mike, son of longtime musician Susie Saunders, he enjoyed a successful career as a Texas attorney.

Looking Backward to 1948

The 1963 vote on the Rotary Cup brought back memories of a similar setting 15 years previously, in 1948, when the name of that year's Rotary Cup was announced. As I sat there on the stage after giving the salutatorian address, I wondered whether it would be Reed Yount, our valedictorian, or me. It never occurred to me that it might be someone else.

So when the name Bill Acree was called out by Superintendent Willie C. Ray, I was not only disappointed but also puzzled. Bill was a nice enough fellow, but I thought his scholarship and activities were just average.

It was only in 1963 that I realized that "attitude," and not scholarship or activities, was the key to winning the Rotary Cup.

A member of that class and close personal friend was Charles Ray Ferguson. Mrs. Ray arranged for him to receive maximum scholarship assistance at Purdue, from which he graduated in engineering in 1952. He became a jet fighter pilot, and flew many missions in Korea. He died in the late 1990s.

Shelbyville High School was competed in 1917. It now houses the administrative offices of the Shelby County Public Schools System.

Newspaper years, 1962-2013

My early time at *The Shelby Sentinel* and the editing and writing jobs I had in Washington, D.C. must have placed ink in my blood.

In the spring of 1962, my brother Ben called me in Washington, D.C. to say that *The Shelby Sentinel* was being placed on the market by the O'Sullivan brothers, Michael and James (Buddy). The newspaper had been in the O'Sullivan family for many years, following the purchase in 1904 by their father, Michael O'Sullivan.

If I was ever going to leave the Central Intelligence Agency, this appeared to be about as good a time as any. I began traveling back and forth from D.C. to Shelbyville in an effort to find out what my chances were of buying the paper.

The biggest problem, of course, was money since everything we owned was tied up in a house that we had bought the previous spring in Alexandria, Va. – and that wasn't much.

The key person in the transaction in Shelbyville was Miss Mabel Oats who had been with the newspaper since her graduation from high school in 1919. Miss Mabel was very much afraid that Bob and Sally Fay, who owned the rival newspaper, *The Shelby News*, would wind up with the *Sentinel* and she would be out of a job. So she and Buddy O'Sullivan conspired with me to withhold his one-half of the *paper* from the sale, knocking the price down considerably and leaving potential buyers with the possibility of having a partner they didn't know or like. Charles Randolph was at the auction bidding on behalf of the Fays, and Jesse Alverson was there trying to buy the paper to go along with his Paris, Kentucky, *Daily Enterprise*.

In the spirited auction that started at $20,000, my winning bid of $40,000 bought the interest of Daniel O'Sullivan. Later that day, Miss Mabel negotiated the sale of Buddy's half to me for $27,500. So the total was $67,500, which was about $65,000 more than I had available.

The next few years were a gigantic struggle. Not only was I short of money, but *The Shelby Sentinel* was operating (and had been operating for many years) with out-of-date, if not obsolete, equipment. Also, the true circulation of the newspaper was only about 1,600 compared to the *News'* 4,000. We were still publishing in what was called "hot type" yet the *News* had already converted to the more modern offset method of printing.

Fortunately, few merchants ever inquired about circulation and the Fays, financially well-fixed, were more interested in the news product than in advertising. So we were able to hold our own, in spite of an enormous gap in circulation numbers.

News versus *Sentinel*

Bob Fay and I rarely agreed editorially. The big topic in the early 1960s was the possibility of consolidating the two school systems. Bob was for it; I was sharply opposed.

The Shelbyville City School District had been bulging at the seams because it had inadequate facilities to accept all the Black students who had to be absorbed following the Supreme Court decision outlawing school segregation. Toward the end of the '60s, city schools were operating double sessions and even Saturday sessions for students in an effort to resolve the building capacity issue and to stay afloat. Thus, city-county school consolidation appeared to be the answer to many.

I opposed consolidation because I feared the quality of education would suffer for both systems. Even the city school board was split. When city voters failed to approve a tax to fund a new high school, the die was cast. With the state serving as the catalyst, consolidation was effected in 1975. As Duanne Puckett wrote in her article on schools in *The New History of Shelby County*, by 1976, "records no longer indicated any reference to the former school system as separate and distinct, suggesting that merger was finally complete."

School consolidation wasn't the only issue Bob and I disagreed about. We generally supported different candidates in both local and state elections. He was a mainstream liberal; I a mainstream conservative.

One day Mrs. Robert D. Shipman came into my office and very firmly said, "Mr. Matthews, you and Mr. Fay should be ashamed. You're not interested in the community; you two just want to sell newspapers." I disagreed with her on the first part of her statement and agreed with her on the second part.

In 1965, Bob Fay approached me about setting up a joint composition shop to compose both newspapers. Naturally I jumped at the opportunity to finally move into the 20th century typographically. The joint operation worked well until Bob figured out that our new relationship benefitted me more than his paper.

Greater Kentucky Publishers

The next two years, 1966 and 1967, turned out to be pivotal years for the newspaper and me.

In the spring of 1966, Lewis Conn and I were inspired by a talk on cooperative printing that Bill Brannen from Milwaukee gave at the Kentucky Press Association annual conference in January. So, we decided to ask a number of publishers if they would be interested in building a printing plant at a central location where we could have our papers printed.

Somewhat surprisingly, we found great interest and about 90 days later, in July, we formed Greater Kentucky Publishers. The original 11 were George Trotter (Lebanon), Jim Edelen (Springfield), Jack Perry (Carrollton), Elliott and Frances Garrison (Lawrenceburg), Jim Goranflo, Gene Armstrong and Tom Manby Sr. (LaGrange), Frank Stanley (Louisville), Lewis Conn (Louisville), and me (Shelbyville).

Each of the eight papers put up $5,000 and we borrowed $60,000 from the Liberty National Bank in Louisville. With this $100,000 we started construction of the plant on KY 55 South in spring 1966 and installed a Fairchild News King Press.

After many difficult days and even weeks of trying to get the plant running smoothly, we finally got all of the kinks worked out by November. Tom Gilbert of Shelbyville was the first plant manager for the first cooperative printing plant south of the Mason-Dixon.

We had numerous publishers and/or delegations from all over the country come to Shelbyville over the next few years to learn about and observe the operation. Many were surprised that we had persuaded men of such diverse backgrounds and different publishing requirements to put their faith in an untried concept.

What made this group interesting is that it contained a Jew (Conn), an African-American (Stanley), four Catholics (Edelen, Trotter, Goranflo and Armstrong), and four Protestants (Perry, the two Garrisons and me).

I served as President and General Manager at a salary of $25,000; Lewis was Vice-president; Elliott Garrison, Secretary; and Stanley, Treasurer. As this book is published, all are deceased except for Jim Edelen and me.

The newspapers owned by the eight owners all showed a better bottom line almost as soon as the plant opened. The reason: we now had control of our printing expenses. Relationships among the eight owners were sometimes tenuous, but for the most part everyone agreed that they were getting a better looking product for less money.

Kentucky Press Association

The Greater Kentucky Publishers start-up was but one of the major happenings in my life during the 1966-1968 period.

From the first days back in Kentucky following my purchase of the *Sentinel*, I had become aware that our professional trade organization, the Kentucky Press Association, was in something of a moribund mess.

It was basically run by two individuals, Victor Portmann and Florida Garrison. Vic, who had been and still was a journalism professor at the University of Kentucky, and Florida held a less-than-vibrant organization together.

At my first convention in 1963, held at the Phoenix Hotel in Lexington, my family was aroused at 3 a.m. by some loud knocking on the doors up and down the hall so we assumed the hotel was on fire. Wrong. What we had were two very drunk longtime KPA board members having some fun at the expense of the hotel guests.

What bothered me more than a couple of drunken KPAers was the fact that the association operated as a personal fiefdom for a few individuals who served as its officers

Russ Metz

Jack Thomas

and directors. For example, Frank Bell from Bedford, which was in our geographical district, had served for more than 30 years as our representative on the board. His paper, the *Trimble County Democrat*, was one of the smallest in Kentucky and hardly representative of the quality papers in our district.

The KPA board was not popularly elected but, rather, was self-perpetuating. There were no limits on how long an individual could serve. Board directors were picked according to the whims of a few insiders who decided who could or could not serve. While the publishers or editors for weekly newspapers had been and continued to serve on the board and were occasionally asked to be the president, the state's daily papers, in fact, ran the association.

In the fall of 1967, Russ Metz, from Owingsville, Jack Thomas from Flemingsburg, Carlos Embry from Beaver Dam, Charles Whitaker from Cromona (in Eastern Kentucky) and I began plotting how we might "reform the KPA" through the popular election of board members and officers. We met with several other publishers of weekly newspapers at Rough River State Park and decided to run Metz for president in the January 1968 election. I agreed to serve as his campaign manager.

We had one simple objective: to make the election of board members subject to popular vote by 10 districts statewide. These popularly elected board members would then decide on officers.

However, Russ, after thinking it over for several days, decided he would rather be a campaign manager than a candidate for office, so the group coalesced behind me. What was then shaping up was the first contested election for president in KPA's 99-year history. Also shaping up was the first and, I believe, only scandal in KPA history.

KPA's 'High Noon' Campaign

In early December 1967, Sandy Van Curon, then KPA president, and Tommy Adams, business manager of *The Lexington Herald-Leader*, came to my newspaper office in Shelbyville and asked very politely that I drop my candidacy for KPA presidency. There were no harsh words but, rather, a plea to drop out so that KPA could have a memorable 100th anniversary celebration at the Continental Inn in Lexington.

I declined, saying that to do so would betray the publishers of many other weekly newspapers who had agreed to support me.

So it was on a Thursday in January 1968 that the representatives of newspapers all around the state began to gather at the Continental Inn for the mid-winter convention. I had my wife, Else, and three of our four children with us.

I was enjoying a swim about 5 p.m. when Don Towles of the *Louisville Courier-Journal* asked me to join some KPA directors in a room close to the pool. I reluctantly agreed.

When I reached the room, I was greeted by several current board members and several past presidents. There was also a bottle of Scotch, which told me that this group knew more about me than I thought. After all, I had been back in Kentucky only about six years and had been little involved in association activities.

What started out as a friendly conversation turned ugly when I indicated my desire to continue my pursuit for KPA president. One of the older members wondered why I thought I was fit to serve as president since I'd been back in Kentucky such a short time. Another asked if I was trying to break up the association. The upshot was that I was given until 5 o'clock the following night to renounce my candidacy or "they" would teach me a lesson. I gathered that the "lesson" would consist of beating me badly in Saturday morning's election.

During Friday's seminars, the tension began to grow as the group of newspaper publishers supporting me affirmed their intention to stand strong.

Once again the next afternoon, at 5 o'clock, I was in the pool when Towles summoned me to another hotel room meeting. This time the mood was different, bordering immediately on ugly. Instead of seven or eight KPA board members, Jack Thomas, Russ and I were confronted not only by many board members but a number of past presidents who had been rounded up from across the state to continue the confrontation. Among them were Tommy Adams of the *Lexington Herald*, Enos Swain of Danville, John B. Gaines of Bowling Green, and W. Foster Adams of Warsaw, and, of course, current president Van Curon. Bennett Roach, formerly of *The Shelby News*, who had been KPA president in 1952, was not among the group.

It was rather like the 1952 movie "High Noon" that starred Gary Cooper as a town marshal facing a gang of killers. Van Curon asked if I had decided to withdraw like a good fellow and throw my support to Howard Ogles, the board's hand-picked successor to Van Curon. Howard was a decidedly fine fellow and I had no quarrel with him.

This meeting was not pleasant. Whatever decorum existed the night before, evaporated. One after another of the participants questioned my credentials as opposed to those of Ogles'. In fact, I was told, those present represented more than 400 years of newspaper experience compared to my measly four or five.

Thomas exploded that his father, a Pennsylvania coal miner with no language skills, had more integrity than all those who were trying to force me out. It was not a happy scene when we departed.

Our "rebel" group enjoyed an evening of frivolity, good eating, and even some dancing as the word began to spread that a vigorously contested election was shaping up on Saturday morning.

One could sense the tension as the two sides prepared for battle in a meeting scheduled to get under way at 9 a.m. With Van Curon presiding, telling jokes and stalling, the meeting did not get under way on time and, in fact, it was nearly 10 a.m. when he finally called the session to order. The reason for the delay became obvious as past presidents from years and years ago began filling the convention hall. Even former KPA President W.L. Dawson (1921), from LaGrange, who hadn't attended a meeting for three decades, showed up, as did several past presidents from the *Louisville Courier-Journal*. According to the by-laws at that time, each past president had a vote.

Russ and I sized up the situation and figured we would lose by about 20 to 25 votes. However, the final vote count, as announced by Van Curon, found us losing by nearly 40 votes. Afterward, Adams, who had been president in 1959, gleefully told me that "I told you we were going to beat the **** out of you. Maybe you've learned your lesson."

For obvious reasons, Russ and I didn't attend the final luncheon.

Shady Election

That afternoon while we were licking our wounds around the pool at the Continental, Russ began wondering how we could have lost so badly. He decided, "Let's go back to the ballroom and see if there is any evidence of the voting." At that point, we had no reason to believe there had been any "hanky-panky" with the voting.

The ballroom was just as we had left it several hours previously. There was the table with the ballot box and a ledger beside it of all those who had voted. As we looked at the names, it appeared that there had been a number of weekly publishers who had attended but had voted for Ogles. However, that came as a surprise since several of those publishers were known to favor reform.

So we got busy and started calling, among others – Zach Justice in Pikeville, "Bud" Perry in Paintsville, and Norman Allen in Prestonsburg. All had been recorded as voting. However, each told Russ and me – as we had now begun to suspect – that they hadn't even been at the convention.

More names, nearly all weekly publishers, showed up on the ledger as having voted, yet, again, upon checking, none had been in Lexington, Kentucky that morning.

What obviously had happened was the ruling group, in their zeal to teach us a lesson, had had various individuals sign in for phantom newspapers and vote for Ogles.

"I think we've got those bastards," said Russ. "We got a great story to tell. The KPA stuffed the ballot box."

Russ said he wanted to pass the story along to the Associated Press but I urged caution, "Let's not get too carried away." I outlined a plan whereby Russ would call Towles and I would call Adams. We would explain what we had found and, barring some plausible explanation, we would ask the board to consider what we had wanted in the first place: an amendment to the constitution calling for the popular election of officers by district.

If the board was not willing to do that, then we would release our story alleging fraud in the KPA voting. Russ put all the election materials in a bank lockbox.

Both Towles and Adams disavowed any knowledge of voting shenanigans, but did acknowledge that some of the individuals we named – Perry, Justice, and Allen, among others – had not been visible at the convention. More importantly we got the two of them, plus Van Curon, to take our interest in the amendment calling for the popular election of board members to the next meeting of the board.

In the meantime, Russ and I decided to take a cautionary route but we fully planned to name names and take the story statewide if we didn't get what we and many small-time newspaper owners wanted.

Our struggle paid off at the summer convention when a member of the board put forward an amendment, Article V, Section 2, calling for the direct election of board members from 10 individual districts, with four at-large members. The board has been expanded over the years to 27, but the concept of popular election has remained in place.

Within a few years of the January 1968 election, several of the old board members had been "retired" and a number of new faces had taken their places. As I look back on that fateful election, many of those who have since served as president would never have had the opportunity to do so if Russ, Jack Thomas, Carlos, many other weekly publishers and I had weakened in our resolve to change things.

Of those individuals who were involved in the 1968 scandal, I am the only one still alive. I believe the story needs to be told of how a group of otherwise honorable people let their zeal for control lead to corruption of the voting process.

Ten years later, in 1977, with a big push from Al Smith from Russellville and Bob Carter from Hopkinsville, I was elected president and Russ was elected president a few years later. Many of the "old guard" had been voted out.

'Where in the Hell is Clay City?'

In January 1968, I went to a KPA convention and, in an ill-advised and whiskey-caused moment, signed a paper obligating Jack Thomas from Flemingsburg and me to purchase

***The Clay City Times* held a luncheon for correspondents and postmasters at Dalton's Restaurant. Seated: Nellie Meadows, Red River Historical Society news; Celia Hood, Virden; Rita Farmer, Bowen; Jerlene Rose, *CCT* Manager; Virginia Rose, Clay City news; standing: Co-Publisher William E. Matthews, (Mrs. Jack) Wilma Thomas, Freda Wells, Trapp; Mrs. Craig Salyers, Airport News; Bethany Chaffin, Poet's Corner; Rev. Elijah Baker, Sermonette; Dick Spaulding, Clay City Postmaster; Jewell Thomas, Library news; Marjorie Gabbard, Stanton; Nannie Schimfessel, Hardwick's Creek; Stanton Postmaster George "Cappie" Billings Jr.; Jack Thomas, Co-Publisher, *Clay City Times*.**

The Clay City Times in Clay City, Kentucky. Jack, publisher of the *Flemingsburg Times-Democrat*, was my drinking companion at the time and had little, if any, recollection of signing his name two days before.

We didn't take our signing too seriously because Curt Cawood, who, along with his sister, Lucinda, was selling the property following the death of their father and newspaper owner Bill Cawood. Curt was asking $125,000. We offered $40,000.

So when I called Jack two days later to tell him we had bought the *Clay City Times*, he responded, "Where in the hell is Clay City?" My response: "I don't know."

Two days later, after we had each published our own newspapers, Jack and I rendezvoused in Clay City, which is about 20 miles southeast of Lexington, Kentucky and were amazed to find that this little paper had 13 employees.

It didn't take us long to terminate 10 of the 13 and put Jerlene Rose, then making $35 per week, in charge and increase her salary to $60 weekly. We kept the ad manager, Shirley Neal, and the bookkeeper, Bonnie Smith. Preparation and printing of the paper was transferred to Shelbyville. Rose became chief reporter, photographer, and editor.

Newspapers Inc.

From March until August, the *Clay City Times* became a highly profitable operation. Based on the concept of centralized composition and printing, I proposed that the eight newspapers comprising Greater Kentucky Publishers merge their entities into a company in which each of us would own stock. The idea gained traction and within two months, a new company, Newspapers Inc., was formed. Each of us received varying amounts of stock depending on the price that each had negotiated for our papers.

I sold my paper, *The Shelby Sentinel*, to Newspapers Inc. for $125,000 in stock, as did Leonard Bean with the *Elizabethtown News*. Elliott and Frances Garrison sold *The Anderson News* for $80,000; George Trotter and three other shareholders, the *Lebanon Enterprise* $125,000; Jim Edelen, the *Springfield Sun* $100,000; Thomas Manby, Gene Armstrong, and Jim Goranflo, *The Oldam Era* for $80,000; and Lewis Conn, *The Jefferson Reporter* $175,000 (it wasn't particularly profitable but it was billing out more than $1 million annually).

Frank Stanley Sr. declined to have *The Louisville Defender* join the new company because he said his African-American constituency would perceive his paper as having been sold to a white-oriented corporation.

Working through the investment house Hilliard-Lyons, we reached out to potential investors for $150,000 in seed money so we could start immediately with computerized bookkeeping, more production employees, and the additional services of an established accounting firm. Among the investors were General Dillman Rash, John Stites and Halsey Sandford with Hilliard-Lyons of Shelbyville, Judge E. Skiles Jones, A. Robert Doll and my brothers, Ben and Bob.

The first 90 days of the new corporation were disastrous. Several of the publishers sat back and expected the money to roll in simply because we had joined forces and were saving money on our printing. We lost about $50,000 and several of the new stockholders questioned whether they had made a wise decision.

With the seed money about gone, accounts receivable declining, and accounts payable climbing, the 14-member board (eight newspaper publishers and six outsiders), decided we needed to have a "rights offering" to raise more capital. We set a target of $150,000 that was quickly exceeded because the Garrisons purchased an additional $50,000, and Bob and Howard Logan of Shelbyville came in for $25,000 each.

By now every publisher knew he had to hit it hard to right the ship and the second quarter ended with a modest profit.

At the end of our fiscal year, we had a net profit of $30,000 and the future looked very promising.

From 1969 until our sale to Landmark Communications Inc. in September 1973, we established central printing plants in Cynthiana and Elizabethtown, as well as Shelbyville, and our gross revenues climbed from under $2 million in the start-up year to about $5 million four years later.

We acquired papers in Munfordville, Horse Cave, Cave City, Irvine (2), Columbia, Flemingsburg, Cynthiana, Campbellsville, Olive Hill, Hazard, Carrollton, Bedford, and Tell City, Indiana. Start-ups in Mount Sterling and Richmond failed. Papers that we had acquired in Corydon and Salem, Indiana were later sold to Eddie Waggoner of Columbia.

Much of our revenue was obtained from the printing of other newspapers, shoppers and circulars.

In 1971, we had a stock split that resulted in an evaluation of each of our shares at $1.50. A few months later, several of our outside investors who were not receiving any compensation began to exert some pressure for us to sell the company since that had been our intention from the outset or to "go public." We contacted one of the better known newspaper brokers, Bob Bolitho, and advised him of our interest in selling the company to a respectable organization.

In the spring of 1973, we were visited by a representative of the Knight-Ridder chain based in Miami. After a few discussions and visitations to several of our properties, the representative decided that we were "too small" for their acquisition.

Landmark Community Newspapers Inc.

In July, Bolitho said he had a serious prospect for us to consider: Landmark Communications based in Norfolk, Virginia.

In August 1973, I signed the papers officially transferring ownership of Newspapers Inc. to Landmark Communications, Norfolk, Virginia. We were officially renamed Landmark Community Newspapers. From left to right are John Colburn, William E. Matthews, J. William Diederick, and Bob Bolitho who assisted in the negotiations.

Frank Batten, in essence, owned Landmark Communications, which owned such media outlets as the Weather Channel and large daily newspapers. A few days after Bolitho's phone call, Batten came to Shelbyville along with Treasurer William Diederick and Acquisitions Advisor John Colburn. They treated my wife, Else, and me along with our corporate treasurer, Larry Coffey, to lunch at Science Hill Inn. A few days after that, Batten sent the company's corporate jet to Louisville to transport Else, Larry and me to Norfolk.

We were treated royally and Batten turned out all of the company's senior officers for a fancy dinner at a local club.

The next day, while Else and I enjoyed the sights of Norfolk, Diederick grilled Larry about our financials.

We had been home only a few days when we received a firm offer of $4.00 per share for at least 90 percent of the shares. This meant that Newspapers Inc. shareholders would more than double their original investment. We agreed to take 29 percent down, 29 percent the second year, 29 percent the third year and 13 percent the last year.

Our management team was asked to stay on as Batten issued the usual "no changes are contemplated" in the announcement about the transaction that appeared in both large and small newspapers across the state.

In fact, in a one-on-one conversation, Batten told me to "keep going like you have been."

Whether it was naiveté or just plain stupidity on my part, I took Batten at his word and assumed I would stay at the helm of the newly-named group, Landmark Community Newspapers Inc., indefinitely since the cooperative concept of centralized printing and bookkeeping and editorial independence for each paper had been mine from the beginning.

One of the reasons that helped push us to sell Newspapers Inc. was the Arab Oil Embargo of 1973, which had caused paper mills to reduce the amount of paper they could deliver to their customers. While we had many of our own papers to print, as well as those of many other publishers, we were a relatively small company when it came to the use of newsprint. The bigger the company, the more anxious the mills were to keep them in business. Consequently we became aware that the rationing of newsprint was a serious possibility. Landmark was a more attractive and lucrative customer for the mills.

My immediate boss became Bill Armistead, who had run the papers in Roanoke, Virginia, prior to their sale to Landmark. We didn't exactly click at the outset and the relationship didn't improve during my brief two-year stay. My best relationship was with Diederick while I only saw or heard from Batten during the monthly meetings in Norfolk that were attended by senior Landmark officials and the heads of all the various newspapers, cable and broadcast properties.

During the two years I was with Landmark, we bought out Jimmy Cravens' paper in Campbellsville, which gave us a monopoly there, and acquired the *Carroll County Times* in Westminster, Maryland. Our bottom line improved because of the acquisitions, reduced competition, and expansion of commercial printing.

Batten preferred his principal operators to maintain an extremely low profile and participate in no activities that could possibly interfere with the job at hand. This was counter to my nature because I had always been heavily involved in community matters in Shelbyville and enjoyed a high profile.

Perhaps the biggest conflict we had was over my ownership of a sports publication, *Reds Alert,* which made its debut in the spring of 1974. Two young men, Pete Alexis and

Dennis Gruelle, had approached me in the fall of 1973 about the possibility of publishing a sports magazine covering the Reds, and the idea appealed to me because I'd been a lifelong Cincinnati fan.

We decided to call it *Pete Rose's Reds Alert* because we had made a deal with Pete that in return for the use of his name, we would give him a percentage of all subscriptions and advertising.

An unhappy Armistead called me in May 1974 after a *Cincinnati Enquirer* front page story reported that Pete Rose had been told by Reds management that he would have to sever his relationship with the publication because it represented a conflict of interest.

I had responded that the Reds were trying to suppress Pete's free speech. Be that as it may, Pete gave up his interest in the publication, which we then renamed simply *Reds Alert.*

I pressed Armistead for more commercial printing presses because I thought the future of LCNI lay just as much in commercial work as it did with newspapers. I lost my case because Diederick was not as enamored with commercial work as he was with newspapers. He called dollars earned from newspaper ads "Hard dollars" and those through commercial printing "Soft dollars."

Two actions that I took upon orders by Armistead bothered me greatly.

The first centered on our printing plant in Cincinnati, which I was directed to close and lay off all of the employees. The reason: Batten hated unions and he was fearful that International Typographical Union #3 would attempt to unionize our plant. Plant Manager Paul Miller was incredulous when I told him to close the plant, but he dutifully complied and we gave each employee one week's severance pay.

The other action that I was directed to take was to close *The Jefferson Reporter,* our award-winning suburban paper in Louisville. Lewis Conn was not only the publisher, but a longtime personal friend dating back to the establishment of our printing plant in Shelbyville.

After firing each of the 19 employees following a one-on-one meeting, my final act was to fire Lewis who at least realized how distasteful it was for me. Although we saw each other several times after that, our relationship was never the same.

I saw the "handwriting on the wall" in mid-summer of 1975 when I was about 15 minutes late meeting Armistead who arrived on the Landmark plane at Standiford Field in Louisville.

When I pulled up to the plane, he asked me for the time and when I said it was 10:15, he said, rather sharply, "I told you to meet me at 10 o'clock sharp."

In late August I was called to a meeting with Armistead and Diederick at the old Ramada Inn that stood at the intersection of I-64 and Hurstbourne Drive. Even as I was driving toward Louisville I knew that the end of my days at Landmark was nigh. That was when I realized that I had been "had." Prior to acquiring Newspapers Inc., I had been told by Armistead, as well as Batten, to keep doing what I had been doing. As it turned out, neither meant a word of it because, in fact, our community newspapers division of Landmark was doing better than the daily in Roanoke, Virginia.

Landmark was nice enough about my "resignation to pursue other interests," as Armistead characterized it for *The Courier-Journal* and other media. I was also elated to receive a full year's salary of $48,000 and retain my very profitable stock until the end of the year.

Over the next two weeks, there were several parties celebrating my time with Landmark. Diederick and Armistead both came from Norfolk to see me off.

Actually I was relieved to be leaving Landmark because my personality was not compatible with Landmark philosophy and I had been smitten by the Reds bug. Making *Reds Alert* successful had become a high priority. Cincinnati was on its way to its first World Series championship since 1940 and the magazine had become a tremendous hit with subscribers and advertisers alike.

I left Landmark in relatively good graces as far as the public was concerned.

Community versus Corporate

Continuing my reflection on the short Landmark period of my life, I might mention again how the corporate world works. John Colburn, whom I have previously given the title "Acquisitions advisor," was also the company's "Hatchet man," "Axe man," "Enforcer," or whatever term you might use to describe the "bad guy" who gets rid of people.

It was John who fired Sally Fay as editor/publisher of *The Sentinel-News* in Shelbyville and Louie Heitkemper in Tell City. I was unaware that we had a problem with either Sally or Louie, but Norfolk thought differently.

Louie's sacking was particularly odious. He was asked to meet Colburn and Max Heath, who lived then and still does in Shelbyville, at a Tell City restaurant. As they were finishing lunch, Colburn said, "Louie, we're going to make a change here." When Louie responded, "Who?" Colburn said, "You."

Colburn introduced Max as the new No. 1 guy, took Heitkemper's keys to the company car, and left him "high and dry" at the restaurant. He had to call his wife, Marcie, to pick him up. When he arrived home, the items from his desk at the *Tell City News* had been placed in a brown paper sack and delivered to his home.

When I talked to Louie 39 years later, he still wondered "Why?"

Buying *Grant County News*

One month after leaving Landmark, I joined my brother Ben in purchasing the *Grant County News* in Williamstown for $100,000. After a few days he decided that I was entitled to the paper by myself and bowed out of the picture.

I was pleased that Susan Arena, also fired by Landmark, had agreed to become editor of the paper. She rented a home in Dry Ridge in the northern part of Grant County.

At the same time I established another newspaper, *The Boone County Leader*, in Florence, Kentucky, a fast-growing city in Boone County. We composed both papers in Williamstown.

Later, in 1976, I established *The Campbell County News* in Alexandria, Kentucky, one of only two Kentucky counties that have two county seats. The other is at Newport.

In setting up shop in Campbell County, the E.W. Scripps Company, a communications conglomerate with vast media holdings throughout the country, took exception and started a zoned edition aimed at forcing me out of business. A zoned edition is an edition with a specific geographic target and generally carries only news and ads for the targeted area. In this case, my competitor became a zoned edition of *The Kentucky Post,* which was an afternoon daily published by Scripps.

While I was discussing a possible lawsuit against the Post with my attorney Ed Perry of Louisville, John Feldman, business manager for *The Kentucky Post*, asked me about having lunch and talking about things of mutual interest. That "mutual interest" turned out to be the possibility of Scripps acquiring my small operation.

A few days later, I met with Jacques Caldwell and Dan Castellini from Scripps' senior management team.

I liked each of the two men immediately and it didn't take long to reach a deal.

Scripps acquired my operation for $140,000 and provided me with a written five-year contract starting at $30,000 per annum. In view of my unfortunate, short stint at Landmark, I had insisted on a written document as an integral part of the sale.

Scripps-Howard acquired the web printing plant owned by Carroll Knicely, Glasgow newspaper publisher, for $300,000.

My bailiwick, then, became the three northern Kentucky papers plus the Louisville printing plant. Subsequently I became publisher of the *Voice of St. Matthews* that Scripps-Howard bought from Bruce Van Dusen.

My five years with Scripps-Howard were not particularly memorable as my small division of papers and the printing plant lost varying amounts of money each year.

The 'Mob' and Me

It was during this stint that I encountered one of the more colorful figures in Northern Kentucky history, a somewhat legendary man called Johnny "TV" Peluso.

Johnny was a leftover from Newport's colorful and criminal days dating back to the Civil War.

In the book *Wicked Newport*, the three authors point out that post-World War II Newport was ruled by the Cleveland Mob and "fueled by government corruption," assisted by "crooked politicians and law enforcement officials."

The city was known as staid Cincinnati's playground where 300 to 500 girls operated in bordellos in the main part of Newport, primarily Monmouth Street. Not only prostitution but illegal gambling provided the mob with millions of dollars, and frequently left naive out-of-towners with only enough pocket money for gas to somehow get home.

It was into this "den of iniquity" that former football star George Ratterman stepped when he announced his candidacy for Campbell County Sheriff in 1961. Frightened by the prospect of losing its franchise on illegal money-making, the mob succeeded on May 9 in drugging Ratterman and putting him in bed with stripper April Flowers.

The attempt to blackmail Ratterman was exposed and even the usually passive voters elected him sheriff. With the help of local informants and federal agents, most, but not all, of the sin was rooted out and Newport, long considered the predecessor to Las Vegas, began electing honest citizens and ridding itself of the "sin city" moniker.

As I said, Peluso was a "leftover" from this period and, as mayor or commissioner, was at the center of what I thought were many questionable activities. I pointed these out in several editorials and even my employer, the E.W. Scripps Co., advised me (but didn't order me) to "ease up" on Johnny who was a rather popular figure.

It was in the fall of 1979, as I was packing my car to return to Shelbyville, that the staccato of gunfire erupted in front of our office in the county seat of Alexandria. When I checked a few minutes later, there were at least 21 bullet holes in my station wagon.

I promptly called my boss in Scripps-Howard who sent out a reporter. When I suggested it was a random shooting, the reporter responded, "Well, there are 21 cars in the parking lot and only yours has been shot up."

I told the reporter that I had "too many enemies" for me to name anyone publicly. *The Kentucky Post*, owned by the E.W. Scripps Company, ran a lengthy article on the shooting.

The station wagon had to be towed back to Shelbyville where Bob Pearce asked me, "Who's that mad at you?"

That Christmas, Peluso and two of his henchmen showed up for our office's Christmas party and he was carrying a brown paper sack.

At the sight of him, all of my employees bailed out of the room. He wished me a Merry Christmas, hoped that we could "get along better" in the New Year, and left the sack. I didn't exactly rush to open it, but when I did, it turned out to be a bottle of Chivas Regal, a high-priced brand of Scotch. I never knew how he found out that I was a Scotch drinker, but it gave me an eerie feeling to realize how much he knew about me.

Peluso was first elected mayor in 1964 and served as mayor or commissioner for 18 years. I have not heard or seen Peluso since that Christmas of 1979. Nor have I wanted to.

Voice of St. Matthews

During my tenure with Scripps-Howard, I was offered the opportunity to buy the *Voice of St. Matthews.* For some reason I jumped at the chance.

We had long since sold, if not given away, the three northern papers to Gloria Bushelman, longtime owner of *The Dixie News,* a shopper, and *The Boone County Recorder*, a weekly newspaper.

My experience with the *Voice* was just as bad as the one that Scripps had suffered. One of the reasons for the *Voice's* failure, under both Scripps-Howard and me, was the *Louisville Courier-Journal's* introduction into the market place of its zoned Neighborhoods editions, which enabled the mother paper to tailor local news and advertising to specific geographic areas, including St. Matthews.

After only eight months of battling the *Courier*, I was fortunate enough to sell it to the late real estate developer John Waits.

KPA President

As I mentioned earlier, through the strong support of Al Smith and Bob Carter, I was elected president of the Kentucky Press Association in 1977. By that time many of those who had been around 10 years previously when we had lost the battle but won the war had been replaced by men and women enjoying their first term as a district director or director-at-large.

My old adversary, Donald B. Towles, was still on the board as was Russ Metz of Owingsville. Russ had resigned from KPA following the squabble in 1968, but I had persuaded him to return several years later. At this time I owned *The Grant County News*, *The Boone County Leader*, the *Tri-City News* in Cumberland, and *The Reds Alert.*

Of particular significance during the 1977-1978 year was KPA's continuing the fight to preserve public notice advertising from efforts by the Municipal Statutes Revision Commission to sharply reduce, if not, eliminate such advertising.

The commission, made up primarily of city officials, was established by legislation enacted by the Kentucky General Assembly in 1976.

The Kentucky Press, a monthly publication of KPA, quoted me as saying that KPA "will do everything within its power to see that the recommendations for statute changes are defeated so long as the public notice requirements remain as drafted."

I was quoted further as saying, "While many members of KPA feel a need for revising statutes dealing with city government, they do not feel that additional authority should be granted to city officials unless or until they are willing to be open and accountable for their actions."

I continued, according to the publication, that "if the commission does not revise its recommendations before forwarding them to the appropriate committee of the General Assembly, KPA will carry the fight to defeat the proposal to the hearing room of the legislature."

The bottom line is that city officials cited the expense of public notice advertising as an excuse to get rid of them. They claimed that "no one reads these notices" and "they're a waste of public tax dollars."

Newspapers countered that the public's right to know was being compromised.

Unfortunately, the General Assembly, which was perhaps more effectively lobbied by the cities than KPA, acquiesced, and many of the public notices that had been required almost since Kentucky became a state, "went by the board."

In my view, the public lost a very big and basic "right to know" what was happening in their towns and cities.

At the January 1978 banquet in Lexington, I handed over the gavel to Carroll Knicely from Glasgow. I named Russ Metz KPA's most valuable member for many of the trips he made with me as we contested the actions of the Municipal Statues Revision Commission.

Attorney General Investigation

The low point of my career came in August 1983 when the Kentucky Attorney General's office filed a lawsuit charging me with consumer fraud. A number of other individuals and I had formed a company in 1981 called Official Publications (also known as Salute Publications) to produce a telephone directory in Hardin County and a Fort Knox map. The suit sought unspecified civil penalties for alleged willful violations of the state's Consumer Protection Law. Actually I owned only 40 percent of the shares in the company but, as president, it was my responsibility to ensure that the directory and map were published.

Unfortunately the man hired to oversee the actual sale of advertising and the production of the map did little of either and we missed several deadlines prior to publication.

My banking records were subpoenaed, as well as those of the company, with the state trying to prove that I benefitted from the advertising sales.

However, after more than two years of investigating me personally and financially, the state had to conclude that not one penny had gone into my pocket, and the action was dismissed. I signed an agreement to insure that nothing similar would happen in the future.

Kentucky Travel Company

Throughout the period between leaving Landmark in 1975 and selling the *Voice* to Waits in 1983, I had retained The Kentucky Travel Co. as a profitable sideline. The travel company had only one employee, Alice Richardson, of Shelbyville, who had been with me since 1963 at *The Shelby Sentinel*.

Alice was unquestionably the best and most loyal employee I ever had.

The company traced its beginning to 1968 when newly-appointed Commissioner of

Kentucky Parks Jim Host approached me about doing a special edition on the reopening of the renovated park at Fort Boonesborough. Alice sold the ads, the state provided the copy, and the edition was very successful, editorially and financially.

I then decided to promote as many of the state parks as Alice's time would allow, and within two years we were publishing up to 12 separate editions annually. Some of the titles included "Exciting Western Kentucky," "Enchanting Eastern Kentucky," and "Cumberland Splendor," just to name a few.

Alice continued to work for me even after her husband, Newton Richardson, retired after many years as manager at the Shelbyville Kroger. She was still on the job selling ads in 1994 when she was killed outside Richmond, Kentucky in a two-car accident that was not her fault. I gave the eulogy at her funeral in Owingsville in Bath County.

The Huntingburg Press

With the sale of the *Voice* to Waits, Alice and I concentrated strictly on the travel magazines from January 1983 to the fall of 1987. It was then that Paula Waggoner, who had been with me as an Administrative Assistant at the *Voice*, and I launched *The Huntingburg Press* in September. We received a $25,000 low-interest loan from the City of Huntingburg and $25,000 from a group of leading citizens in Huntingburg who wanted a paper to concentrate on what was happening in the newly-reenergized city.

The Jasper Herald had a virtual "lock" on the Dubois County market but, somehow, we generated enough advertising from Huntingburg and Jasper merchants that we survived from 1987 to our sale of the paper to Chris McGehee in 2000.

Huntingburg is populated largely by folks of German descent and someone once asked me seriously if I had considered changing my name from the Anglo-Scotch Matthews to the more Germanic Matheis.

I commuted every week for those 13 years from Shelbyville to Huntingburg where I enjoyed a spacious apartment on the second floor of a Fourth Street building. The newspaper was on the ground floor.

It was during this period that Huntingburg became famous for hosting three movies: *A League of Their Own, Soul of the Game,* and *Hard Rain.* I appeared as an umpire in the first movie, a photographer in the second, and a consultant on the third.

Paula died in 1993 and Jerlene Rose became my new partner the following year.

Jerlene and I operated the paper from 1994 to November 2000 when we transferred ownership of the paper to Chris McGehee of Louisville. The sales price was $200,000.

In a farewell luncheon hosted by some Huntingburg citizens, I received a beautiful plaque in the shape of the State of Indiana stating, "With appreciation to Bill Matthews for Thirteen Years of Service to the Citizens of Huntingburg as Editor of the *Huntingburg Press*. Gail Kemp, Mayor, December 2000."

Individuals that I remember with great affection from those 13 years in Huntingburg include "Rosie" Rosenblatt, Gail Kemp, Dr. Michael Warren, his hygienist Jane (Olinger) Fritch, Mike and Steve Uebelhor, Bob Steffe, Cecil Buerckley, Sue Fraze, Tina Cyrill, Donna Blessinger, Rosemary Suters, Joyce Deel and the late Jack Davis.

Back Home in Kentucky

Jerlene and I bought *Back Home in Kentucky* in the fall of 1999 for $70,000 from Bill

Smith of Franklin, Tennessee, and brought the publication back to Kentucky the following year.

We published *Back Home in Kentucky* from 1999 to the sale of her half-interest in April 2009 to Mae Peniston of New Castle.

While *Back Home in Kentucky* magazine was profitable, Mae and I decided to suspend publication of the magazine following our spring 2012 issue. The decision was based, in part, on the decline of print advertising and our decision to reduce our staff to just the two of us.

The magazine went out on a high note, as the 96-page issue featuring Pikeville and Pike County was the largest ever published dating back to 1977 when *Back Home in Kentucky* was launched by the Cockrel family in Bowling Green.

I am especially pleased *Back Home in Kentucky* won the Media Award from the Kentucky Historical Society three straight years (2003-2005).

Historic Kentucky continues to publish the popular *"Discover Shelby County"* travel guide in the spring of each year. It has increased the number of pages and the amount of information each year since it was started in 2007.

Shelby County Life

Jerlene and I successfully launched the monthly full-color *Shelby County Life* in the summer of 2007. Former *Sentinel-News* Editor James Mulcahy signed on as the editor; Marilyn Major, Harold Thom, and Margaret Yates worked with the advertisers; and Stephanie Dunn handled circulation and the office. The publication filled an important niche in the community with its eye-catching layout and hometown human interest content, which drew much praise from readers and advertisers alike.

We concluded in the spring of 2009 that we had "too much on our plate," and decided to sell the magazine to Mulcahy and some of the community's leading citizens.

Publishing Books

Mae and I formed Historic Kentucky Inc. on January 3, 2008. Our first and highly successful project was the publication in September of that year of *Portrait of the Past, A Pictorial History of Shelby County, Kentucky from 1865 to 1980.* Jim Cleveland and I partnered on the production, with Jim supplying hundreds of images for which I wrote most of the captions. The photos included family portraits from various sources as well as historic events and buildings.

In 2012, Historic Kentucky published *A Living History – Shelby County, Kentucky, 2011*, featuring Greg Biagi's photos, which mirrored the earlier book except that images were from the current era. In the future, this will serve as an historic outlook on the community.

In 2013, we produced *Historic Kentucky Postcard Art – 1900-2013 – Shelby, Henry, Spencer Counties.* There are about 135 pages of postcards that feature images of community settings… some still in existence, others lost to what is considered progress.

Newspapers Today

The newspaper industry in 2014 is a very pale shadow of what it was in the 1960s through the early years of the 21st century. Daily newspapers, in particular, have been hit hard as the Internet, Facebook, and other advanced technological means of transmitting news and advertising, have caused both readers and advertisers to look somewhere other than the printed page.

Community newspapers such as *The Sentinel-News* have not been hit quite so hard, but they too have suffered serious losses in circulation and revenue. Classified ads, once the backbone of most paid newspapers, have largely gone out the window because "free" papers offer them at little, if any cost, because it helps drive readership.

Landmark Communications, the parent of my old company, has sold off dailies in Roanoke and Greensboro, N.C. Landmark scored big when it sold The Weather Channel to NBC for a reported $3.5 billion in 2008. It continues to have the community newspapers, including *The Sentinel-News,* up for sale. As part of the change of focus for Landmark, the printing plant that was originally built in 1966 with the formation of Greater Kentucky Publishers was closed in 2013. *The Sentinel-News* and other publications that were printed in Shelbyville were sent to neighboring plants.

The three men for whom I worked in 1973-1975 are all deceased: Frank Batten Sr., William Diederick, and Bill Armistead along with John Colburn.

Batten Sr., at the time of his death, was judged by Forbes magazine to be worth $2.3 billion, making him 190th on a list of 400 of the wealthiest people in the United States. His son, Frank Batten Jr., succeeded his father in 1998 and made the decision to start selling components of the company in 2007. His father died in 2009 at the age of 82.

When I came back to Kentucky in 1962, it marked the beginning of a new era for newspapers, switching from the old linotype set-up to offset printing. That was considered a technological breakthrough for the companies. As we move into the digital age, newspapers will still be relevant in society but will no longer occupy the primary position of communication for American households that they have for 200 years.

Tom Sawyer (later Dr. Sawyer) and Van Monroe (center) have been lifelong friends since our days at Michigan and were groomsmen in Else's and my wedding on Friday, June 13, 1952.

Interns under my watch

Each of us has played a role – some important, some not so important – in the lives of others, be they family or friends or folks we barely know. These experiences count for something, big or small, in the lives of those we touch.

I was blessed to have had a small part in the career development of three wonderful and talented young ladies. In the following pages you will learn how their experiences in the newspaper or magazine business helped mold their lives.

Here is a very brief bio of each of these outstanding individuals.

Dr. Carol (Tipton) Aitcheson was the valedictorian of her Shelbyville High School class of 1966. She interned at the *Sentinel* seven summers, from 1966 to 1972. Quite remarkable is the fact that she also was the No. 1 graduate of her University of Kentucky class of 1970, and of the Tulane Medical School Class of 1974.

She is an internist/rheumatologist with the Piedmont Physicians Group in Atlanta, Ga.

She and her husband Frank have two daughters, Nancy and Beth, both of whom are pursuing careers in medicine.

Carol earned several honors, including the Hamilton Watch Award for her 4.0 GPA at the University of Kentucky, and the Isadore Dyer Memorial prize for graduating first in her medical school class at Tulane. She received her board certification in Internal Medicine in 1976.

A member of Phi Beta Kappa, an honorary academic society, Carol was president of the Tulane Chapter of Alpha Omega Alpha Medical Honorary Society.

She is the daughter of Truman and Louise Tipton, both of whom are deceased.

Quite simply Carol did it all at *The Shelby Sentinel*. She set the standard for every other intern who ever worked at the newspaper. The only two who lived up to the high standard she set were Libby Fraas and Laura Biagi.

Dr. Libby (Duffy) Fraas was valedictorian of her Shelby County High School class of 1967. She interned at *The Shelby Sentinel* in 1968 and 1969.

She retired as professor emerita from Eastern Kentucky University in 2006. She taught journalism at EKU for 27 years and was the faculty adviser for *The Eastern Progress*. In back-to-back years, the paper was named Best All Around Campus Newspaper by the Society of Professional Journalists. In 1994 she was recognized as Society of Professional Journalism's National Outstanding Campus Chapter Adviser.

A member of Phi Beta Kappa at the University of Kentucky, she graduated with a B. A. degree in 1971, and received her M. A. Degree from UK in 1976.

She edited *The Public Papers of Governor Martha Layne Collins*, published by the University Press of Kentucky in 2006. She was the first graduate of the doctoral program in communications from the University of Kentucky in 1984, writing her dissertation on "Keen Johnson: Newspaperman and Governor."

She and her husband Bob, also a retired professor from EKU, now live in Lancaster County, S.C., close to their grandchildren, Sophia, Kade, and Livi in nearby Charlotte. They are the children of Kerry (Fraas) and Bobby Lindauer. Libby is the daughter of Mary Ann (Biagi) Duffy and Tom Duffy, both of whom are deceased.

Laura Biagi is a full-fledged literary agent for the Jean V. Naggar Literary Agency in

New York City where one of her primary duties is to acquire, edit and negotiate deals for adult literary fiction and young readers' fiction. She worked at *Back Home in Kentucky* in 2006 and 2007 as a writer, interviewer and researcher. She wrote more than 20 articles on featured counties, people and events for *Back Home in Kentucky* and *Shelby County Life* magazines.

She graduated magna cum laude and Phi Beta Kappa from Northwestern University in Chicago, Illinois in 2009.

She received the Kentucky Emerging Artist Award for 2012-13 for Excellence in Fiction. An essay which she wrote was published in *USA Today* in July 2011.

She is the daughter of Robert and Marcia Biagi.

Carol Aitcheson

I had just graduated from Shelbyville High School and needed a summer job to help pay for college. I had taken typing in school and thought I would try to get a job in an office. I put in applications at several businesses in town. When I was hired by *The Shelby Sentinel*, I didn't realize that my world would be opened up in many new ways.

Over the next seven summers, not only did I type, but I made up newspaper pages, did feature articles, wrote a weekly column called "Teen Scene", covered news stories including a rape trial, called lists of women for news for the Society Page of the paper, and was all around Girl Friday. One year I typed all but the front page of the paper on a justowriter that was like a typewriter but made the left edge straight so that it would form columns. When the first personal computer came out, I was sent to IBM in Louisville to learn how to use the computer so I could type the newspaper on this new invention. This was in the very early days of the computer when no one had a personal computer at home.

Carol Tipton Aitcheson was the No. 1 student at Shelbyville High School, UK, and Tulane Medical School.

Bill Matthews owned the credit bureau so part of my job was calling credit references and making credit reports.

How did I know how to do all these things? I didn't. What I learned was to not shy away from new tasks, to do the best I could, and to learn to take criticism and correction without taking it too personally. I learned to say yes to challenges and believe I could do things. I gained confidence in myself as well as multiple skills that would subsequently serve me well in my profession as a physician. Interviewing all kinds of people, making sure the facts were right, and learning to solve problems were all important skills that I learned. Even my typing has served me well in the days of the electronic medical record.

One of my most memorable (and embarrassing) experiences was the summer day that Mr. Matthews asked me to drive the mock-up of the paper to be printed in Georgetown, Kentucky. I wasn't really used to driving to places that were new to me, and I was apprehensive. I got on an isolated, country road and had gone some distance before I realized that I was on the wrong road. Suddenly a young man, attired only in khaki shorts and no shirt, signaled for me to stop the car. I didn't know what he wanted and I was scared. I didn't pay much attention to what he said – I just wanted to get away from him. He handed me something through the window and I just laid it down on the seat and drove on. I went on for several miles until I could find a good place to turn around. I started back along the road and came to a place where all the cars were stopped. We all sat there at least an hour in extreme afternoon heat – not able to use the air-conditioning because we were stopped for so long. No one knew what was causing the delay because there was no sign of an accident. I was concerned that I wouldn't get the pages to Georgetown to be printed on time. I finally called the man who was stopping the cars back to my car. I told him that I had to get the paper through. He said he couldn't let us go until he received a red flag from the other side letting him know that they were holding the traffic going the other way since this was a construction site with one-way traffic only. I looked down beside me at the red piece of cloth that had been given to me and said "Could this be what you are looking for?" I will never forget his expression.

One of my favorite times every week was when the weekly paper was coming out on Thursday and we stayed to fold the papers and get them ready for distribution. There were no prima donnas at *The Shelby Sentinel*. Everyone, including Miss Mabel (the office matriarch), C.L. Love, the photographer, and Mr. Matthews himself all stood around a large table getting ink on hands and clothes and got the job done. I learned the real meaning of teamwork in getting that paper out every week.

Bill Matthews was my mentor in every way. He taught me to think big, to go after my dreams, and to believe that I could accomplish whatever I wanted to do. I doubt that I would be a physician today without the influence of Bill Matthews.

Libby Fraas

For some reason, a note I penciled to myself on April 28, 1968 — as I was finishing up my freshman year at the University of Kentucky — remains in the clutter of clips and stuff that a person collects over a lifetime and can't bear to toss away until someone has to do it for her: *"Today I wrote my summer employer and accepted the job I had written to him about, 'hoping that I could contribute something to the Sentinel.'"*

The break that Bill Matthews gave me as an intern at *The Shelby Sentinel* that eventful summer was the first job on my resumé and contributed to a career in journalism education and writing about Kentucky history and politics.

One of my first assignments occurred on the morning of June 5, as the world was waking to the news that another Kennedy had been shot. The editor wanted the reaction of Main Street, Shelbyville. JFK, MLK, now RFK; this 18-year-old reporter ached as much as the folks who were nice enough to talk with me.

That summer brought the anti-Vietnam movement and the Eugene McCarthy campaign to a Democratic Party caucus in the Shelby County courthouse. *"Long hair, sideburns and even a mini-skirt mingled with the bald heads and gray hair of the party hierarchy,"* I reported. My story – headlined '*Courthouse Rumble*' – documented futile protests that none of the delegates selected were female or young. Both the Democratic Party and journalism underwent changes after that year. The Society of Professional Journalists, an organization that I later worked with as a chapter adviser and board member, didn't allow women to join in 1968. Fortunately *The Sentinel* did.

The world of journalism and politics was changing, but straddling the transition were people like Mabel Oats, who enforced deadlines and showed by example how to properly use our before e-mail lifeline: the telephone. Details and accuracy were important whether it was the type of taffeta on a wedding veil or the time and place of a funeral. Gerry Johnson taught the importance of advertisements and the patience needed to jigsaw together a Kroger ad with glue and an X-acto knife.

When I worked for *The Sentinel*, there were two weekly papers in my hometown. Although the staffs sometimes shared ad copy and press releases, I fiercely bought in to the concept of delivering the better product on Thursdays. It might be the dairy farm tour, but I wanted our story to be the best. Thus was nourished a competitive streak associated with the practice of journalism that was sustained even when newspapers merged and combined into chains.

The Sentinel also was undergoing changes, becoming part of a community newspaper chain that pooled printing presses and business staffs. One of my jobs was to transport the "flats" from places like Springfield to the printing press in Shelbyville. I learned the geography of those communities around Shelbyville and many of my students at Eastern Kentucky University went to work for those papers as interns, reporters or editors.

Libby Fraas

Today, perhaps ironically, I live in a community in South Carolina, which depends on a weekly newspaper for its local news. That newspaper is owned by Landmark Communications, of which *The (Shelby) Sentinel-News* is affiliated. At some point, a person looks back and thinks about choices made and opportunities given. I blush now at the arrogance of writing a column, egotistically named "libby duffy", which appeared one summer in *The Sentinel.* I marvel that the publisher let me write a signed editorial urging a new Shelby County jail, even though he disagreed with my view. I don't go back and look at these clips often. I have moved on. And yet, most of my career ended up working with young adults in college journalism. Giving young people the opportunity and the tools to communicate isn't a bad calling. Seems like that summer job I was given in 1968 "contributed something" to me.

Laura Biagi

I began interning for Bill Matthews as a journalist at *Back Home in Kentucky* during my first summer in college. It was my job to write articles about various counties, businesses, people, and events throughout the state and to interview business owners and the like as necessary for these articles. Upon learning what I would be doing all summer, I was mostly thrilled to have a job that involved writing… but I was also a bit terrified of interviewing strangers. Under Mr. Matthews' mentorship, however, I quickly learned to not let my fears get in the way of exciting, new experiences. Over the course of that summer and the summer that followed, I would gain a much deeper sense of confidence in not only my interviewing skills but also my work ethic, my writing, and myself.

Some of my favorite memories from *Back Home in Kentucky* involved getting to see slices of life I never would have on my own. One day in the middle of that first summer, Mr. Matthews suggested I go around the corner from his office and interview Dottie Spaulding Gordon, founder of Dottie's Beauty Shop. Dottie had opened her business in 1940, a time when very few women were business owners. In 2006 she was 89 and still coming in to get her hair styled every Thursday. She maintained she would return to practicing cosmetology herself once her arthritis improved. I admired her tenacity.

Later that summer, Mr. Matthews and I attended the old-fashioned "social" portion of Lincoln Institute's reunion. Between 1911 and 1966, during the segregation era, this high school in Simpsonville served as the only source of higher education for African-Americans throughout the state. Many of the alumni in attendance had made great successes of themselves. There were teachers, engineers, lawyers, and doctors among them. Their enthusiasm at reuniting to celebrate the school that had given them their start was infectious.

Laura Biagi

I also wrote articles profiling noteworthy Kentuckians. Among them, of course, was Colonel Harland Sanders. The man famous for creating Kentucky Fried Chicken had always seemed larger-than-life to me. In researching his history, however, I learned the real-life, rocky story of how hard he had to work through the Great Depression, World War II, the 1950s, and the 1960s to achieve success. His persistence was extraordinary. It is a quality I believe must flourish in Kentucky, as I saw it in each of the noteworthy Kentuckians I profiled. It is a quality I saw in Mr. Matthews, too – molded into the very way he conducted his businesses and mentored his employees – and it is something I strive for myself now as a literary agent in the publishing industry.

During my second summer interning for Mr. Matthews, my time was primarily devoted to his new publication, *Shelby County Life*. A special issue would focus on the Shelby Industrial and Development Foundation, and I was to write most of the articles profiling the county's industries for the issue. To this end, I toured nearly 20 different industries and interviewed employees and managers at each. They ranged from the family-owned Purnell Sausage Company, founded in 1932, to the Japanese-owned Katayama American Co. Inc., founded in 1988 to manufacture trim moldings and sashes for automobiles. I had never before realized how robust Shelby County's industrial sector was, nor how critical it was to the health of our economy.

I also wrote general articles for *Shelby County Life* about residential, commercial, and industrial real estate trends. This was the summer the words "national housing crisis" began cropping up in the news, or what would later become known as "the Great Recession." Toward the summer's end, Mr. Matthews asked me to write an article about the housing crisis and its outlook for the future of the county. I interviewed a residential Realtor, a commercial Realtor, two bank representatives, and the county commissioner in charge of foreclosure auctions in an effort to better understand the issue that had the entire country flummoxed. Eventually I concluded that, though the residential real estate market had slowed, the county's conservative lending practices and expanding commercial and industrial sectors would help it avoid the worst of the downturn. I'm still not sure how off base I was.

In looking back on my time working with Mr. Matthews, perhaps what I remember most is the great responsibility he gave me. I was the one accountable for portraying well the counties, people, businesses, and events I profiled. I thrived on the confidence Mr. Matthews had in my ability to succeed. His confidence in me, in turn, gave me confidence in myself. It is this confidence that has helped me forge my paths in the publishing and writing worlds. I will never forget the summers I spent learning from Mr. Matthews.

Reds Alert

The first ever national sports magazine dedicated to a single professional team was *Pete Rose's Reds Alert*. It made its debut on March 28, 1974. For the next few weeks this magazine created about as much commotion and excitement off the field as the team it was covering on the field

The magazine resulted from some conversations that I had, beginning in the fall of 1973, with two young men, Pete Alexis and Dennis Gruelle. They had been partly inspired by a magazine published seasonally by former Green Bay Packers' great, Ray Nitschke. Seed money for the publication was provided by the two young men's mothers, Jean Alexis and Ruth Gruelle, both of whom passed away in 2012.

While the magazine was enthusiastically welcomed to the greater Cincinnati area by thousands of avid Reds fans and readers, controversy struck almost immediately. It was triggered by my "Full Count" column that ripped reserve infielder Darrel Chaney as not being fit to be a Red.

Before it was over, the controversy embroiled Team President Bob Howsam, several of the Reds players and me.

A May 16, 1974 article by *Kentucky Post* sportswriter Ed Menaker quoted Howsam, generally credited with being the architect for the "Big Red Machine," as saying that the magazine has "run a series of articles that have ridiculed and unfairly criticized various members of the Cincinnati team."

Howsam, who died in 2008, continued that, "while I affirm the right of any publication to say what it likes, within legal bounds, I do not believe it is right for a publication that is known as Pete Rose's paper to attack Rose's teammates, even though Pete has not authored such articles."

The statement continued that Rose had agreed "to relinquish his relationship with the paper."

Contacted at my home in Shelbyville, I was quoted by Menaker as being "completely flabbergasted."

I told Menaker that "In seven issues we have had over 200 action photos and countless articles wholly favorable to the Reds. We've had four or five articles that have been objective, reflecting the independence of the tabloid. Chaney's was one of them."

At the time I considered taking legal action against the Reds, but thought better of it if the magazine was to continue.

The problem with the magazine basically was that Johnny Bench didn't like the attention that was being focused on Rose. The two players didn't get along off the field but, fortunately, never allowed their antagonism toward one another to affect their play on the field.

It was Bench who complained to Reds' Vice President Dick Wagner and Howsam that the magazine was hurting team morale.

This was simply not true as the players, almost to a man, liked the magazine and the publicity which it was showered on them. Manager "Sparky" Anderson was also a great fan of the publication.

Bench's Criticism

Here's what Bench had to say in his book, "*Catch You Later*":

"Pete (Rose) and I did have a fight about something called Pete Rose's Reds Alert. It was a kind of a fan newsletter about the team. Pete put his name on it, but it was written by a guy named Bill Matthews. It seemed to me that Matthews never even showed up at the ball park but once or twice a year, but that didn't keep him from writing some cheap shots about some of the guys.

"Finally it got out of hand, and a lot of players had hard feelings. We decided freedom of the press was fine and dance until it went as far as allowing a rag like this, with Pete's name on it, to rip a guy.

"I went to the front office and told them it shouldn't be. Pete had his name on the front of it and was getting paid for it, and it was hurting the team. He and I went at it one day before a game, and I told him that if he was going to have a newspaper and use it to cut his teammates, then it wasn't much of anything.

"Management agreed and said they were no longer going to tolerate it. Pete was pretty burned up about it, and he went for a long time without saying a word to me. That old square jaw was thrust out farther than ever. But we still played the game together and executed like we had to. We didn't say anything to each other in the dugout, and walked by in the locker room. But that passed after a while. Pete is Pete, and I knew who I was, and we both had jobs to do. After 1971, that involved getting the Red Machine running again.

Johnny Bench

Morgan's Perspective

Here's how second baseman Joe Morgan saw the "dust up" in his book, "*Joe Morgan: A Life in Baseball*":

"There was always a thin line between the absolute togetherness we had developed on the field and the potential for bad feelings behind the scenes.

"During that time, we had a reserve infielder on the ball club, Darrel Chaney. Chaney was not having a particularly good season and a local newspaper put out by fans called Red Alert (sic) lit into him. When the paper later came to Johnny Bench for an interview he told them to get lost, because he thought they'd gone too far against Chaney.

"None of that would have mattered except that Red Alert was heavily underwritten by Pete. To most of us, it was Pete's paper – and so John and Pete got into it over John's refusal to grant an interview.

Joe Morgan

"The argument started at the batting cage when the four of us were there to hit. Pete asked John to cooperate with Red Alert. John replied that he wasn't about to cooperate with any group that blasted Darrel Chaney.

*"'That's pretty chicken****, ya know!' Pete said.*

"'Why? John snapped. Darrel Chaney's just trying to make a living like everyone else.'

*"'And so f*** the fans, huh? They don't have a right to say what's on their mind, huh'?*

"'That's okay for you to say but Darrel Chaney isn't making your kind of money!'

"When we walked back to the dugout, everyone within earshot knew something was wrong, everyone except Tony Perez, who somehow thought Pete and John were just kidding around.

*"'Hey, you know what?,' Perez chimed in, 'F*** the Red Alert!'*

"Rose turned livid.

*"'F*** you, you're just like Bench, he's selfish, and so are you.'*

"Tony now caught on, saw that Pete was furious, and that save for his body interposed between John and Pete, there was an actual chance of physical confrontation between them.

"'You know what,' Tony said, 'I'm going to do the interview.'

"John and Pete both looked at Tony with exasperation, but, once, again, the Dog (Perez) had done just enough to take the edge off. We returned to the dugout without a fight breaking out.

Rose's Connection

Exactly how Rose got involved in the publication is spelled out in the book, "*Charlie Hustle*", written by *Cincinnati Enquirer* sports writer Bob Hertzel.

Here is a March 23 entry in the book:

"I became, of all things, a newspaperman today. A real journalist.

"It all started when I came back from the ball park, my tail dragging. Two guys were there with my wife, doing an interview. Karolyn has made herself into quite a celebrity, doing her own radio show and the like. They even want her to make speeches.

"These two kids – Pete Alexis and Dennis Gruelle – are from a new sports weekly paper in Cincinnati that's going to be call The Reds Alert.

"I remember the kids. Back in January they contacted Ann Smith, who works as my agent. They asked her if I'd be interested in lending my name to the paper, and doing a column. She said we ceretainly were.

"So they started negotiating. They were from Illinois, but they'd come to town and talk, First thing you know we were ready to go to spring training, and they couldn't get together with Ann.

"Ann's always reaching for the moon. She always wants front money and they couldn't come to an agreement.

"So now I recognize the kids.

"'I thought you were the guys I'm supposed to be in the newspaper business with,' I say, and they say 'Yeah, but they couldn't get together with Ann. She was asking for financial statements and things like that.'

"'Goddamn,' I said. 'I'm not signed exclusively with Ann. You guys should have come to me. I'd be happy to talk with you.'

"So, we talked. I mean these two kids, early 20s, were optimistic as hell. They wanted to do it with pictures, interviews, offbeat stuff.

"'Look, get some kind of contract together and talk to me,' I said.

"The next day I met with them and Bill Matthews, president of Landmark Community Newspapers, and I decided to sign with them. No front money. I'm going to be the good guy, do a column, all that jive and get nothing up front. It's settled."

Pete Rose

The next entry is dated March 25:

"Today, I find out that they offered Ann five grand up front. I mean I'm mad. I'm trying to help and they screw me out of five grand.

"'How come you guys offer Ann $5,000 front money and you talk to me and won't give me any front money?' I say.

"'We decided we just didn't have the front money,' they say.

Now I call Ann. I tell her about it.

"'Look, I know I signed the damn thing, but see if you can't call Bill Matthews and renegotiate. Get the front money,' I say

"She got it all. The front money. 20 percent of advertising. A dollar per subscription. A newspaper empire is born.

"All I do is give them a column a week. I pick out which one of the guys goes on the cover, and one of the wives will be interviewed.

"'Look,' Pete Alexis says, 'What if the newspaper wants to take a stand that anti-Reds?'

"'Okay with me, as long as you make it plain that I'm only responsible for my column.'"

The next entry is dated May 9:

"Pete Rose's Reds Alert came out today, our seventh issue. And, oh, hell. First, Bill Matthews has taken off after Darrel Chaney again. First it was Cesar Geronimo who Matthews went after. Now Chaney. I'm in for it. I remember when Matthews started getting on Geronimo's cases. I kept telling him not to do it.

"One day he gets on Geronimo for a bad throw. The day before the article came out, Geronimo threw out two runners in one game. He throws out two, three guys and here's Matthews writing about a bad play he made a week ago.

"He's on Geronimo, and at the time, Geronimo's hitting .300, our only .300 hitter. 'How the hell can you be talking about how bad he is when he's the only .300 we got?' I ask him.

"But Matthews isn't listening. He believes statistics don't lie, and he states Geronimo's statistics in the minor leagues, in the big leagues, with the Reds. He thinks he's an expert and he doesn't like Geronimo as a player.

"'Hell,' I say, 'why don't you rip me or Bench? Bench is only hitting .150. but you gotta pick on Chaney.'

"Chaney's had troubles, true. But he isn't the reason we've been losing. Hell, he has a tough job, going in for defense in the late innings with the game on the line and with little chance to get the feel of things.

"The story hurt me as much as it did Chaney. I mean, he's my teammate. I didn't want bad things written about Chaney.

"Darrel was mad at first. So were a couple of other guys. But mostly they laughed about it, just like they do about all rips that show up in the paper.

"And, believe me, no one in the clubhouse thought I had anything to do with it."

The next entry is dated May 15:

"Today a journalistic empire crumbled. Crushed to the ground by the heavy hand of management.

"It started with a phone call from Dick Wagner, vice president and hatchet man of the Reds.

"'Pete,' he says, 'You don't have authorization to have your name on The Reds Alert. We'd like for you to take you name off the paper.'

"I was a little stunned, didn't answer at first. That was all Wagner needed.

"'We can take legal action,' he says, 'You're going to take it off there.'

"'Hey, Dick,' I said, 'I'm worried about catching the Dodgers and playing ball. I don't want to be worried about going to court with you. Sure, I'll take my name off. If you want me to, I'll take it off.'

"Bob Howsam stated the Reds took action because of 'a series of articles that have ridiculed and unfairly criticized various members of the Cincinnati team.' The statement went onto say that the Reds didn't believe in censorship but that they didn't believe 'it is right for a publication known as Pete Rose's paper to attack Rose's teammates, even though Pete has not personally authorized such articles.'

"It didn't exactly bother them when the paper printed 200 action photos or when it ran free full-page ads for the Reds in the first eight editions.

"Matthews was fuming. 'I very much deplore that honest, objective journalism has been termed 'ridicule' by the management of the Cincinnati Reds,' he announced to the media. 'This would appear to be a classic case of an effort to muzzle, however delicately, the efforts to report the day-to-day happenings of a major league team as they actually happen.'

"To me, Bill merely said, 'Pete, I just can't come out and say Pete Rose is gone.'

"I got on his tail about the articles and he wanted to fight it some. So, we arranged a meeting."

The final entry about the controversy is dated May 16:

"It was meeting time: Dick Wagner and the Reds' public relations director Jim Ferguson, who has become a house shill.

"I went through the whole spiel about how I got my name on the paper. It seems they got approval for the name Reds Alert, but they were so pressed for time when I entered the picture that they didn't go to get approval for Pete Rose's Reds Alert.

"Wagner had a negative attitude going in. I wasn't going to get anywhere. 'Damn, Dick, you think they aren't hurting me when they write bad about my paper?' I said.

"'Sure, I do,' he answered, 'but people who pick that paper up will think you wrote the articles.'

Founders of *The Reds Alert* included editorial specialist Pete Alexis, left, and Dennis Gruelle, photographer. I served as the publisher.

Matthews 'flabbergasted' over furor

From *The Kentucky Post,* May 16, 1974

Pete has a pressing problem

BY ED MENAKER

Pete Rose has been caught in the middle of a flap between the Cincinnati Reds' management and a newspaper publisher in Shelbyville, Ky.

Rose's name has been connected with an infant sports tabloid that has been published once a week for the past eight weeks. The paper is called Pete Rose's Reds Alert and is a compilation of columns and viewpoints about the Reds.

Yesterday that paper came under severe criticism from Reds' president Bob Howsam who issued a statement claiming it had run "a series of articles that have ridiculed and unfairly criticized various members of the Cincinnati team."

THOUGH HOWSAM affirmed the right of any publication to say what it likes, within legal bounds, he said he "did not believe it is right for a publication that is known as Pete Rose's paper to attack Rose's teammates, even though Pete has not authored such articles."

Howsam stated that Rose received $1 for each subscription sold as well as 20 per cent of advertising and newstand sale revenue.

The statement went on to say that the Reds had requested Rose to relinquish his relationship with the paper and that Rose had agreed.

Rose, who in addition to having his name associated with the paper also has his own column, was unavailable last night for comment.

However, Bill Matthews, the publisher of the tabloid was and expressed surprise from his home in Shelbyville that such a furor had erupted.

"I was completely flabbergasted," Matthews said.

MATTHEWS BELIEVES that it was a column written by him about Reds' infielder Darrel Chaney in the May 9 issue that triggered the incident. In that article Matthews said that the Reds had acted too hastily in trading former Red Dennis Menke, leaving Chaney as the prime infield utility man. Matthews catalogued Chaney's misplays this season, called Chaney's fielding mediocre, said Chaney "lacked proficiency at the plate, and posed the question, "So why is Chaney still a Red?"

"In seven issues we have had over 200 action photos and countless articles wholly favorable to the Reds," Matthews said. "We've had four or five articles that have been objective and reflecting the independence of the tabloid. Chaney's was one of them.

"But personally I think the whole thing could have been handled a little bit more quietly by the Reds' management," Matthews said.

Matthews indicated that he had first learned of the Reds' unfavorable reaction about three days ago. He had arranged to meet with Howsam this afternoon before Howsam's statement was ever issued.

Though Matthews denied that he was thinking of suing the Reds, he did not entirely rule out the possibility.

"A lot of course will depend on our meeting," the publisher said. "However, I think this is a classic case of the right of a newspaper to publish in a free and wholesome climate."

MATTHEWS, 44, IS the president of Landmark Community Newspapers, a subsidiary of Landmark Communications Inc. centered in Norfolk, Va., and publishers of that city's two daily newspapers. The relationship between Rose and the tabloid was contracted the first week in March when Matthews visited Rose at the Reds' spring training base in Tampa, according to Matthews. Matthews said the original idea was the brainstorm of Dennis Gruelle, 22, and Pete Alexis, 24, whom Matthews said were both graduated from Illinois State University last June. Alexis is the actual author of Rose's column although Rose furnishes the material and proofreads the copy before it is published, Matthews said.

Matthews said that 25,000 issues of the tabloid had been published each week and that the last two weeks the paper had been sold out.

"I think we've got a real winner here," Matthews said last night.

"'I disagree. I don't think anybody who reads an article that carries the name, "Full Count by Bill Matthews" is going to think I wrote it.'

"'Now understand this. Every edition of the paper carried this disclaimer: "Pete Rose's Reds Alert is not a publication of the Cincinnati Reds Professional Baseball Team," and it said I was responsible only for what ran as my column.'

"'People don't read that,' said Wagner. 'They only know it's your magazine and think you're writing about your players.'

"That is just how this man thinks of the public, too. Doesn't give them much credit. He added he was worried about the bad publicity and, even more important, about hard feelings among the players.

"There no hard feelings. Quite the contrary, Chaney was really upset when he learned I was going to lose the paper. He thought it would cost me money and, worse yet, hurt the two kids running the paper. 'I really like them,' he said.

"If the front office would just get down to the locker room and sit around and chew the fat with the guys and get to know the life, they might realize what the hell's going on. I've been trying to tell Howsam this for years.

"But it's over. I am out of the newspaper business."

So, eight issues after Reds Alert began, Pete was forced off the magazine by Reds' Vice President Dick Wagner who gave him no alternative.

Still, Rose remained a primary supporter of the publication and was always accessible to Pete Alexis and Dennis Gruelle as they continued to cover the Reds for what was officially now called The Reds Alert.

The End in Sight

In retrospect, 40 years after that first issue, we undoubtedly remained true to the magazine's mission, which was set forth in Volume I, No. 1. It stated, in part:

"We want to state at the outset that if Reds Alert has a bias, it is probably our favoritism for the fan. We will do our best to keep the fan informed of events on and off the field. We intend to do this in a direct, no nonsense style. Reds Alert will not be cheap, sensational or ridiculously controversial. We will, however, meet the issues head on with honest reporting and analysis. Alert's staff feels that baseball fans are entitled to a "tell it like it is" approach and we will do our utmost to deliver just that!"

1974 was a great year for the magazine and a poor one for the Reds. The Los Angeles Dodgers won the National League pennant before losing to the Oakland A's in the World Series. Despite winning 98 games, the Reds finished 4 games behind the Dodgers. *The Reds Alert* had more than 12,000 paid subscriptions by the end of the season and eagerly awaited the '75 season.

It's hard to believe, in these days of vast sums of money being paid for naming rights, that we originally paid only $1 for the right to use the term *Reds Alert.*

However, when it came time to start talking in February about rights for '75, Dick Wagner was waiting for me.

When I met with him at his office at Riverfront Stadium, I thought for a minute that he might deck me. He chastised me sharply and actually accused me and/or the magazine of "losing the 1974 National League pennant for the Reds. We would have beaten the Dodgers if it hadn't been for you and that damn magazine."

This was such a ridiculous position that I didn't bother to respond. And this made him even madder.

Finally, he simmered down and, surprisingly, agreed that for one dollar we could use the title one more time. He made it plain that the agreement was for one year only and would have to be renewed annually.

The 1975 and 1976 seasons led to world championships for the Reds and the magazine grew to nearly 20,000 paid circulation. Howsam became a good fan of the magazine and, it is regrettable that, as of this date, he has not been voted into the Baseball Hall of fame.

The high points for both seasons were *The Reds Alert* weekends at the Netherland Hilton where we welcomed up to 300 subscribers from throughout Reds' country. One gentleman even attended from Japan. The weekend included two nights at the hotel, three games, plenty of beer, and two catered meals. The cost ranged from $149 to $199 per person. Several Reds' players always attended and fan favorites were Rose, Tony Perez, George Foster, and "Cactus Jack" Billingham and his wife Jolene.

A surprise guest one year was World Heavyweight Champion Mohammed Ali, who just happened to be in the hotel.

After both championship seasons, Pete Alexis, Dennis, and I collaborated with two Baseball Hall of Fame writers to produce a bestselling book.

The Relentless Reds was the first book. The text was by Hall of Fame writer Hal McCoy and foreword by Hall of Fame writer Earl Lawson. It came out in the spring of 1976 with the following spring offering *The Royal Reds*, with text by McCoy and foreword by *Louisville Courier-Journal* sportswriter Ron Coons. Pete provided profiles of each player for each book and Dennis provided his spectacular photography. Each sold more than 20,000 copies.

We had book signings in Louisville, Cincinnati, Dayton, and several other cities. Rose was the principal signer, and he always got a minimum of $500, as in five $100 bills. He always arrived in a Rolls-Royce. Although I explained to him that I would have to report the stipends on a Form 1099 to the IRS, I realized at the time that he had no intention of reporting the income. Later, Pete went to prison for income tax evasion, but I don't believe it involved our particular payments to him.

I had a good offer from a Reds' follower to buy the magazine after the '76 championship season but, unfortunately as it turned out, I turned it down. Cincinnati got off poorly in 1977 and the Dodgers won 22 of their first 26 games to put so much distance between the two teams that the Reds never seriously contended.

The Reds' downfall after their second straight World Championship Title in 1976 actually began during the offseason when they traded fan favorite and future Hall of Famer First Baseman Tony Perez to Montreal for a couple of run-of-the-mill players, including southpaw journeyman pitcher Woodie Fryman. The deal, made to give Dan Driessen an opportunity to play first base regularly, went down as perhaps the second worst trade in Reds' history. The worst was the trade in the fall of 1965 that sent another future Hall of Famer, Frank Robinson, to Baltimore for pitcher Milt Pappas and Harry "Suitcase" Simpson. All Robinson did in 1966 was win the baseball's Triple Crown in leading the Orioles to the World Series title.

Cincinnati's decline continued with the trade of Pete Rose to the Philadelphia Phillies after the 1978 season and Joe Morgan to the Astros after the 1979 season. Rose helped the Phillies win their first-ever World Series in 1980. Rose, Morgan, and Perez were on the Phillies' National League pennant winners in 1983.

The magazine lost ground steadily, beginning with the Reds' collapse in 1977. I sold it for next to nothing after the 1978 season. It faded out shortly thereafter.

Prior to its demise, the magazine covering the Cincinnati Bengals NFL team and Cincinnati Stingers ice hockey team. Its name had been changed to *Cincinnati Sports Alert*.

Tony Perez

Casey Stengel played first game in Shelbyville

Shelbyville and Shelby County are known for many things – Saddlebred horses, Wakefield-Scearce Antique Galleries, Col. Harland Sanders' home, and Harry S. Truman's grandparents' homes… but did you know that Shelbyville was the home – for a short time – of New York Yankees Manager and legendary baseball great Casey Stengel?

And, further, did you know that Casey played his first game as a semi-professional player at the old Coots Park just off Second and Washington near Clear Creek? Coots Park still exists without that name and it is no longer a ballpark but community soccer fields.

Coots Park had its origins as a ball field dating back to the late 1800s and, in modern times, was the scene of many a Little League and American Legion game in what was then known as Stratton Field.

The park was originally named after a man named Coots who owned the land. The park was not particularly distinguished except for one thing – it had a small creek wandering around its outfield perimeter, serving as a forceful, if not very wet, barrier for overly-zealous outfielders trying to track down balls hit into deep left field.

Stengel, himself, told about his start in Shelbyville, in an article in *Sports Illustrated* in 1962.

What he didn't relate was the hi-jinks he played to help Shelbyville win his first game as a baseball player.

Stengel, who died in 1975, was a great storyteller, and one of his greatest involves his debut.

It was the spring of 1910 and Shelbyville was a town of about 2,500 souls. It was also the home of a semi-professional team, nicknamed the Millers, which played in the old Bluegrass League that included teams from Frankfort, Lexington, Paris and Maysville.

Stengel took a room in a boarding house that stood on the corner of Seventh and Main Streets, a building that stood until 1923 when it was torn down to make way for a U.S. Post Office.

He was 20 years old, single and a player of undetermined ability who was assigned to play left field where he was destined to make his highly controversial debut.

As the story goes, and it has been passed down at least three generations, Casey Stengel had two hits and was playing left field on that fateful day when his team had forged ahead, 5 to 2, going into the top of the 9th inning.

The invading Lexington club then loaded the bases on a couple of hits and a walk. A strikeout and pop fly out reduced the tension somewhat, but the excitement – mostly from the Lexington fans – surged anew as the visitors' clean-up hitter, a first baseman named Phillips, stepped up.

On a two-ball, two-strike count, Phillips drilled the pitch way, way back to left field and, as the crowd roared, Stengel disappeared over the bank and was lost from sight.

The umpire signaled home run, and, suddenly, Lexington had moved ahead 6-5 and the local crowd fell silent.

But…wait! Here comes young Stengel up over the bank racing toward the infield. He's holding what appears to be a baseball high over his head.

His Shelbyville manager, whose name has been lost to eternity, and the two umpires conferred quickly at home plate, and, suddenly, the crowd roars as the umpire signals that Phillips is out. Shelbyville wins!

Why the "out" sign from the umpire? Because Stengel, wet uniform and all, is proudly cradling a dry… that's it… a dry baseball. He had somehow caught the ball on the fly – at least that's what he claimed – as he fell into the creek

Needless to say, a melee threatened. However, the home plate umpire, mindful of a potentially explosive and huge hometown crowd, never wavered. The 5-2 score stood then as it still stands today… a zany beginning for a legendary player and manager who started it all in Shelbyville, Kentucky.

*Years later, Stengel confessed that he had hidden a dry ball just over the bank and out of the sight of the umpires for just such an occasion.

*Some of Casey's teammates were Emil Huhn, shortstop Ed Glenn, Bill Cramer, and Paul Long. Long later ran the Greyhound Bus Lines Depot in Shelbyville during the 1930s and 1940s. He led the league in hits (82) and runs (60) in 1910.

*Later, on August 24, 1910, the Shelbyville team moved to Maysville, where the team was renamed the Rivermen. Statistics found on the Internet reflect game results from both towns in 1910.

*The Bluegrass League operated from 1908 to 1912. Shelbyville finished 5th out of six teams in 2008, last in 2009, and the combined operation last in 2010.

Dan McGann only Shelby Countian in World Series

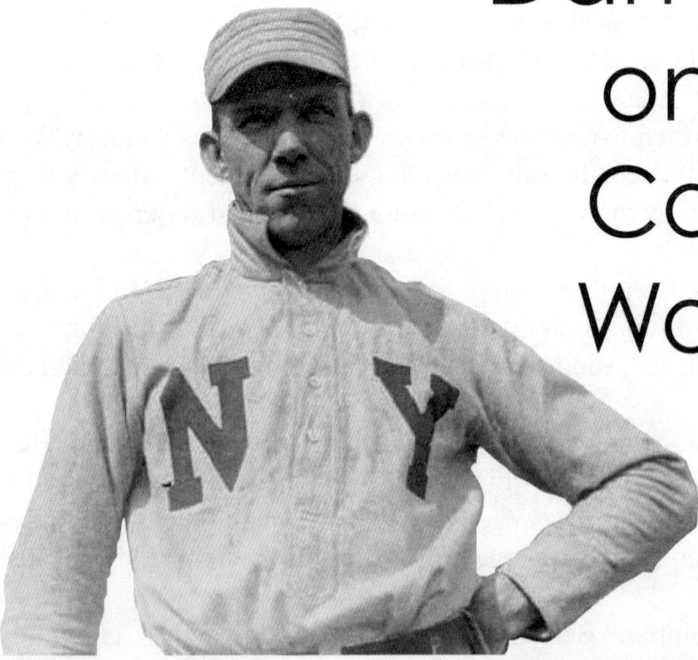

When I was working in the summers of 1948, '49, and '50 at *The Shelby Sentinel*, I took notice of a beautiful gold watch carried and referred to daily by James "Buddy" O'Sullivan who, along with his brother Daniel, owned the newspaper. He told me that it was a family treasure, and he had inherited it from his uncle, J. Michael Casey, a close relative of baseball legend Dan "Cap" McGann.

While "Buddy" downplayed the watch's significance, I later learned through some research that the watch had been given to McGann as captain of the Giants' World Series champions of 1905. At that time, the league didn't give individual rings as it does now, but only the captains of the two teams were awarded something of value.

I have valued the watch since "Buddy" was thoughtful enough to earmark it for me in his will. The watch contains McGann's initials and the year it was presented.

McGann was the only Shelby Countian to ever play in the World Series. His grave at Grove Hill Cemetery was at one time marked with a staked baseball tribute that was eventually given to relatives. His story and burial site are typically included in the Friends of Grove Hill tours.

Born in Shelbyville in 1871, McGann played professionally for the first time with the local Shelbyville Bluegrass League team. Other stops on the minor league trail included Harrodsburg, Lexington, Maysville, Norfolk (Va.) and Lynchburg (Va.)

He broke into the big leagues on August 8, 1896, with the Boston Beaneaters. His final game was on October 7, 1908 with the Boston Doves.

Other teams for whom he played included the Baltimore Orioles (two stints), Brooklyn Superbas, Washington Senators, and St. Louis Cardinals.

He finished with a batting average of .284, 42 home runs, and 727 runs batted in.

He played in 1909 and 1910 with the minor league Milwaukee team, batting only .225 in his final year. He was reportedly prepared to play with Louisville's minor league team in 1911.

Hall of Fame Manager John McGraw's New York Giants bested the Philadelphia Athletics in the 1905 World Series. McGann had three hits in Game three of the classic.

McGann achieved his greatest success in 1904 and 1905 with Hall of Fame Manager John McGraw's Giants. For years he and McGraw not only gave it their best on the diamond, but they were great "drinking buddies" off the field. McGann was called a "fielding genius" by one writer, and during his prime he was considered the best first baseman of that era.

McGann was only 39 years old when he shot himself to death in a Louisville hotel on December 13, 1910. While his death was officially labeled a suicide, McGann's two surviving sisters told reporters that he had not committed suicide, but, rather, had been murdered. A ring valued at over $20,000 by today's standards was missing from the body. One of the sisters claimed he was well, physically and mentally, and had no reason to kill himself.

The McGann family cemetery plot

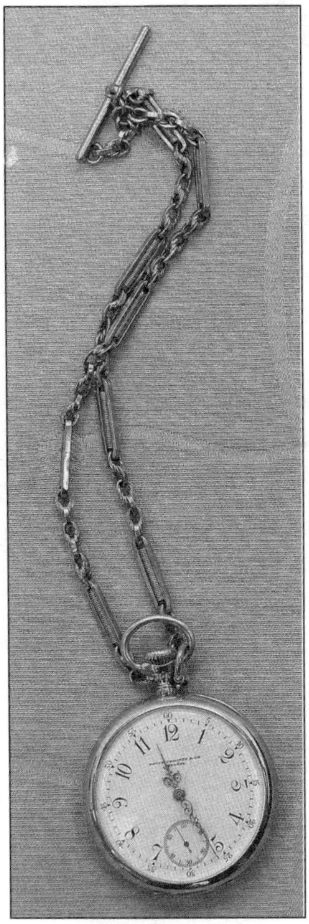

McGann's World Series gold watch

There had been a series of family tragedies: One of McGann's sisters committed suicide in 1890 after their mother died. On New Year's Eve in 1907, one of McGann's brothers died as a result of an accidental shooting. In 1909, another one of McGann's brothers committed suicide.

However, Dan McGann was known as a solid defensive player and a "clutch" hitter. He was also a renowned base stealer, and set a record by stealing five bases on May 27, 1904, while playing for the Giants. That record stood for 70 years until Davey Lopes stole a similar number of bases in 1974 and Otis Nixon stole six in 1991.

In the Giants' 1905 World Series championship over Connie Mack's Philadelphia Athletics in five games, McGann batted .235, but accounted for four RBIs on three hits in a Game Three victory.

McGann finished first in National League fielding from 1903 through 1906. He also served as team captain.

McGann was a relatively wealthy man when he died. In today's terms he would be considered a millionaire since his estate of approximately $40,000 would translate into $1,002,143 in 2014. I keep the highly valuable artifact in a bank lockbox.

The bus trip in *A League of Their Own* provided a lot of laughs as well as drama for moviegoers. In the bus itself, left to right, are Robin Knight, Renee Coleman, Rosie O'Donnell, Madonna, Betty Schram, Anne Elizabeth Ramsay, and Ann Cusack; standing are Pauline Brailsford, Neezer Tarleton, Patti Pelton, Connie Pounds-Taylor, Kelli Simpkins, Megan Cavanagh, Geena Davis, Lori Petty, Freddie Simpson, Tracy Reiner and Tom Hanks. (Photo courtesy of Columbia Pictures)

Lights! Camera! Action!

Growing up in Shelbyville, I loved attending the downtown theater where we could see the "picture show." My favorite movies were always on Saturday when Buck Jones, Tom Mix, and Ken Maynard rode for years before giving way to Gene Autry, Hopalong Cassidy, and Tex Ritter.

Later on, John Wayne and Cary Grant became my male favorites and Barbara Stanwyck my female star.

I remember the 1957 movie *Raintree County* being filmed in Danville and how those residents were able to see Elizabeth Taylor, Montgomery Clift and Eva Marie Saint up close and personal. Another movie filmed even closer to home was George C. Scott's *The Flim Flam Man* in Lawrenceburg. Little did I know how leaving Shelbyville would allow me a similar experience.

A League of Their Own

It was while publishing a newspaper in Huntingburg, Ind., that I received the chance that nearly every one on earth only dreams about … to be in the movies.

I learned about *A League of Their Own* when Mayor Connie Nass invited me to her office one day to meet someone. That someone turned out to be Penny Marshall.

Since I didn't then and still don't watch sitcoms, I didn't know who Penny Marshall was when we were introduced. When Marshall asked if I watched a sitcom called *Laverne & Shirley.* I responded, "I tried to one time but it was so silly I turned it off." While the mayor was very embarrassed and said so, Penny Marshall thought it rather amusing and shrugged off my lack of interest in her highly-rated TV hit.

Huntingburg was chosen as a site location for the movie being directed by Marshall because of the city's ownership of what remained of an old-time stadium dating back to late 1800s. The film tells a fictionalized account of the real-life All-American Girls Professional Baseball Team. Columbia Pictures was looking for a logical companion stadium to go with historic Bosse Field in Evansville, only about 50 miles away.

The movie's cast included Geena Davis, Tom Hanks, Madonna and Rosie O'Donnell. When the casting call went out for extras in *A League of Their Own*, little did I realize how fate would intercede and propel me into the experience of a lifetime.

I just happened to be in the wardrobe area in Evansville working on a story about the film when one of the extras managers asked if I knew anything about baseball. A lifelong fan of the sport, I nodded "yes" and dismissed the matter from my mind.

Umpires Jim Milton and William E. Matthews

Several weeks later, when filming was about to begin in Huntingburg I received a call from the extras director giving me the dates and sign-in times for my debut as an umpire.

Talk about starting at the top! I suppose, I could have indicated that my only umpiring experience had been during Little League days of years ago, but what the heck, if they needed umpires, why not me?!

When we reported to wardrobe that next-to-last Monday in August 1991, there were eight, all with some degree of professional or semi-professional experience … that is, all except me.

By the third day, we had lost three of the eight umpires for various reasons, reducing our number to five for the round-the-clock (including night) filming sessions.

Actually most of the time we just stood around, either waiting for the sun to shine just right, or for the "doubles" to work through their lines while Marshall and her associates fine-tuned the scene for the actual filming.

It was shortly after lunch on about the eighth day of filming when Marshall yelled, "Hey you!" (The umpires never seemed to have names.) Since the temperature was in the mid-90s with no wind, I looked around in the hope that her finger might be pointing elsewhere. It wasn't.

So behind the plate I went wearing a massive balloon chest protector, an oversized steel mask, and all the authentic trappings that accrued to an umpire in the 1940s.

The scene itself (that does appear in the movie) consists of catcher Geena Davis trying to catch the ball behind her back after batter Madonna has swung and hit a high foul pop-up. In reality, the ball is dropped by a member of the crew from the top of a ladder off screen.

The action started around 1:30 and for about two hours the batter swung, Davis ripped off her mask and raced toward the backstop, and I struggled to keep up.

First, I had trouble getting the mask off … and then I had trouble getting the mask off while keeping my cap on. Also troublesome was trying to endure the intense heat of an August afternoon. Worst of all, I had overindulged at lunchtime on crab meat and steak in the celebrities' tent, adding substantially to my discomfort.

If you've ever hyperventilated, you know the feeling that I began to experience as time went by. My face got redder and redder, and I felt dizzier and dizzier. Finally, after what seemed like an eternity, Marshall sensed that one of her extras was about to "stroke out" at home plate and called for another umpire.

Sadly, dejectedly I was assisted from the field, with an ammonia ice pack around my neck.

For the rest of the weekend I brooded about my misfortune. I almost prayed for another opportunity to redeem myself.

So it was on the following night that the cameras were again rolling and I guess Marshall decided that it would be safer to station me on the bases rather than at home plate.

Fate again got into the picture. On that night, the cameras were rolling for two purposes: to pick up some crowd noise and to get some unrehearsed images of players sliding, batting, pitching and fielding. In short, they were just letting the cameras roll.

So it was that in an exceptionally close play at second base I called a Racine (Wisconsin) Belles runner out. I then reversed the call when I saw that the second baseman had juggled the ball, then let it slip away despite her best efforts to conceal the action from me. So I signaled the runner "Safe!"

I had hardly turned around when Rockford (Illinois) Peaches Manager Tom Hanks was in my face, letting me know in no uncertain terms (his language wasn't genteel) that I had blown the call.

In very uncomplimentary words and gestures, he said, "That's probably the first and worst call you ever made!" Well, he was certainly right on the one hand because it was the first major call I'd ever made in my entire life. As for the "worst" call, the Peaches' second baseman confessed later that, yes, she had muffed the ball.

My encounter with Hanks was used nationally to help promote the film.

Did I appear in the film? The answer is "yes" … for about 12 seconds: once behind the plate and the other on the bases.

By the time the filming had ended in Huntingburg on Labor Day 1991, only three of the original eight umpires were left. Maybe the pay wasn't good enough ($50 for a 12-hour day), but as I look back at 14 days of filming *A League of Their Own,* they have to rank right up there with the most exciting time for any community of its size (about 5,500) in America. And it made me a "big man" in Huntingburg since no one else from the city had such an important "extras" role.

Would I do it again? For $50.00 a day? You bet!

A League of Their Own turned out to be a huge financial and artistic success. Budgeted at around $40 million, it earned $107 million in the United States and an additional $25 million overseas.

In 2012 it was selected for preservation in the U.S. National Registry by the Library of Congress for being "culturally, historically, or aesthetically significant."

The stadium in Huntingburg where the movie was filmed cost Columbia more than $500,000 to renovate and enlarge. Rather than dismantling it after filming was completed, Columbia presented the beautiful stadium as a "permanent gift" to the citizens of Huntingburg for their support and interest in making the film.

Of the three primary actors in the film – Tom Hanks, Madonna, and Geena Davis – Hanks was everyone's favorite. He drank beer at night at the local pub and seemed to enjoy visiting with folks around town and at the ball park. Madonna was a pill, to put it mildly, frequently going out of her way to show her disdain for the English language. She didn't appear to be able to put together a coherent sentence without including an obscenity. Davis was rarely visible, spending most of her time in the fancy mobile home that each of the primary actors had.

Soul of the Game

HBO's *Soul of the Game*, which was originally titled *Baseball in Black and White*, told the story of baseball's integration in the mid-1940s. It starred Blair Underwood as young Jackie Robinson, Delroy Lindo as Satchel Paige, Mykelti Williamson as Josh Gibson, and Edward Herrmann as Brooklyn Dodgers owner Branch Rickey. Jerry Hardin portrayed A.B. "Happy" Chandler who, as baseball commissioner, approved the Dodgers' contract with Robinson, making him the first black man to play in the Big Leagues.

Because the recently enlarged stadium in Huntingburg still had the vintage 1940s feel from five years previously, that Indiana community was the natural choice for the film.

Unlike *A League of Their Own* that operated behind a closed set, *Soul of the Game* was filmed on an open set that enabled local residents to watch the actors and actresses as they said their lines and played the game.

When the call went out for "extras," I sent my resume in to the casting director, playing up my experience in *A League of Their Own*. I didn't realize how fortunate I was to get chosen until we began filming.

I'm in the film on three different, but very brief, occasions, and, in case you're wondering how to find me, that's easy. There are eight photographers and only one of them white.

The 94-minute *Soul of the Game* was released in 1996 and was both criticized and praised. Critics called it historically inaccurate. For example, while the movie indicates there was an inter-relationship among the three men, there is no evidence that Gibson ever knew Robinson in real life. Also Paige was actually a loner and a carouser and was never Gibson's close friend as portrayed in the film.

Other reviewers liked the movie's overall approach as being true to the movie's main theme of how baseball was integrated.

Blair Underwood shot to fame with the TV series *L.A. Law,* and Williamson played "Bubba" in the movie *Forrest Gump,* which won the first of two academy awards for Tom Hanks, who I had met previously in my first movie role.

Actress Salli Richardson-Whitfield visited with me on the set of *Soul of the Game* where I played the role of the only white photographer in the movie assigned to cover baseball's integration and the rise to fame of Jackie Robinson.

Mykelti Williamson portrayed famed black slugger Josh Gibson in *Soul of the Game.* He was also featured as "Bubba" in the movie *Forrest Gump* which won the Oscar statue for its star Tom Hanks.

Famed television and movie star Ed Asner was a frequent visitor to *The Huntingburg Press* during the filming of *Hard Rain*. The movie also starred Morgan Freeman, Christian Slater, and Minnie Driver.

Hard Rain

Huntingburg was the scene of still another film in 1998 that starred Morgan Freeman, Ed Asner, Christian Slater, Minnie Driver, and Randy Quaid. This was a crime thriller involving a bank heist and the effect that the bursting of a dam and monumental rains has on that robbery.

This was an open set movie with local residents able to observe many of the scenes. The film was also partially shot in a warehouse-type building full of water in California. The building was reportedly three times the size of a football field, and had been used to build B-1 bombers at one time

Downtown Huntingburg was also filled with water and, after the filming was completed, residents were able to take home the hundreds of sandbags that were used to help hold the flood waters back.

Asner was the most visible actor during the filming. He visited several times with our staff at *The Huntingburg Press*. Readers may remember Asner's role as a TV producer on the *Mary Tyler Moore Show*.

One of the movie's highlights involves a fight between two of the main characters on top of a church. Most of us watched in awe as a helicopter crew flew dangerously close to the church steeple repeatedly to film the scene.

I was offered a role as an "extra" but declined because of the immense amount of work involved in putting out a special edition on the movie.

Stories ... funny, not-so-funny, and sad

"Hitting the Sawdust Trail"

Mother was quite a singer as a teenager and into her 20s, so she was frequently invited to sing at church revivals at which church members and visitors were urged to "hit the sawdust trail." The term harkens back to the early 1900s, but it gained its greatest prominence during the evangelistic revivals conducted by the famous Billy Sunday.

Sawdust was used to deaden the sound of shuffling feet on the ground inside the tent, and also because of a perceived pleasant odor that it emitted.

Most churches had a revival at least once a year, generally featuring an itinerant minister. Tent revivals were not only good for reenergizing the brethren, but also served as popular social events in the summertime.

Mother began singing at various churches in her home county of Madison at about the age of 14 or 15.

She moved into the Finchville community as a 19-year-old school teacher in 1921 and sang at her first revival there at the Finchville Baptist Church. Her beautiful soprano voice caught the attention of the senior pastor of one of Louisville's larger churches and he invited her to sing at an upcoming four-night tent revival.

All went well the first three nights but, at the outset of the fourth night, the minister told her that he had arranged for two connecting rooms at the Seelbach Hotel after the service. She politely declined his offer and headed home after the service.

As for "the rest of the story," she had married my father only a few months previously and they were living in a small apartment on Bland Avenue.

A few evenings later, she casually mentioned the minister's proposal to my father and, without a word, he stormed out of the apartment at about 9 o'clock and didn't come back within a reasonable amount of time. She became quite alarmed at his continued absence until he finally showed up at 3 a.m.

He explained that he had been thinking and walking all that time. He finally looked at her and said resolutely, "I've decided not to kill him."

Blackmail Business

About 1935 or 1936, a young Shelbyville lawyer, who had had too much to drink, was enjoying himself at the Shelbyville Country Club when one of the young women present gave him a "come hither" look. So, without too much thought, the lawyer followed the young woman home and up the stairs to the apartment she shared with her husband. Naturally, since the young woman had been so beckoning, the lawyer assumed that the husband was not home. As the lawyer began undressing, he was confronted by the husband who stepped suddenly out of a closet, slammed the door, and turned the key.

The price to not tell anyone, certainly not the lawyer's staunchly Baptist parents, was $5,000.

The lawyer came to see my father at his law office the next day and explained that while $5,000 was a lot of money, paying the money was a lot better than having his parents find out. "It would kill my mother," he said… To which Dad responded, "Once you start paying, you will just keep paying. Don't do it."

So, the lawyer didn't pay the blackmail; his parents never knew about the incident; the couple left town a few years later; and the attorney went on to have a highly successful career and became a much admired figure in the community.

Now, please fast forward 45 years to the time when I was editing and publishing the *Voice of St. Matthews*. I received a call one day from a former employee who said she and her husband wanted to talk with me at the local Frisch's restaurant. They said it was "confidential."

When we got together, the young woman said she wanted her job back at one of the northern Kentucky papers that I published. I told her that was not going to happen because she had already been dismissed once. But she responded, "Unless I get my job back, I'm going to accuse you of sexual harassment." Naturally a chill went through me because, while I was not guilty of the crime, a simple charge to that effect would be enough to ruin my career.

I began sweating and realized that my life, in a way, "literally hung in the balance." Deciding to take a big chance, I called what I hoped was her big bluff. I said, "The St. Matthews police station is just four blocks away, so we'll all go there together. You file your action and I'll respond with a 'defamation of character' suit."

She and her husband thought it over for a few minutes and then walked out of the restaurant. They went back to Texas from whence they had come.

"Funny Money"

In the fall of 1963, I was desperate for a printer – someone who could make up ads via the old-fashioned hot type process, and run our similarly old-fashioned flatbed press. I advertised in our trade press, *The Publishers Auxiliary*, and received a response from what appeared to be a well-qualified candidate. The only problem, he said, is that he wouldn't be available until April of the following year.

I didn't wonder why he would take so long getting to Shelbyville because I was so pleased that a good candidate was apparently available. So I waited until April and, sure enough, in walked a man by the name of Petey Peterson. Within a few weeks, Petey had turned into a first-class employee and, as a bonus, he was accompanied everywhere he went by a beautiful solid white German shepherd.

All was going well until one Sunday afternoon when, for no particular reason, I decided to drop by the office and check the ad log for the upcoming week.

When I opened the door, I could hear the steady clicking of our 1250 Multilith press, which was unusual because no one in the back shop ever worked on Sunday.

So when I opened the door between the front office and the back shop, I was amazed that a steady stream of $20 bills was flying off the Multilith and into a waiting basket. Some missed the basket and were lying on the floor.

In that split second, I realized that the reason Petey couldn't take the job offer for seven months was because he was a counterfeiter! He had been in prison!

Surprised to see me, Petey said he hadn't passed any bills yet. So, within a few minutes I had retrieved all of the "funny $20s" and Petey and the dog were on their way out of town.

I never heard from him again. Prior to burning all the bills, I checked one out. I could tell no difference between a "funny" one and the real one. Petey was a well-qualified printer… just of the wrong product!

Cows and Daylight Saving Time

Winford Thomas was a longtime friend of mine, primarily through our relationship in the old Upper Room Bible Class at church. There were many stories that one could tell about this very eccentric man, who died in August 2011.

My favorite has to do with Winford's strong, if not bitter, dislike of Daylight Saving Time. He railed about it from sun-up to sun-down. Beginning in the 1950s and '60s, one of the ways he protested was to slip into the graded and high schools and set the big clocks in the hall back one hour while no one was looking.

When Superintendent Willie C. Ray finally caught him in the act one day, he bellowed, "You don't understand and the cows don't understand. They do not like Daylight Saving Time and never will!"

Winford claimed that cows not only didn't understand DST, but that they didn't perform well during this time of the year when the clocks were moved forward. Yet, he offered no proof, one way or the other.

Gardiner and the Golfers

In between the Rev. Glover Daniel, who served the First Presbyterian Church from 1942 to 1963, and the Rev. Gayle Threlkeld, who served the same church from 1966 to 1982, there was one Dr. William Gardiner, who was called as its minister in early 1964. This was still at a time when most of Shelbyville and Shelby County were closed on Sunday, and only the drug stores were permitted to be open. Retail stores were shut tight. But one thing that residents could still do without restriction was play golf.

Thus it was on a Sunday morning in the summer of 1965 that Gardiner, noticing that several of his more prominent male parishioners were frequently absent on the Sabbath, took a trip out to the Shelbyville Country Club and made note of those who were favoring the fairways to the pews. That might not have been so bad except that on the following Sunday he made reference to these golfers by name from the pulpit. And the names included at least one church elder.

Needless to say, Dr. Gardiner's tenure at the First Presbyterian Church was brief. He was gone within a few months.

"My Number Wasn't Called"

Many of us have heard the expression, "His time was up," or "His number was called," and a good friend of mine, the late Roy Lyons, said this thought ran through his mind as he prepared to be part of still another landing in the Pacific during World War II. He had survived the first three, jumping from an LST and wading ashore under heavy enemy fire.

Roy was scheduled to be the 40th man to jump as the craft approached the beach at Okinawa. But, as he watched his buddies jump, the first 39 fell dead in the water, cut down by Japanese snipers operating a few yards inland from the beach.

His last thought as he jumped, Roy said, was "My time is up this time." But, almost miraculously, the bullet glanced off his steel helmet, and he charged ashore. "His number hadn't been called."

It is no wonder that men such as Roy Lyons were part of what Tom Brokaw called "The Greatest Generation."

Naming Road and School

Prior to the opening of a new second high school in our county, a committee of 15 people, including townspeople, school personnel, and students, was appointed to recommend a name for the new boulevard leading to the school and the school itself.

The committee was chaired by Duanne B. Puckett, public relations coordinator for the school system. Members included retired teacher/historical society member John Graham, County Judge/executive Rob Rothenburger, neighbor to the school property Martha Hall, and me. There were representatives of an elementary, middle, and high school.

We bandied about several names for the boulevard but finally settled, very proudly, on Edwin Powell Hubble (or Hubble for short) for the boulevard. During the summer of

928 Bland Ave.

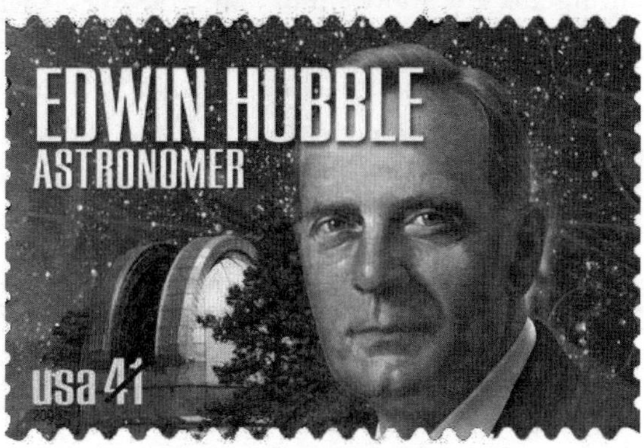

1910, Hubble lived with his parents at 928 Bland Avenue in Shelbyville. He was a Rhodes Scholar – one of five with Shelby County connections. The committee even had the idea, if the name were approved by the School Board, to plant trees along the boulevard to recognize all five of the Scholars. Hubble was recommended for the road name since he is the most famous of the 20th century astronomers since his name was chosen by NASA for the renowned telescope that has made many, many enlightening discoveries.

However, when the recommendation was presented to the School Board, member Doug Butler immediately "scotched" it, saying, "We're not going to name anything that rhymes with Bubble." And so went our chance to put a Shelby County road on a world map right now. The name "Discovery Boulevard," suggested by a seventh-grader, was eventually adopted.

As for the high school's name, the committee's recommendation was approved by the Board to honor Martha Layne Collins, a native of Bagdad, who became the first – and only – female governor of Kentucky in 1983. The public doesn't know how close the school almost came to be named for the late Shelby County Teacher and first African-American Kentucky Education Association President Marnell Moorman, or one-time slave turned educator Elijah Marrs. Graham argued very persuasively that naming the school after Marrs would do wonders to show how far Shelby County has advanced racially.

Attendance records

On graduation night in 1948 I was recognized for almost 12 years of perfect attendance. I missed one day in the 5th grade because of sickness. Actually, the teacher, Sara Belle Waters, and my mother didn't agree that I was sick when the teacher sent me home because I complained of being "sick at my stomach." When I explained the situation to my mother, she responded, "You look perfectly fine to me." But she reluctantly accepted the teacher's decision, and I got the day off.

I thought missing one day in 12 years was remarkable until I read an item in the 60 Years Ago column in *The Sentinel-News* that "Male High School Valedictorian of the Senior Class of 1915 Robert F. Matthews of Shelbyville attained a perfect attendance record at the Louisville school. He did not miss a single day while riding the Interurban between Simpsonville and Louisville for four years between 1912 and 1915."

"Having a baby"

In 1982 when I was publishing the *Voice of St. Matthews*, one of our employees, Patti Hoddinott, came to my office and said, "Bill, you and I are headed to the hospital right now." When I asked, "Why?" she replied, "Lynn is going to have a baby." That seemed strange, if not impossible, to me because Lynn worked just two doors down from me in our bookkeeping office. Lynn was a little on the heavy side and did have wide hips, but the idea seemed absurd to me since I hadn't noticed anything.

But Patti insisted, saying, "Look, her water has already broken, and unless you want to have the baby in your office, I suggest we leave NOW." So, grudgingly, I grabbed the car keys and headed to my car where Patti and Lynn were already seated in the backseat. We headed to University Hospital going as fast as good sense would permit and pulled into the parking lot just as Patti cried out, "We're just seconds away."

As Patti and Lynn were welcomed by a nurse, I was welcomed by the receptionist who asked, "Are you the father?" When I responded that, to the best of my knowledge, the father had skipped to Alaska, she said, "I've heard that one before." But I knew I wasn't paying, so there the matter rested.

Unfortunately, while I was away, my wife, Else, called the *Voice* and when she asked to speak to me, she was told, "Bill has gone to the hospital to have a baby." This was particularly upsetting to her because she was opening that night in *"The Matchmaker"* at the Shelby County Community Theatre.

Also, my boss, Gil Champagne, from Scripps-Howard called and was told the same thing, except that it got shortened to "Bill is having a baby."

One can imagine how much explaining I had to do a few hours later when calm had been restored.

Frugality in the family

My sister-in-law Betty has long been known for her conscientious attitude toward spending and saving money. Years ago when Else and I had just returned to Shelbyville, she and Bob invited us for dinner. The meal was good, and there were only four butterbeans left in the dish when she said, "Bill would you have some butterbeans and pass them?" So I took two and passed the dish.

Local lynching thwarted

When I was growing up, each summer a rather swarthy, black-haired woman with far too much makeup would visit our house on Main Street. She was usually accompanied by my aging second cousin, Katie Goff, who lived in a big, beautiful red brick home at the corner of 1st and Main streets (later torn down to accommodate an A&P store).

When I was grown, my mother told me the story of this seemingly mysterious lady.

In 1904 William Morris Goff, one of two brothers of Cousin Katie, was reported around town to have impregnated Fannie Lynch, the daughter of Dr. Meredith Lynch, who operated Lynch's Drug Store on the southwest corner of 6th and Main streets. Fannie was very popular.

When word of Fannie's alleged pregnancy became known, a number of townspeople reportedly grabbed Morris and rushed him down Jail Hill to the bridge where they planned to lynch him. At the last minute, Fannie's father arrived and pleaded with the mob to spare Morris's life. Finally, the crowd yielded to Dr. Lynch's plea and Morris was spared. He was taken to Louisville and placed in protective custody.

Several weeks later Morris Goff and Fannie Lynch were married in Louisville and from this union in a few months came a child who was named Katherine Goff, undoubtedly in honor of Morris's sister. The couple divorced a short time later.

The years passed and the child grew up, and in 1931 she was officially adopted by Cousin Katie, a longtime Sunday school teacher at First Christian Church.

Morris and his brother, Thomas, both lived dissolute lives and died early. Morris, who owned the second licensed automobile in Shelby County, died in 1911 at age 28. Thomas Lewis Goff died in 1906 at age 35.

Cousin Katie (1872-1963), who never married and was as prim and proper as her brothers were "wild and wooly," lived to be 91. No one knows what happened to Fannie Goff's daughter and Cousin Katie's niece, but it is believed she died and is buried in Tulsa, Okla., where she made her home. I do know that she received and acknowledged an invitation to our daughter Lisa's wedding in 1973.

Political arena

Dating back to my paternal great-grandfather, Absalom T. Matthews, and my maternal grandfather, Junius Gaines Baxter, our family has been closely aligned with Kentucky's Democratic Party.

Absalom was a longtime Democratic magistrate in the western part of Shelby County, and Grandfather Baxter was both a county judge and county road commissioner in then heavily Democratic Madison County.

I first became aware of our family's Democratic affiliation in the late 1940s when Lawrence B. Wetherby of Louisville ran for governor and defeated Republican and Court of Appeals Justice Eugene Siler by about 58,000 votes. He was the last man from our state's largest city to sit in the governor's chair.

Alben Barkley was campaigning in 1954 for his old U. S. Senate seat when he came to Shelbyville. He had served as vice president under Harry S. Truman (1948-1952). Barkley died while making a speech at Washington & Lee University in 1956. Here he greets local Democratic chairman Howard Pearce, right, and Carol and Laban Jackson, left. Charlene Anderson Kresin peeks over Barkley's right shoulder.

In the 1940s, Wetherby and one-time senator Earl Clements and Alben Barkley headed up one wing of the Democratic Party while their principal adversary, A.B. "Happy" Chandler, headed up the other. Chandler resigned his seat in the U.S. Senate to become baseball commissioner from 1945 to 1951. After he was fired by the baseball owners, he returned to Kentucky and was elected governor in 1955. He lost his bid for additional terms as governor in 1963, 1967, and 1971.

Bad blood had existed between Barkley and Chandler since well before 1938 when Chandler challenged the Senate Majority Leader and lost by 71,000 votes in the Democratic primary.

My father, Robert F. Matthews, who had aligned himself with the Wetherby-Clements-Barkley faction, served as the finance chairman for the Democratic Party in the 1950s.

Dating back to the 1930s, it had become tradition that the Democrats would begin their fall campaigns at the Shelby County Fairgrounds and, as mayor, it was frequently my father who welcomed the candidates, their supporters, and the general public.

It was at the fairgrounds in 1939 that Democrat Ralph Waldo Emerson Gilbert, my father's first and only law partner, was stricken and died a few hours later on July 30 while campaigning for the office of lieutenant governor. Gilbert was a five-term U.S. Congressman, two-time county judge, and state legislator.

Alben Barkley was a frequent visitor to Shelbyville, including 1949, when, as vice-president of the United States, he introduced his new bride, the former Jane Rucker Hadley, to a group of leading Democrats at our home on Main Street.

Later, in 1954, he came to Shelbyville on behalf of his candidacy to regain his old seat in the U.S. Senate against leading Republican John Sherman Cooper. He won narrowly.

While there are many campaigns that I recall, I will mention only three here because they had lasting significance for our family.

Lieutenant Governor's Race

The key race for my family involved the Democratic primary in 1967 when my brother Bob faced Wendell Ford for lieutenant governor.

Bob, a graduate of William & Mary College, had experienced considerable combat as an officer in the U.S. Navy in World War II. He had graduated from Shelbyville High School in 1940 and received his law degree from the University of Virginia.

He served as chief administrative assistant to Gov. Bert Combs before becoming State Finance Commissioner. In 1963, he defeated Republican Jean L. Auxier by about 19,000 votes for the office of attorney general.

In addition to Matthews and Ford, there were two other candidates, A.J. Jolly of northern Kentucky, and Harry King Lowman of Ashland, competing for the job as lieutenant governor.

Former Governor Combs maintained his neutrality during the race since both men had worked with him as his chief administrative officer. Governor Edward "Ned" Breathitt also proclaimed his neutrality since he was a supposed friend of both men.

The polls gave Bob a narrow lead as Election Day approached. Then Breathitt, according to a book by longtime Democratic consultant Fontaine Banks Jr., threw his support to Ford; both men having their roots in Western Kentucky.

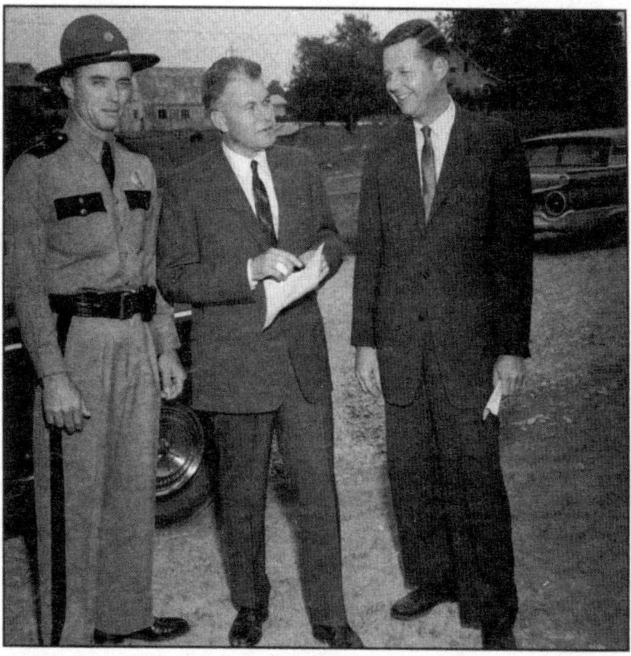

Governor Bert Combs, center, and State Finance Commissioner Robert Matthews Jr. were the principal speakers at the dedication of the new Shelby County High School. The trooper is Robert Howser, father of longtime Circuit Court Clerk Kathy Nichols. Matthews became the first and only Shelby Countian to serve as Attorney General, from 1963 to 1967.

Here's how Banks, Breathitt's chief of staff, recalled his involvement in the race in his book, *Memoirs of a Political Legend:*

"The campaign proceeded and I watched its progress with interest. Then on a Thursday morning, two and a half weeks before the primary, I was given a copy of the opinion polls on the race. A member of Wendell's campaign staff had recently told me that he expected to lose the election. I spent several hours studying the polls. Wendell was right. He was headed for defeat at the hands of Bob Matthews.

"That afternoon I sent for Bill Leonard of the Department of Highways to come to my office. I explained the situation to him and, after some lengthy discussion, we decided the best thing we could do for Wendell was to quickly raise some money over the weekend and then leave on Monday morning for Eastern Kentucky where Wendell was trailing and spend the next two weeks prior to the election working to pull out a win for him. It was a formidable task and we knew it would take working day and night and on weekends over the next weeks if Wendell was to have any hope of winning. We kept our plans secret until Monday morning and then we took off for the mountains.

"But before leaving Frankfort I had one important matter to attend to. That Monday morning, I went to Governor Breathitt's office and, fortunately, found him alone working at his desk. In my coat pocket was the letter of resignation. Before I pulled it out of my pocket and handed it to the governor, I said, "Governor, I can't stay neutral in the lieutenant governor's race any longer. I'm for Wendell and he's behind, and I've got to help him.

"Gov. Breathitt jumped up from his chair, clicked his heels together, saluted me and said, 'Major (he always called me 'Major,' my Marine rank at the time), what can I do to help?'

"I said, 'Governor, you can organize Christian County for Wendell.'"

Banks then worked overtime and with the help of county highway department chiefs in Eastern Kentucky and some county chairmen, whom he converted into Ford supporters, Ford prevailed by a few hundred votes out of several hundred thousand cast.

The final totals were: Ford 104,566; Matthews 103,619; Jolly 52,153; and Lowman 27,866.

While Banks claims in his book that his efforts helped Ford prevail, and this is undoubtedly true, it was actually Breathitt who double-crossed my brother on the eve of the election. None of those county highway chiefs or county chairmen would have switched sides without Breathitt's blessing.

When Breathitt died in 2003, I asked Bob why he planned to attend his funeral in Hopkinsville since he had betrayed him in 1967. His only response was, "Bill, it's all about politics." I have no idea what he meant.

And what did Banks get out of it? According to his book, Banks says, "At no time from election day to this day, did Wendell Ford or J.R. Miller, his campaign manager, ever say a word of thanks to either Bill (Leonard) or me."

Losing the election, in retrospect, may have been a blessing for Bob. While he said he loved politics, many of his friends thought he was too nice a person for the "down and dirty" tactics it sometimes takes to win.

He went on to have a successful career as a corporate lawyer with the Louisville firm of Greenbaum, Grissom, Wood, Doll & Matthews, which has now evolved into Greenbaum, Doll & McDonald.

Upon Bob's death in 2010, the law firm released the following statement: "Matthews set the standard for what all lawyers should strive to be. He was knowledgeable of the law and a skillful advocate, while always being professional, civil, and respectful of all."

As for politics, my brother managed to get seriously involved only one more time. He managed Combs' hugely unsuccessful campaign to win back the governorship in 1971 against the man he mentored and Bob's onetime adversary, Wendell Ford. As Bob said later, he should have "left well enough alone."

As for Ford, he went on to become Governor in 1971 and then served four terms in the U.S. Senate.

Had my brother defeated Ford in 1967, we can speculate that he might have followed a similar path. We will never know.

Mayor's Election

The other election was much closer to home. In 1965, a group of businessmen began meeting regularly with the idea of finding a candidate to run against incumbent mayor Jesse Puckett who had been first elected in 1958 and was completing his second term.

The principal business leaders included, among others, Mark J. Scearce, H.A. "Gus" Barnett, and Laban Jackson. While I was not directly involved in the committee's planning and fund-raising, I attended the meetings on a regular basis and was perceived to be a member of the group. Puckett's principal advisor was Louis Ruben, longtime owner of Ruben's Dry Cleaning.

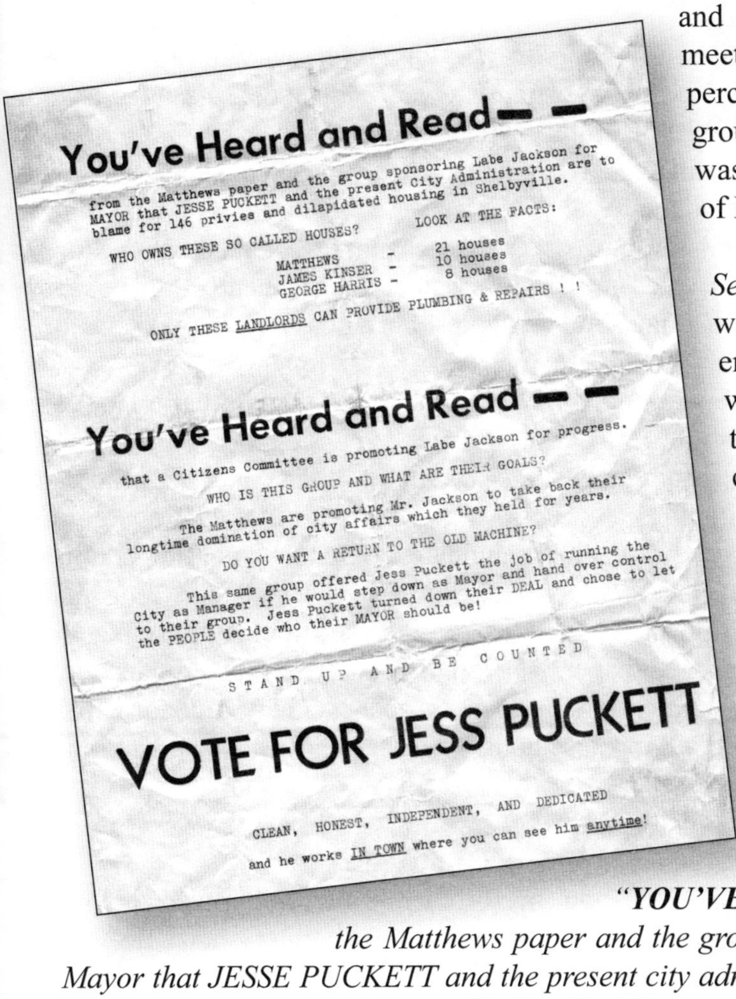

Neither my paper, *The Shelby Sentinel,* nor Bob and Sally Fay, who owned *The Shelby News,* endorsed a candidate. However, we benefitted from the ad dollars that flowed in on behalf of both candidates.

On the night before the election, the Puckett group distributed to every home in Shelbyville a flyer, which may have contributed to Puckett's one vote win (600 to 599) in the election. Puckett was nicknamed by many as "Landslide Puckett" after that vote.

The flyer proclaimed, *"**YOU'VE HEARD AND READ** – from the Matthews paper and the group sponsoring Labe Jackson for Mayor that JESSE PUCKETT and the present city administration are to blame for 146 privies and dilapidated housing in Shelbyville. Who owns these so-called houses? Look at the facts:*

Matthews – 21 houses; James Kinser – 10 houses; George Harris – 8 houses.

Only these landlords can provide plumbing and repairs!!

***YOU'VE HEARD AND READ** that a Citizens Committee is promoting Labe Jackson for progress. WHO IS THIS GROUP AND WHAT ARE THEIR GOALS?*

The Matthews are promoting Mr. Jackson to take back their longtime domination of city affairs which they held for years. DO YOU WANT A RETURN TO THE OLD MACHINE?

This same group offered Jesse Puckett the job of running the city as manager if he would step down as mayor and hand over control to their group. Jesse Puckett turned down their DEAL and chose to let the PEOPLE decide who their MAYOR should be!

The flyer says, *"STAND UP AND BE COUNTED"*

Vote for Jesse Puckett

Clean, Honest, Independent, and Dedicated

And he works IN TOWN where you can see him anytime.

Puckett's one vote win led to a lawsuit filed by Jackson and his supporters. Both sides subpoenaed individuals whose votes they wished to challenge.

Circuit Judge Coleman Wright, strong Democrat, was no friend of Jackson. The judge and many other Democrats were angered that Jackson had switched his allegiance from the Democratic to the Republican Party.

One person who was subpoenaed was Betty Carter, then a secretary for attorney Ted Igleheart. She joined several others waiting to be interviewed. The first person interviewed by Judge Wright was Ernie Fultz. When he refused to answer the judge's question, he was marched off to jail on a charge of contempt. What happened to him so shook up the others that each quickly told the judge how they voted.

Betty had married the same month, but, rather than changing her registration to the precinct where she now lived, she voted in the old precinct. Consequently, her vote for Puckett was disallowed. Both sides gained and lost votes, but in the end Puckett's victory was sustained.

Jesse went on to serve a third term as mayor before losing to Wyman Porter in 1970. He continued his public service by serving 15 years as city clerk.

The Puckett's group decision to run against the Matthews, rather than the candidate himself, Laban Jackson Jr., is nothing new. It is similar in our times to Republicans campaigning against Obama instead of the actual candidate in Kentucky politics.

How truthful was the flyer? Not very. Robert Matthews Sr. had died four years previously; my brother Ben was a local lawyer with no interest in politics; brother Bob was the attorney general; and I ran a newspaper. None of us had any desire to run the town.

On the other hand, my mother did own more than 25 houses, many of them without plumbing. Before five years passed, all of those houses had been sold and she was out of the rental house business.

1983 Governor's Primary Campaign

The third and final election in which both my brother Robert and I were involved was 1983 when Bagdad native Martha Layne Collins ran against former Louisville Mayor Harvey Sloane in the Democratic primary for governor. At the time, I was publishing the *Voice of St. Matthews* in Jefferson County, so I had to consider whether I should support editorially the Jefferson County candidate or the candidate representing my own Shelby County.

Complicating the issue was the fact that my brother Robert was heading up Sloane's campaign in Jefferson County.

To his credit Bob never lobbied me to support Sloane because he realized it was a "tough call" for me to make.

It really wasn't a difficult decision for me, not because of the family situation, but because

I genuinely felt that Martha Layne was the better candidate and was more committed to the state's welfare and development.

Events proved me right as she went on to win the primary rather convincingly, did a good job as governor, and has devoted much of her post-gubernatorial life to making the Commonwealth a better place to live. Sloane, on the other hand, left Kentucky shortly after the election and has rarely been heard from since.

Gov. Martha Layne Collins

Shelbyville Rotary

It is doubtful that any civic organization has done as much to benefit mankind as Rotary International. The organization's stated purpose is to "bring together business and professional leaders in order to provide humanitarian services, encourage high ethical standards in all vocations, and help build goodwill and peace in the world."

Rotary, in a collaborative effort with Microsoft founder Bill Gates, has been credited internationally with the virtual elimination of polio from the planet.

Several years ago Gates challenged Rotary to raise $200 million to match the $200 million he would give in the fight against polio. Rotary oversubscribed the issue, and the relentless effort to make polio obsolete is drawing to a successful conclusion. Only a few pockets of polio remain, and, for the first time, in 2011, India was declared polio-free.

Not only has Rotary contributed millions of dollars for a number of years to wipe out one of civilization's most deadly and despised diseases, but it has given freely to bring fresh water to millions, render free medical service to those in Africa and the Asian continent, and provide enhanced education tools to the uneducated wherever they might be globally.

The Shelbyville Rotary Club was chartered with 18 members in 1927. The first president was Ben B. Cozine.

My first experience with Rotary was in 1939 when, as a nine-year-old, I had the honor of meeting Harold "Pee Wee" Reese of Louisville, destined to become a Hall of Fame shortstop with the Brooklyn Dodgers.

Not only did he stand tall as the ballplayer, but he gained additional fame for standing up for Jackie Robinson in 1947 when he made his debut as the embattled second baseman for the Dodgers. There is a sculpture outside Louisville's Slugger Field depicting Reese with his arm around Robinson who was the first to break baseball's color barrier.

The Rotary Club, at that time, was meeting at 1108 West Main Street in a boarding house operated by a Mrs. Zaring. The house was actually owned by my father who had bought it during the Great Depression in 1930 for $4,500. Three years later we sold our home at 1122 West Main and moved three doors down the street to that building.

I joined Rotary in 1963 and served as the club's president in 1969. The only injunction I received upon assuming charge came from longtime member and county extension agent J.W. Holland. He told me, "Whatever else, Bill, keep everything to one hour. You understand, one hour. We meet at 6:30 and everybody is going home at 7:30. Make sure the speaker knows that."

Although we now meet in the middle of the day on Tuesday, the one-hour rule has continued to be the club maxim. Even the District Governor found out about the understood time frame. He was about half-way through his remarks a few years ago when several members bailed out. More followed. He apparently either hadn't been told about the one-hour limitation or chose to ignore it.

For almost 10 years, from 2002 to early 2012, David Mathis did a whale of a job as program chairman. We had speakers on local topics such as education, health, Shelby County Fair, Shelbyville Horse Show, election prognostications, and other topics. Then there were speakers who brought us information about state and national issues and problems.

Pancake Breakfast

The one incident I remember from my presidency was triggered when I recommended doing away with the annual Pancake Breakfast. This had become a club tradition going back to the early 1950s. Morton Webb Sr., of Lee-McClain Clothing Co., had chaired the event…forever. I had come to the conclusion that the pancakes weren't too good and this impression gained more credence when in 1968 a lady came into the assembly hall at the First Presbyterian Church where we held the breakfast event. She said, "Here's $4, you can keep the pancakes."

W. Coleman Wright, an active Rotarian, was judge of the 12th Circuit Court of Kentucky from 1952 until 1970.

Two of our Rotarians, Rev. J. Edward Cayce and Judge Coleman Wright, had fun flipping the pancakes high into the air and hoping that they would hit the skillet on their return trip. For the most part they did, but a few didn't. Those got brushed off and served anyway.

The motion to do away with the Pancake Breakfast drew a near unanimous vote. Only Morty voted against it.

After the meeting that night, he lit into me, saying that overseeing the Pancake Breakfast had become one of the highlights of his life. He said that I had violated one of the tenets of Rotary's 4-Way Test, the one that says, "Is it fair to all concerned?" He said, "You certainly weren't fair to me."

He had very little to say to me for the remainder of his life.

Later on, the club revived the Pancake Breakfast with much success…and better pancakes.

Insight into Treasury

My other recollection from 1969 involves the club's treasury. From the time I joined the club until I took over as president, neither I nor anyone else in the club ever knew how much we had in the treasury. However, when I asked Club Treasurer Wright how much we had, he smiled benignly and replied simply, "Enough," He thought that was cute. I didn't.

Community Projects

The club has been involved in many community projects, some of which were fund-raisers, some not.

For many years, under the direction of Briggs Lawson, the club worked closely with the Easter Seals state organization to send handicapped children to Camp Kysoc, Camp Green Shores, and Cardinal Hill. It has also supported the Boy Scouts, Cub Scouts, Red Cross, and the local hospital.

Perhaps it is best known for the Rotary Cup that is given each year to the "Most Outstanding Senior Boy" at high schools in the county. The award was first given in 1937 to a senior at Shelbyville High, and later to county schools at Gleneyrie, Finchville, Bagdad, Simpsonville, and Waddy.

One of the biggest changes in club membership came with the introduction of female Rotarians. Joyce Dudley, director of nursing at United Medical Center (now Jewish Hospital Shelbyville), was the first lady Rotarian. Presbyterian Minister Lynn Williamson (2003) was the first lady president. Erin Ratliff is the president for 2013-2014.

Another very visible program of Rotary is handling the front gate at the Shelby County Fair. Dating back to the 1940s, the club has earned anywhere between $3,000 and $7,000 annually collecting admissions at the fair.

Another crowd-pleaser has been the annual dinner-auction the last Saturday night in February which has raised more than $20,000 on several occasions. George Brinkhaus was the ramrod for the dinner-auction for many years. Sherman Riggs has been the bellwether of the event more recently.

Student Loan Program

Shelbyville Rotary has gained widespread recognition for its Student Loan Program. Over the years, since it was established in 1985 through the foresight and dedication of Max Avery, the club has provided more than $400,000 in loans to 70 students. Loans are typically made for four years, with the maximum now being $4,000 per year. Loan recipients are required to maintain at least a C average and take a minimum of 12 semester hours. The interest rate is 1 percent.

Riggs succeeded Avery as the longtime overseer for the program. Erin Ratliff recently succeeded Riggs. Lee Shannon is the treasurer.

Longtime members

Bill Shannon holds the record for the longest active period of membership, 68 years, beginning in 1946 and extending into 2014. Others who have been members for at least 40 to 50 years include Ted Igleheart, Bob Pearce, Brinkhaus, Riggs, Mathis, and the late Briggs Lawson, Phil Moesser, Stewart McBrayer and undoubtedly several more from the club's early years.

Bill Shannon

Colorful memories

On the night of December 31, 1999, Else and I, along with more than 325 people, gathered at Floral Hall to celebrate the Fantasy Ball's salute to the New Millennium. The combination dinner-auction held annually to benefit the Shelby County Community Theatre, raised more than $50,000 for the theater that evening. Else served as the General Chairman for the event.

The Shelbyville High School class of 1948 gathered at the Executive Inn in Louisville to celebrate the class's 50th anniversary. On hand were Bill Green, the late Bob Logan, late teacher and Kentucky State High School Hall of Fame Basketball Coach Evan Settle, and me.

Every year the Painted Stone Settlers Group re-enacts the Long Run Massacre which occurred in September 1781. The event is held annually at Red Orchard Park and attracts an increasing number of local residents as well as re-enactors and visitors.

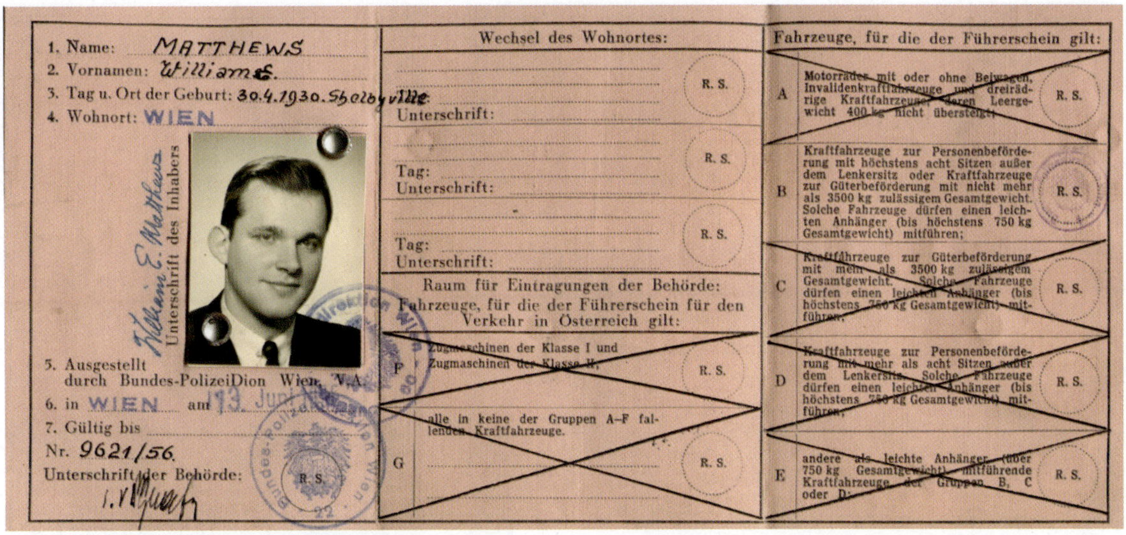

1. Name: MATTHEWS
2. Vornamen: William E.
3. Tag u. Ort der Geburt: 30.4.1930. Shelbyville
4. Wohnort: WIEN

William E. Matthews
Unterschrift des Inhabers

5. Ausgestellt durch Bundes-PolizeiDion Wien, V.A.
6. in WIEN am 13. Juni 1956
7. Gültig bis
Nr. 9621/56.
Unterschrift der Behörde:

R. S.

Wechsel des Wohnortes:

Unterschrift:

Tag:
Unterschrift:

Tag:
Unterschrift:

R. S.

Raum für Eintragungen der Behörde:
Fahrzeuge, für die der Führerschein für den Verkehr in Österreich gilt:

F Zugmaschinen der Klasse I und Zugmaschinen der Klasse II; R. S.

G alle in keine der Gruppen A–F fallenden Kraftfahrzeuge. R. S.

Fahrzeuge, für die der Führerschein gilt:

A Motorräder mit oder ohne Beiwagen, Invalidenkraftfahrzeuge und dreirädrige Kraftfahrzeuge, deren Leergewicht 400 kg nicht übersteigt; R. S.

B Kraftfahrzeuge zur Personenbeförderung mit höchstens acht Sitzen außer dem Lenkersitz oder Kraftfahrzeuge zur Güterbeförderung mit nicht mehr als 3500 kg zulässigem Gesamtgewicht. Solche Fahrzeuge dürfen einen leichten Anhänger (bis höchstens 750 kg Gesamtgewicht) mitführen; R. S.

C Kraftfahrzeuge zur Güterbeförderung mit mehr als 3500 kg zulässigem Gesamtgewicht. Solche Fahrzeuge dürfen einen leichten Anhänger (bis höchstens 750 kg Gesamtgewicht) mitführen; R. S.

D Kraftfahrzeuge zur Personenbeförderung mit mehr als acht Sitzen außer dem Lenkersitz. Solche Fahrzeuge dürfen einen leichten Anhänger (bis höchstens 750 kg Gesamtgewicht) mitführen; R. S.

E andere als leichte Anhänger (über 750 kg Gesamtgewicht) mitführende Kraftfahrzeuge der Gruppen B, C oder D; R. S.

Our family spent more than four years in Austria when I was employed by the CIA. This is a copy of my Austrian driver's license which was issued on June 13, 1956.

The Shelbyville Rotary Club, which was chartered in 1927, includes (front, from left) "Chip" Chiappetta, Jennifer Way, Bill Shannon, Ted Igleheart, Don Armstrong, Erin Ratliff, Geoffrey McGillen and K.C. Crahan; second row are Teresa Pager, Joe Piccini, Secretary Lowell Keene, Leon Mooneyhan, Jason Fowler, Mark Smith and Tom Sorrell; back row are Wade Hembree, Lowry Miller, Lindsey Logan, Lani Basberg, Jerry Tracy, David Mathis, Theresa Atha, then-President Tim Lee, Bob Pearce and Bill Matthews. Shannon joined the club in 1946. This photo was taken in 2011.

During one of my Amtrak trips, a cook responded to my complementary remarks about the food with a big hug.

I was an obviously happy "Henry Clay" during one of the summer camps sponsored by the Shelby County Historical Society.

Former Gov. Martha Layne Collins, right, was an honored guest at a 2012 book signing in the atrium at the Shelby County Public Library, which marked the release of *A Living History, Shelby County, Kentucky, 2011,* published by Historic Kentucky. Greg Biagi provided the photographs and I wrote the copy. The group also included, left to right, Ernestine Jennings, who contributed a survey to the book, Greg, Co-publisher Mae Peniston, and me.

The Friends of the Library donated more than $3,000 to the public library for the purchase of this new book drop. Officers pictured, left to right, front, are Mae Peniston, Sue Baker, and retired treasurer Bill Adams; rear, President Bill Matthews, Vice-President Kerry Johnson, and Treasurer Bill Logan. The annual Bookfests in 2012 and 2013 at the Stratton Center raised almost $10,000 divided between the Friends and its partner, *The Sentinel-News*, which uses its share to help underwrite its Newspapers in the Classroom program.

Dressed in a yellow rain slicker I welcomed theater-goers to the movie house in Jasper, Indiana, where *Hard Rain* was making its national debut in 1997. You will notice that the movie *Titanic* was playing on alternate nights. Filmed in part in Huntingburg, Indiana, where I owned the local newspaper, *Hard Rain* told the story of a bank heist which went sour due to an avalanche of rain which caused a dam to break, thwarting the thieves' getaway. The movie starred Christian Slater, Ed Asner, Morgan Freeman, and Minnie Driver.

I kept these two tickets for the World Series, one in 1964 and the other in 1976. I didn't get to use the 1964 ticket because the Reds didn't make it into the Series. Note that a premium field box seat for the 1976 Series, in which the Reds swept the New York Yankees, 4 games to 0, was only $15.

Mae Hall Peniston, co-owner of Historic Kentucky, is a Bagdad native who lives in New Castle. She is the widow of attorney and longtime state legislator L.T. Peniston. She is past president of the Democratic Woman's Club of Kentucky (1982-84). She was Executive Secretary of Newspapers Inc. from 1968 to 1972. She was the first woman clerk of the Henry County Baptist Association (1975-82) and is also a four-term Regent of the Bland Ballard Chapter of the DAR.

2011 Miss Kentucky Ann-Blair Thornton is the granddaughter of Bill and Ann Borders of Shelbyville.

Our daughter, the late Lisa Matthews, joined me in 2004 when *Back Home in Kentucky* received the Media Award from the Kentucky Historical Society for an outstanding Civil War map that Lisa prepared.

Veteran television and movie star William Shatner is a frequent participant in the Shelbyville Horse Show.

"Barnaby," a miniature schnauzer, has been a part of our family for more than 10 years.

Sue Grafton, center, a writer famous for her alphabet series of books such as *A is for Alibi,* and her latest, *W is for Waste,* spoke to a large crowd at the Shelby County Public Library as part of the Friends of the Library's "One Book, One Community" program. Else and I enjoyed talking with her prior to her appearance.

In San Diego, Kerry Magan stands in front of the USS *Carl Vinson* which served as the ship which transported Navy Seals on their mission to hunt down and kill Osama Bin Laden in his Pakistan hideout in 2011.

Shelly Hirsch has helped manage Bill and Else's household for 23 years. She is married to Steve Hirsch. They have a daughter, Samantha.

Historian and retired Brigadier General Ronald Van Stockum visited with retired District Court Judge Mike Harrod and Duanne Puckett before the Memorial Day ceremony in 2011 at Grove Hill Cemetery. Harrod and Puckett conducted a tour. They touched on many of the cemetery's beauties and unique features, and noted the many individuals, some more distinguished than others, who are buried there.

John Hackett, Jeff Disponette, and Shelby County Judge-Executive Robert Rothenburger cut the ribbon for the new Kroger store in 2011. The store was the second largest Kroger store in Kentucky.

Over the course of 10 years I interviewed many outstanding presidents of colleges and universities in Kentucky. Michael Carter, left, president of Campbellsville University stood out as No. 1. His unequaled enthusiasm for his school set him apart from the others. When I first interviewed him in 2001, the school had only about 1,000 students and "I'm hoping that we eventually get to 2,000," he said. Today the school has 3,600 students and has developed a national reputation for academic excellence. Vice president John Chowning, right, vice president for church and external relations and executive assistant to the president, has been a wonderful spiritual force for the university; Joan McKinney, news and publications coordinator (former staff writer for *The Sentinel-News*), and Linda Waggoner, marketing and media relations coordinator, have been especially helpful in working with me to make sure I get the facts straight.

Jim Cleveland, left, and Kentucky Journalism Hall of Famer and renowned columnist Byron Crawford joined me at the 2008 Kentucky Book Fair in Frankfort. We introduced *Portrait of the Past, A Pictorial History of Shelby County, Kentucky from 1865 to 1980.* Jim provided the photos, I wrote the cutlines, and Byron wrote the introduction.

Project Manager Jerry Miller, John Graham, Henrik Oetinger, Olivia Sherrod, Austin Dupre and Diane Coon (left to right) gathered at a historic massacre site near Simpsonville in 2011. The headstones honor 22 black Union soldiers who were killed by Confederate guerrillas in January 1865. Miller and the Shelby County Historical Society were honored as the "Best Community Volunteer Project" in 2011 by the Kentucky Historical Society.

A near record crowd turned out in 2011 for the Shelby County Historical Society's annual dinner meeting at Science Hill Inn.

Anna and Ed Warren raised these six beautiful, high-achieving daughters at their home on Clay Street. Seated are Wanda and Barbara; standing are Joan, Jeanette, Jennifer, and Vivian. The majority graduated from Lincoln Institute due to segregation and could not swim in the city pool their father helped construct.

These eight Cincinnati players constitute the nucleus of what is considered one of the greatest baseball teams of all time. In the front is catcher Johnny Bench, immediately behind are Pete Rose, Davey Conception, Joe Morgan, and Tony Perez; in the back are George Foster, Cesar Geronimo, and Ken Griffey. Bench, Morgan and Perez are in baseball's Hall of Fame. Rose would be in the Hall except for the lifetime suspension for gambling. Manager Sparky Anderson is also in the Hall.

Hall of Fame writers Hal McCoy, who wrote the text, and Earl Lawson, who wrote the foreword, helped produce *The Relentless Reds,* a Pressco book which I published following the Reds 1975 World Series victory. Pete Alexis profiled the team and Dennis Gruelle produced the photographs. The book is out of print.

Hal McCoy wrote the text and Ron Coons of the *Louisville Courier-Journal* wrote the foreword for *The Royal Reds* in 1976 following the Reds victory over the New York Yankees in the World Series. Pete Alexis again profiled the players and Dennis Gruelle provided the photographs. This book is also out of print.

Nick Clooney, accompanied by his lovely wife, Nina, talked to the Shelby County Historical Society about efforts to restore and maintain the home of his sister, Rosemary Clooney, in Maysville.

Blair Underwood, star of the television hit "L.A. Law," portrayed Jackie Robinson in the HBO hit "Soul of the Game." He and I became good friends on the movie set. The film was shot partially at Huntingburg League Stadium in Huntingburg, Ind.

Church life: Then and now

First Christian Church (1865-1969)

The world of religion has grown dramatically more secular since I was fortunate enough to grow up in the First Christian Church, located until recently at the corner of Fourth and Main streets.

As a youngster, I was doubly fortunate to have as our minister two of the most gifted pastors in the history of our brotherhood. One went on to become the president of the Lexington Theological Seminary, and the other was called to larger churches in Louisville and Birmingham, Alabama.

Thomas Giltner

Thomas M. Giltner came to Shelbyville as our minister in 1936 with the country still mired in The Great Depression and our church on life support. The church roof leaked; the furnace worked spasmodically in the wintertime; there was no such thing as air conditioning; and the church budget was never fulfilled. The parsonage was barely livable. My mother, Zerelda, became the unpaid choir director in 1935 and my father was one of the Elders.

First Christian was Tom's first ministry, having recently graduated from the seminary. He was short, red-haired, and full of life. One of his first acts was to establish a Cabinet that included committee chairpersons and their assistants. One of his next steps was to revitalize the youth program. Another decision he made was to help establish a budget that could be met. And, finally, he put a premium on bringing in new members, the younger the better.

As for his sermons, they were, as they say, "short and sweet." As the last item on

Sunday's church program, they never exceeded 20 minutes, which emphasized his saying that "No souls are saved after noon on Sunday."

In the summer, our young people went off to Camp Shantituck where Tom was not only the leader and inspirational speaker but also very apt to ram the ball down your throat during a game of volleyball.

Spurred by strong membership growth and inspired by his leadership style and community involvement, the church, by 1940, was able to fix the roof, reopen the parsonage, buy a new furnace, and meet its financial obligations. Tom and his wife, Margaret, and their two children, Jane and Betty Brents, became community favorites.

Tom stayed until 1942 when he went off to World War II to begin service as a U.S. Army chaplain. He was decorated for heroism under fire and became an even more inspiring figure to those of us on the home front.

Wayne Bell

Tom was succeeded by another young man just out of the seminary, Wayne H. Bell, who was accompanied to town by his wife, Virginia.

Wayne inherited a much better situation than did Tom in 1936. During his tenure, the church continued its rapid growth and First Christian continued being the church where most of the "who's who" in young people from all the other churches in town came together on Sunday morning.

Virginia and Wayne Bell were instrumental in helping Shelbyville's First Christian Church grow between 1942 and 1951.

It was during Wayne's tenure that the Upper Room Chapel was dedicated in 1948. Wayne was one of the sparkplugs who helped focus interest on the chapel that had long been the dream of Upper Room founder and its teacher, my father, Robert F. Matthews.

Tom Giltner's return from active service in 1946 marked a very emotional service at First Christian. Tom said only a few words as Wayne delivered the principal address, but there were few dry eyes that Sunday morning as the choir sang "My God and I" to welcome him home.

Wayne stayed on as our pastor and Tom responded to a call from Douglas Boulevard Christian Church in Louisville. He went on to become senior pastor at the First Christian Church in Birmingham, Alabama.

Wayne Bell stayed with First Christian until 1951 when he answered a call from the Seventh Street Christian Church in Richmond, Virginia, and, later, from the Vine Street Christian Church in Nashville, Tennessee. It was from Nashville that he was elevated to the presidency of the Lexington Theological Seminary. He served the Seminary from 1974 until his retirement in 1986.

My father was on the pulpit search committee that traveled throughout Kentucky in 1951 in search of a new minister. The committee agreed that whoever came to First Christian would find the going tough because we had had two great ones in a row.

"Brother Ed"

The committee finally decided on J. Edward Cayce who was then the senior minister at the First Christian Church in Madisonville, Kentucky. He was accompanied to town by his wife, Martha, who, unfortunately, was destined to die of cancer just a few years later.

Rev. Cayce's tenure extended from 1951 to 1976 years, which, based on whom you talked with, was probably about 10 years too long. The church, which had experienced such dynamic growth during the Giltner-Bell years, lost its appeal for youth and young couples, although, to be fair, "Brother Ed" was much beloved by many of the older parishioners.

He ended my mother's 22-year stint as choir director in 1957 simply by calling her on the phone and telling her she was out as Worship Chairman. He replaced her with an individual who barely knew the difference between a musical note and a baseball bat, yet he was one of Ed's allies.

"Brother Ed" systematically eliminated the church's intelligentsia from key positions, replacing these men and women with men and women with whom he was more comfortable intellectually. Those ousted, who represented the church's theological giants, included W. Boyd Roe, Ben Allen Thomas Sr., School Superintendent Mrs. Willie C. Ray, Bert Smith, George Pilcher and Robert F. Matthews.

I thought of that situation from church in the late 1990s when I had the opportunity to interview Dave Thomas, founder of Wendy's. I asked him a rather simple question: "To what do you owe your success?" He answered, "That's easy. I have always surrounded myself with people who are smarter than I am. You don't learn anything from people who are dumber than you are."

Col. Harland Sanders

"Brother Ed" did bring us perhaps the most famous man who ever attended a church anywhere. He became fast friends with Col. Harland D. Sanders of Kentucky Fried Chicken fame. The Colonel always came five minutes late and proceeded down the main aisle to the front row where he listened to his dear friend's sermons.

The Colonel also played matchmaker for Cayce after his first wife died.

Ed had been widowed for several years when the Colonel introduced him to a Texas lady and singer named Eleanor. It wasn't long afterwards that they were married and Eleanor started attending our church.

With a Pentecostal background and claiming that she could talk in tongues, Eleanor was a distinct opposite from Ed who came from a conservative background and preached a very unemotional, Biblically-based sermon.

For all the good that Eleanor claimed that she wanted, she split the church badly. Even after she left the church years later because of ill health, her influence was still being felt.

As for Col. Sanders, he was a very generous patron of the church and most of the members were quite aware of that status. One of board members questioned the Colonel's parking in the handicapped zone in front of the church (he wasn't handicapped) and was immediately reminded of the sizeable checks that the Colonel left in the collection plate. The practice continued.

The Colonel was also great friends with another church member, barber Paul Johnson. Paul, Ed and the Colonel went on many a fishing trip, with another friend, C.L. Love, handling the driving.

"Brother Ed" persevered for 25 years before finally retiring in 1976. He was succeeded by interim pastor Arthur Landolt (1976-1977).

James Collins

He was followed by James Collins from a church in Georgia. He sparked new life in a church suffering from a long period of stagnation. It was during his ministry that Child Town was born. This was a wonderful daycare ministry of the church that reached out to families who needed a nurturing facility for their children while they worked at jobs locally and out of town. Nearly 100 new members were added to the rolls, most of them young.

However, as so often happens, good things don't last and Collins left in 1982 for a church in Lubbock, Texas. Disaster followed when the church called the Rev. Bruce Merton from a church in Florida. Bruce was more of a clown (his hobby) than a minister. The church lost many of the same young people whom Collins had brought into the fold. For the first time in the church's history, the board fired its minister but gave Merton a generous severance package.

J. Howard Griffith

J. Howard Griffith became minister in 1986 and served for more than 20 years. Under his leadership, the church relocated from its historic location at the corner of Fourth & Main to 1000 Eminence Pike. Although many of us in the Upper Room Bible Class were among those who favored keeping the church downtown, events have proved that this was a good move and has served to attract many new members.

It was during that time, elders and deacons had to be invited to return to their positions following their sabbatical. June Davis, Jimmie Adams, and I, along with several others from the Upper Room, were among those who did not receive the required invitation. In 2013, however, J. William Hundley Jr. and I were elected to the position of Deacon Emeritus.

Howard said he buried virtually an entire congregation, 215 people, during his ministry. Child Town also found a new home at the Clay Street Baptist Church on U.S. 60. Howard became much more involved in the community than had any of his predecessors.

David Charlton

David Charlton, who had been the senior minister at the First Baptist Church in New Castle for 22 years, brought new energy to the church when he became minister in October 2009. Dave had actually received his training in the Disciples of Christ seminary and

Fr. Mike Tobin

decided to "come home" to his roots. Church attendance has climbed to nearly 200 each Sunday.

Dave Charlton

Our Director of Music David Pilkinton has drawn many accolades for his musical leadership over the past 26 years, particularly for the concerts his festival choirs have performed at Easter and Christmas.

Edwin Hisle

Other ministers, from the past and present, whom I remember fondly include Brothers Charles Elsey and Fred Moffatt from First Baptist Church, Edwin Hisle at Centenary Methodist, Gayle Threlkeld at First Presbyterian, Rev. Mike Tobin at Church of the Annunciation, Ron Holder at Clay Street Baptist Church, William George at Highland Baptist, and Wayne Ward at Finchville Baptist.

There have been significant changes in the worship service since I was a youngster.

While the sermons haven't changed much (Baptist ministers still preach about sin and redemption), the music certainly has...in most churches.

First Christian Church today

Observations which I have made during our various book signing trips to many of the churches include:

Clapping and Singing

First, most church congregations now love to clap, whether it's for the little people's choir, the big people's choir, individual solos, or just about anything else. All this clapping is a distraction for some.

Second, many churches, but certainly not all, have gotten away from traditional music, and, in trying to gather in the young people, have come up with what I call a syncopated be-bop sound. In short, much of the music sounds alike from one Sunday to the next.

This sound is preferred to what I call the "sweet classics," such as "When the Roll is Called Up Yonder, I'll be There," "In the Garden," "In the Sweet By and By," "Blessed Assurance," and "Amazing Grace."

John Shannon at First Baptist says that attendance at the early contemporary service parallels that of the later traditional service as the guitar and drums enjoy equal status with the piano and organ.

All things change and contemporary music certainly has its place as long as the congregation halfway understands the words and can comprehend the beat. Some congregations have gotten into what is called praise singing at the beginning of the service. This is sometimes called 7-11 music, meaning the congregation sings the same 7 words 11 times.

Third, most congregants now dress down rather than up for Sunday worship. At one church, I have observed an elder in shorts serving communion; in another, the song leader was wearing shorts with a WKU T-shirt. When I suggested that the poor attire reflected the casualness of our times, the minister said, "I'd rather call it laziness."

I like what veteran baseball coach and former Baptist moderator J.C. Wiley said: "If you don't dress up for the Lord, whom do you dress up for?"

Fourth, some churches are having a lot more luck attracting young people than others. It appeared to me that the average age of the congregation at one church was mid-70s; at another it was in the mid-40s.

Fifth, the diversity trend is also impacting our local churches. It would have been almost impossible to find a Black or bi-racial face in a white church 25 years ago, even 10 to 15 years ago. This certainly isn't true in 2014. Virtually all churches now welcome minorities to their brotherhood … a very positive change as the nation continues to become ever more diverse. This is causing concern to Black congregations as they see many of their professionals (lawyers, doctors, teachers) changing their affiliation to a mixed Black and White church.

Sixth, neckties for men have almost gone the way of the Dodo bird. At First Christian, Bill Hundley Jr., Mike Coleman, Dean Cantrill, Dr. Edward Sames, Neil Hackworth, Greg Buekley, Herman Moore, Eddie Kingsolver, Tony Carriss, James Clark, Bill Ploetner, Dave Charleton, several others and I can still be spotted wearing neckties on a regular basis. Jeans are not exactly the norm today, but I am reminded that the demise of the once popular Lee-McClain Clothing Company in Shelbyville was triggered by drastic changes in men's clothing tastes and styles, from suits and sport coats and quality trousers to just about anything that covers the body.

To their credit, most of the ladies at First Christian still enjoy looking their best.

Upper Room Bible Class (1925-2005)

The establishment of The Upper Room Bible Class in 1925 in the basement of the old church at Fourth & Main Streets fulfilled a dream that my father had upon his graduation from the University of Michigan.

He had met a man at the university steeped in the Disciples of Christ faith who his followers had called "Father Iden." During his undergraduate and law school years, Dad was one of those who "hung around" Father Iden's house for ideas and inspiration. He continued to correspond with his mentor after he came to Shelbyville and decided to follow in his footsteps by starting a class of young men interested in studying the Bible.

Those six men were W.P. Anderson, John Grubbs, Ellis McGinnis, Albert Ramsey, Bernard Tackett and Robert Yount. Dad was the teacher.

The class' first undertaking was an Easter Sunrise Service in 1926. Members of the class gave the invocation and benediction, the Easter prayer, and told the story of the

The final photo of what was once a class of more than 100 men was taken in the late 1990s. In the first row are Jack Langley, longtime organist Wanda Rayburn, Tom Barker, John Lyle Miller, Herman Moore, and Ben Allen Thomas Jr.; rear, Herman Whitaker, unidentified, Bill Matthews, James Casey, Gilbert Jennings, Winford Thomas, and Ben G. Matthews. John Lyle made the cross which is part of the backdrop. The photo was made in the Upper Room Chapel, part of the church at 4th & Main streets. Of the individuals in this photo, Langley, Barker, Whitaker, Casey, Jennings and Winford Thomas are deceased.

Resurrection. They also had to do it from memory, as Dad frowned on the use of notes. Most of the men had never been on a speaker's platform before. Dad gave the message, usually about 15 minutes.

Within a few years, the Easter Sunrise Service became a community tradition because no other church at that time was holding an Easter Sunrise Service.

The music also featured choir members from those other churches. Mother directed the choir and was frequently the soloist. Many others with exceptional voices were featured as soloists, including Lewis Mathis Jr. and his wife, Jan; Harvey Sutherland from Bagdad; Cliff Brooks and Carol Shirley. Two songs that were nearly always included were "The Holy City" and "My God and I."

When the featured soloist failed to show up for the Sunrise Service in 1995, the Upper Room class accepted it as a sign it was time to turn the service over to the church. After all, a run of 70 years was something about which we could be proud.

The Upper Room Class was non-denominational and guest speakers included leaders of the Baptist, Presbyterian, Methodist and Catholic faiths.

The class lost three of its members – Robert Newton, Bailey Cowherd, and Jesse Maddox Jr. – to enemy action during World War II.

Dad taught the class from its beginning until shortly before his death in 1961. Bob Yount, June Davis, Bill Chenault and I rotated teaching for a good many years until it became a challenge for the younger set including Mike Miller, my son Bland, and my late daughter, Lisa. The class, which had included 123 on its attendance book in 1947, disbanded on Easter Sunday 2005. At its last service, the five remaining members sang, "In the Sweet Bye and Bye," a song which the class had sung every year since 1939 as the class president called out the names of those who "had crossed to the other side."

My mother had originated the Keystone Class during the 1940s, and when she left for the First Presbyterian Church during the latter part of the Ed Cayce era, her role as teacher was filled by Eleanor Cayce, "Brother Ed's" new bride.

Not long afterward, Eleanor decided to make the class co-ed so she raided the Upper Room for potential members.

One Sunday when Eleanor was out of town, Roy Beatty Smith took over the class and started talking in tongues. At this point, Bessie (Jack) Langley, Virginia (June) Davis, and Ruby (Delbert) Wainscott walked out. They were joined by Loyd Caudill and Grace Proctor who became the new class' first teacher. It was called the Steadfast Class.

Today's Steadfast group includes "walkout survivors" Bessie and Grace, as well as Libby Miles, Sue Bottom, Mae Peniston, Alva Lee and Nell Smith. It is an honor for me to be their leader.

The Future

The First Christian Church has enjoyed good times and weathered bad times. With all the young people who have joined the church in the past few years, and men such as the learned and charismatic Dave Charlton at the helm, its future looks bright.

But, as I said at the beginning, as America becomes increasingly secular, it will take dedicated Christian families, and many of them, to make First Christian, or any church, a beacon for Christ very long into the future.

The Shelby County Historical Society sponsored its second annual Black Tapestry Event on Saturday, Feb. 8, 2014 at the Settle Gym. Mitchell Payne, son of Hattie Lee and Llewellyn Payne, was the principal speaker at the event which brought out a large crowd of Black citizens, as well as whites, who enjoyed viewing scrapbooks, photographs, and other historical artifacts of local Black history from the late 1800s to the present day. On hand for the event were, front row, Sharyn Mitchell, Willie Fleming, Mattie Bray, Brenda Jackson, Maureen Ashby, Daisy Dale, Etta Murphy-Coleman, Laura Moorman, Lily Roland, Tina Hurt, Mitchell Payne, and Sarah Kirtley; 2nd row, Natholee Harris, Inez Harris, Sue Ellis, Janice Harris, Teretha Beckley, Wandella Dorsey, Kevin Crittenden, Roland Dale, Juanita White, Lura Roland Jr., Sanda Jones and Laverne Stoner.

Race relations

Dating back to Civil War times, black citizens represented about 25 percent of the county's population. Many lived on farms, but the majority lived in Shelbyville. From the end of the war to the 1930s, the percentage slipped to about 12 percent as Shelbyville developed a reputation for being "unfriendly" to those of color.

My father started buying property in the mid-1930s to rent to the "colored", which was the term used in earlier days. Following his death in 1961, my mother inherited 25 rentals. Most of the rentals were in Martinsville, an area of about 10 acres bounded by Washington Street on the south, the railroad tracks on the north, Ninth Street on the east and High Street, now called Lee Nor Mack, on the west. I had personally bought two houses on north College Street in 1953.

Our other rentals, which had indoor plumbing, were principally on Henry Clay between 10th and 11th Streets.

Few of the houses in Martinsville had running water; most of the residents had to carry water from a cistern located at the top of the hill on 10th Street.

Houses rented from $5 to $25 per week.

When I returned to Shelbyville in 1962 from my job with the Central Intelligence Agency, I inherited the job of collecting rents, finding someone to clean out the privies in the backyards of the houses once a year, and recruiting new renters when someone moved out or died.

The houses paid for themselves in less than four years, making them an excellent investment.

As the Civil Rights movement began to evolve in the early '60s, I advised my mother to sell all of her houses. I had sold mine in 1960 and they were demolished a few years later. She initially balked, wondering how she could replace the substantial income they represented.

In 1968, mother sold all of the rentals, the majority of them to one individual and the remainder to another person.

However, long before the sale of our rentals, blacks and whites had co-existed in strictly segregated Shelbyville and Shelby County on a non-hostile basis.

Young whites and blacks played together in pick-up games on the football field and in our back yard. We had a wonderful cook and babysitter, Mary Bates, who lived on Henry Clay Street, just a few yards from our house on Main Street. She was very instrumental in raising two of our children, Ellen, born in 1962 and Bland, born in 1967.

When school integration came, black parents petitioned to have Lincoln Institute, the school for black students near Simpsonville, remain a segregated school because they believed their children were receiving a superior education to those attending white schools. They lost the battle and the school was closed in 1966.

Lincoln Institute teams won the state's high school basketball tournament for black schools on several occasions and Lincoln football teams were renowned for their prowess.

About the only evidence of our segregated community that I became aware of as a young person revolved around the movie house where white patrons sat in the downstairs part of the theater. Blacks were forced to sit in the balcony, which was clearly marked with a sign declaring "for colored" at the doorway.

The effects of segregation were brought home to me more forcefully when I "listened in" to a conversation between my father and a black delegation, headed by Mose Dale Sr., in the summer of 1948. The delegation appeared on our front porch – this in itself was surprising, since most people, other than those we knew socially, came to the back door.

According to Mr. Dale, possibly the black community's most influential citizen and "go-to" person, they were there to propose a deal: Blacks would not try to integrate the swimming pool when it opened in 1949 if the City Council would vote to move the city dump out of Martinsville where it occupied an area equivalent to a large city block.

The dump was not only an eyesore, but a mess of garbage, old tires, trash, pollutants, and yard waste that smoldered all day and all night … 365 days of the year. The smell was particularly odoriferous in the summer.

Since we lived only about 1,000 yards from the dump, Dad was anxious to accommodate the request since it would not only rid the city of a long-festering problem, but would, at least temporarily, improve the lives of those who lived within its proximity and, at least, defer the possibility of pool integration.

Dad took the proposal to the City Council and, based on his recommendation and strong feelings, the council voted unanimously to accept the black delegation's proposal.

However, pool integration did become an issue in 1963 when 14-year-old David Spencer Jr. and two other "Negroes" (as they were called by local reporters) arrived at the pool and were allowed admittance.

Mayor Jesse L. Puckett was credited with policies which, in time, would give way to full integration.

Puckett said that it was a matter of economics as pool revenues were only $41.50 on

Longtime attorney and community activist Willie Fleming reviews local black history and the civil rights movement with Katy Harden and Olivia Sherrod, as part of an internship program sponsored by the Shelby County Historical Society. Fleming was instrumental in bringing about the integration of the city swimming pool in 1964.

the day that Spencer and his friends were admitted. An interim agreement between black attorney Willie Fleming and Puckett provided for whites to swim on Mondays, Wednesdays, Fridays, and Sundays; and blacks on Tuesdays, Thursdays, and Saturdays. What had been a $100.00 dollar-a-day business dropped to $2.50.

Later, when 17 blacks attempted to use the pool on a Friday, they were refused admission by Puckett, Councilman Harry Long, and three city police officers.

The issue was not resolved until Memorial Day 1964 when the pool was fully integrated without incident.

It is interesting that several of the blacks (and their children) who helped build the pool, including Ed Warren, were not allowed to swim in it.

Depending on with whom you talk, race relations are either "greatly improved," according to Willie Fleming who will be 87 years old in August… or "it's about the same as it used to be," according to retired teacher Roland Dale, grandson of Mose Dale Sr.

Fleming graduated as valedictorian of the senior class at Lincoln Institute in 1947. He was one of the first two Negroes (using his own descriptive word) to graduate from the University of Louisville Law School (1954). He believes strong improvement has been made in education, transportation, and health care. Fleming still has his own civil law practice in Louisville.

Fleming says that as far as he knows blacks are being treated equally with whites, except, possibly for some "high-end" department store clerks in Louisville who don't respond as quickly to blacks as they do to whites.

Roland Dale says that after he integrated to the Shelbyville school system, one of his favorite teachers at the high school was Richard Greenwell who treated him and other black students like "gentlemen." Another favorite was George N. Busey, who at one time was chairman of the county school board.

Roland Dale

A graduate of Kentucky University, Dale worked as an industrial arts teacher six days a week for 27 years, and has substituted in the local school system for 12 years.

He remarked how that prior to integration, black teachers earned about one-half of what white teachers earned. Today he believes the school system continues to be deficient for a number of reasons, including the small number of black teachers that are employed.

Although Dale says that integration has helped black citizens generally, he claims that it also "destroyed black culture."

Roland's wife, Minnie, a native of Ohio, is also retired from the local system and she agrees with her husband's comments.

Their daughter Bridgett was the first black girl to win the title of Shelby County Fair Queen. She is now a consultant at Humana. Their other daughter Ashley is employed by the University of Louisville.

Mitchell Payne

Beyond the educational realm, Dale says that the "poor" but not the "rich" go to jail for the same offense. He is also distrustful of the local police who, he says, "don't treat black and white people the same."

Another perspective on the school system and the race relations scene was offered by Mitchell Payne, son of Llewellyn and Hattie Payne of Henry Clay Street. Payne was the first African-American state finance commissioner. He is presently the Interim Vice-President for Business Affairs at the University of Louisville. The department that he oversees at U of L has a budget of $55 million, and more than 700 individuals.

He was one of six black students in the initial first grade class in Shelbyville that was integrated in 1956. He attributes his success to loving parents, a nurturing neighborhood, a good Shelbyville school system and a strong sense of community.

He also has a very warm place in his heart for a fellow white classmate, Duanne Puckett, who was especially welcoming during the early years and remains a friend today.

Hattie Payne acknowledges being "spoiled" by her

parents, Johnson and Nora Cottrell, and says she has no hard feelings about the way black people were treated during the period of segregation. "I always got everything I wanted," she says, "so why should I not have been happy?"

I can testify that integration came slowly to Shelbyville. In 1967, three years after the National Civil Rights Law was passed during the administration of President Lyndon Johnson, my good friend, Johnny Buckner, organized a fast-pitch softball league, primarily as a way of selling and promoting his "Coaches Choice" bats and balls and other equipment.

I sponsored a *Shelby Sentinel* team and at that time we had two black employees, Sonny Sullivan, pressman, and Alex Chambers, general maintenance. (Both Sullivan and Chambers proved to be not only great employees, but also wonderful citizens. Large church turnouts marked their funerals. Sonny died in the early 2000s, and Alex in 2013.)

When our team arrived at Daniel Field for the first game, I had penciled in Alex for left field.

One of the other team managers pointed out that it was a "whites only" league. When I protested, he said, "Let's leave it up to the managers." Whereupon Hubert Briscoe spoke up and said very forcefully, "Times have changed, fellows. Alex Chambers plays or you can count me and my Briscoe Tire Service team out. Let's play ball!

And we did!

Miss Hattie Mae Cottrell (now Payne) was voted "Miss Lincoln" in 1947 during her sophomore year at Lincoln Institute. She was the first sophomore to be named "Miss Lincoln" since 1941. Other contestants were Evelyn Bradford, Ollie Fleming, Rosaline Strickland, Audrey Sullivan, Helen Hill, Marcella Jones and Mary Riddell.

Shelby County Historical Society

The Shelby County Historical Society traces its beginnings to 1963 when Chamber of Commerce Executive Director Joe Tucker proposed its establishment. Mrs. Purcell Lee was the first president; Col. (Ret.) Roger Green is now serving as its 15th president. Several individuals have served more than one two-year term as president, including Ted Igleheart, William Alwyn Miller, George Ann Carpenter, Sherry Jelsma, Betty Matthews and Charles T. Long. Others who have served as president include Jack Youngman, Lewis Cottongim, Gen. Ronald R. Van Stockum, Judge John David Myles, Jack Brammer, and me.

The Society has accomplished much since 1963 to engage its members in preservation and educational projects while making the community aware of the rich heritage this area has to maintain.

In 1979 it published *Cemeteries in Shelby County*, which involved countless hours by individual members combing farm sites for family cemeteries as well as smaller established

The 2014 board includes, from left, standing: board member Jim Cleveland, Treasurer Darwin Foley, Vice President James Mulcahy, board member David Mathis, and President Roger Green; seated are Secretary Julie Mulcahy, left, and board member Sarabeth Farabee. Not pictured are board members John Graham, Nancy Hill and Masha Miller.

burial grounds in the outlying towns. It is out of print but the public can still access the materials at the Shelby County Public Library.

Historical highway markers were researched and obtained through the proper state guidelines. The bronze tablets can be seen even on Main Street where one learns about the downtown fountain as well as in Simpsonville where Old Stone Inn is noted as a pioneer roadside inn.

A major undertaking was identifying city and county structures for inclusion on the National Register of Historic Places. It also awarded Shelby County Landmark plaques to identified property owners in conjunction with celebrations marking the state and county bicentennial in 1992.

Perhaps its biggest challenge was restoring the historic home on the northwest corner of Third and Washington of Augustus O. Stanley (May 21, 1867 – August 12, 1958), Kentucky's 38th Governor. The Society purchased the home in 1984, then owned by Joe Casey and his sister, Mary Kate Casey whose father was a tinsmith. The long, tedious and arduous task of restoring the home to pristine condition was accomplished shortly after the new millennium. It was used as the Society's meeting place until its sale in 2005 for $172,000 to a group of lawyers with the understanding that they would maintain it properly. That sale has enabled the Society to establish an endowment fund of $150,000 which, with interest, has grown to $164,318.

Bill Matthews unloads boxes containing copies of *The New History of Shelby County*, published in 2003 after six years of hard work by many.

The decision to sell the Stanley-Casey House was actively supported by immediate past president Jelsma and me. This did not go well with the entire membership. The vote was 7-1, with two abstentions. Igleheart cast the lone dissenting vote. Those who opposed the sale said it represented a betrayal of the many people who had worked for so many years to bring it back to life.

Those who favored the deal pointed to the substantial amount of money it took each year to maintain the property. Most of the money from membership dues was going into the house's upkeep.

Over time, whatever hard feelings existed in 2005 have given way to a new sense of unity. That unity is reflected in the massive amount of work so many members have put into the successful development of a Society Museum on the second floor of the Welcome Center at 627 Main Street.

In 2003, a highly notable accomplishment was publishing *The New History of Shelby County*. Publication of this book culminated a six-year effort and represented the efforts of more than 120 authors who contributed articles representing their knowledge and/or expertise on a particular subject.

Igleheart served as chairman and assistant editor of the Book Committee. I served as

Unveiling the new historical marker noting the passage through Shelbyville of Meriwether Lewis from his historic expedition (1803-1806) with William Clark are James Holmberg of the Filson Historical Society, local historical society President William E. Matthews, and James Mallory of the Lewis & Clark Trail Heritage Foundation.

associate editor. Other members of the committee were Vivian Overall, Gen. Ronald Van Stockum, Emily Thomas, Duanne Puckett, Charles T. Long, and Judge John David Myles. Well-recognized Kentucky historian John Kleber was the editor.

Lewis & Clark Celebration

The Society did its part to help recognize the Bicentennial of the Lewis & Clark Expedition of 1803-1806.

On Sunday, October 1, 2006, the Historical Society, in cooperation with the Kentucky Historical Society's Highways Marker Program, dedicated two markers commemorating the expedition, one at the Shelby County Courthouse and the other near Clayvillage.

It was in Shelbyville on October 28, 1809, that William Clark read a newspaper telling of the probable suicide of his expedition partner Meriwether Lewis near Nashville, Tennessee. Later that night he wrote a letter to his brother, Jonathan Clark, in Louisville expressing his grief over Lewis' death. The letter was penned at Shannon's Tavern in the small community of Graefenburg in eastern Shelby County.

Among those who gave remarks at the courthouse celebration in 2006 were Jim Holmberg, Curator of Special Collections, Filson Historical Society; Jim Mallory, Lewis & Clark Trail Heritage Foundation; and Nelson L. Dawson, Kentucky Historical Society. Holmberg and Mallory unveiled the marker.

Adding to the festivities were proclamations issued by Shelbyville Mayor Tom Hardesty and Shelby County Judge/Executive Rob Rothenburger. Each of the proclamations referred to October 1, 2006, as "Lewis & Clark Bicentennial Day in Shelby County."

Recognizing Black History

A wonderful Black History Tribute at the Stratton Center in 2013 and at the Settle Gym in 2014 attracted many citizens of both races. Much credit is due Sanda Jones and Kerry Magan who were the principal planners and who oversaw the collection and display of the many items.

Silversmith Exhibit

An exhibit featuring the skills of at least 13 silversmiths from Shelbyville during the 19th century opened at the Wakefield-Scearce Galleries during its annual Christmas opening in early November 2013. Past President and always enthusiastic Sherry Jelsma organized the exhibit, and has been the Society's main sparkplug on many other exhibits. The display then rotated to Commonwealth Bank and Citizens Union Bank with the brochure that outlined each silversmith's biographical information and expertise in the field of silver.

Five Decades of Duty

In 2013, the Society also observed its 50th anniversary and looked back on many achievements aside from those enumerated above. Members who are deceased were acknowledged as current members reflected on their roles and the roles of others who have kept history and its stories alive in Shelby County.

Others who have played prominent roles during my time with the Historical Society include Jim Cleveland, Charles T. Long, Nancy Hill and Jack Brammer. From an earlier period, Ted Igleheart, Judge John David Myles, Duanne Puckett, Emily Thomas, Betty Matthews and Gen. Ronald R. Van Stockum made extraordinary contributions to the Society's work.

Shelby County Historical Society President Sherry Jelsma, left, welcomes the opening day crowd to the official release of *The New History of Shelby County*. The 671-page book with hundreds of photos took almost seven years to prepare, and contained the writings of more than 120 individuals who wrote about a topic with which they were particularly familiar. Above, right, former Gov. Martha Layne Collins, who wrote the foreword to *The New History of Shelby County,* visits with the late Bill Strode, whose Harmony House company produced the award-winning book.

Shelby County veterans

Each Memorial Day in Shelbyville, the VFW Post places a wreath on a soldier's grave. Countless times it has been at the cenotaph for Benjamin McMakin of Shelbyville who was killed off the coast of Formosa while being held prisoner of war aboard a Japanese ship in 1945. He was 32 years old.

Next to placing a wreath at a veteran's grave, nothing brings home the sacrifice of our nation's veterans as much as a visit to a veterans' hospital at Christmas time. That's when you realize who the real American heroes are.

I realized this anew before Christmas when I provided some very minor assistance to two ladies, Phyllis Koch and Mae Peniston, who were distributing fruit baskets to those who have served us so well since World War II. The distribution was part of the mission of the Bland Ballard Chapter of the Daughters of the American Revolution.

It's hard to believe that veterans at the Rex Robley Veterans Center off Zorn Avenue in Louisville could be so appreciative of a simple fruit basket. Yet, each one was effusive in his or her gratitude.

In this photo from 2011, on the occasion of Veterans Day, VFW Post 1179 members gathered to recall their service to our nation. From left to right, seated, are Arvin Bowman, Bruce Wells, Col. (Ret.) Roger Green, Charles Turner, and Roy Hardesty; back row, standing, are Morris Adams, Jim Morris, Noble Roberts, Ed Myles, Danny Moffett, Barry Campbell, Charles Higgins, and Scott McClain.

Veterans Day in November 2011 at the County Extension Office was observed by a large crowd and these 40 veterans of wars dating back to World War II. The appreciative audience saluted each group of men and women as they recited their stories.

Not only did we visit 25 to 30 veterans, but we concentrated on also giving fruit to their spouses, mothers, or children who were biding their time in the many waiting rooms at the hospital.

As you look at and talk to these men and women, one realizes how almost flippantly we send men (and now women) off to war. It was particularly bad that we sent so many soldiers to Vietnam with insufficient training. High casualties were the result. I knew two of those killed, Stanley Lawson and Tommy Thompson, who were exceptionally bright young men from Shelbyville with wonderful prospects.

All told, more than 58,000 didn't come back from Vietnam – including seven from Shelby County. The parents and spouses of those who died must have been really incensed when former Defense Secretary Robert McNamara said after the war that he had had doubts all along that we could win the conflict.

My military career consisted all of 19 days in the summer of 1952 prior to my selection to become part of the Central Intelligence Agency. However, my two brothers, Bob and Ben, did their part during World War II and our father, Robert F., in World War I. All three served in the U.S. Navy.

What has troubled me for years is our seeming compunction to be at war, that we actively seek out times and places to fight, whether it be Vietnam, Afghanistan, Iraq, Yemen, or other points on the globe. We're becoming increasingly active even in Africa and are "strengthening" our defenses in the Pacific to counter the Chinese threat. All told, we have soldiers in more than 100 countries.

In looking at American history, there's hardly a conflict that we didn't initiate or find a reason for-getting involved. We have been the aggressors in more than one war. In our zeal to add Texas to the United States, we provoked war with Mexico, and we jumped into the Spanish-American War with a "Remember the Maine" cry, although it has never been proven that the Spaniards had anything to do with the Maine's destruction.

We also love to talk about "just causes" in which to embroil ourselves. We shouldn't really talk about "just causes" when we consider the plight of the thousands of American Indians who died on the "Trail of Tears" following their eviction by President Andrew Jackson from their legally-owned homes and farms in Georgia and Alabama during his presidency.

Only World War II and the Korean War represent instances in which we were forced to respond when enemy forces attacked us or our Allies.

The problem, of course, with starting and even winning a war, is the human debris left behind in terms of American deaths, quadriplegics, and broken lives. Consider this: In the war on terrorism since 2001, there have been 57,614 killed or wounded.

How, also, do we justify having an American drone kill 13 Afghans heading for a wedding party because our trigger-happy military "thought it was an al-Qaida convoy?" Afghan President Karzi has said more than once that, "Americans cannot roam the world looking for somebody to kill!"

Just as Adolf Hitler had 14- and 15-year-old boys fighting for Nazi Germany as the war wound down in 1945, we ask too many young men and now women to do the dirty work from which smarter and older men shy away.

I felt sad seeing how many veterans, older veterans, at the Louisville hospital are battling their illnesses, diseases, and loss of limbs. However, I felt good seeing how well we are taking care of them. They were being treated with great respect. Their morale was incredibly high.

I can probably understand their high morale if their medical care equals that provided by a longtime Shelbyville doctor. Alfred Deaderick Doak completed his career as a physician at the veteran's hospital in Johnson City, Tennessee. The good doctor Doak and his wife, Evelyn, were two of Shelby County's most beloved citizens.

The reason for his departure from Shelbyville? Too many local patients took advantage of his wonderful nature and didn't pay their bills. So, to survive as a doctor and a father of four children, he was forced to look to the government that would rightfully guarantee him a paycheck for his treatment of the veterans… treatment that was provided with care and compassion.

I was told at the hospital that we're already running out of enough doctors to take care of our veterans, so, perhaps, the answer to that problem is negotiating more and killing less.

Veterans Memorial Park contains this dramatic sculpture memorializing those who gave their lives for their country dating back to World War I. The park was dedicated on Jan. 11, 1983. Quintin Biagi was the architect and Barney Bright the designer and sculptor. Other individuals instrumental in bringing about the memorial were C.L. Love, Kenny Mitchell, George Pigg, Carolyn Hyatt, and John Paul Martin.

Medical engagements

Long before plastic surgery became such a routine practice, I became its first "victim" way back in 1935.

That year my mother decided that my ears "stuck out." While a more pleasing word might be "protruded," the fact is that both of my ears especially, my right one, jutted out too far for my very thin frame. I was also enduring a lot of kidding from my buddies, one of whom called my ears "wind stoppers."

So my mother decided to enlist the help of Dr. E.S. Allen who, to the best of my knowledge, was one of very few surgeons, if not the only one, who operated at the old King's Daughters Hospital on Henry Clay Street. He did everything from routine tonsillectomies to tumor removals and other more complicated procedures.

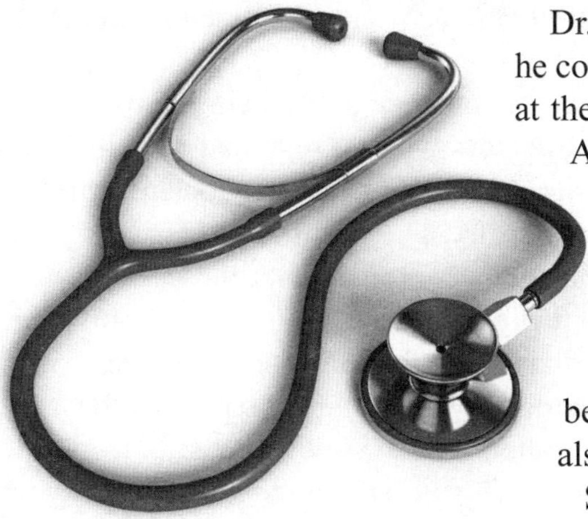

Dr. Allen apparently never met a medical challenge he couldn't handle surgically. Although I was only five at the time, I remember how terrified I was when Dr. Allen said something like this to mother, "I've never done this before, but let's see what I can do." One might call his statement hardly reassuring.

The operation was partially successful and my ears still don't match exactly, but they're better than they were. Filling out my physical frame also helped greatly.

Shelbyville's routine medical needs in the 1930s-1950s were met by, among others, Drs. A.D. Doak, Harmon Nash, William P. Hughes, Livingston Wahle, Max Klein, Willis McKee, A.C. Weakley. Later came Drs. Don Chatham, Bill Powers, Ron Waldridge Sr. and Jr., and by Drs. Kenny Gravett, James Smith, David Wallace, Edward Sames, Kenneth Gardner, David Jones and Alan Honaker.

You cannot overlook the females who were dedicated nurses like Germaine West, Bernice Graybill, Margaret Hornback and Doris Ruble. It was reported at the funeral of Mrs. West that she even removed a fish hook from a young man's hand without the assistance of the doctor on call at the hospital. Miss Hornback provided medical care in World War II, became director of nursing at the hospital and even served as a medical missionary in Gaza after her retirement.

These names represent only a partial listing of the men and women who have cared for Shelby County residents – and we are grateful for all.

Dental

Dating back to the Williams' twins and Dr. C.C. Risk, Shelby Countians have enjoyed good dental treatment. This was a blessing since long-ago treatment could have included a parent wrapping a string around the sore tooth and attaching the other end of the string to a doorknob. The door was then opened and then slammed shut, thus extracting the tooth.

Great examples of good care I received in the hands of a professional are the two gold inlays that Dr. Rodney Whitaker inserted in my teeth in 1950. They're still there. The cost: $88!

Whitaker's office was at 11th and Washington in a structure designed by architect Quintin Biagi that won an award. Dentists occupying that space now are Dennis Long, Gerry Buecher and Jamie Coleman.

Medicare

Medicine has changed mightily since the 1930s as the government and the insurance companies have deprived doctors of their long cherished decision-making roles in patient care.

Even if you're about to drop dead as you enter the doctor's office today, you will still be asked, "May I have your insurance card?" And if you're gasping for air or suffering from an almost unbearable pain as you check into the hospital emergency room, you will still be asked, "May I have your insurance card?" before you see a doctor or receive treatment.

Back in the early 1960s when Medicare was still being debated, I interviewed Dr. Max Klein, a particularly able and committed Shelbyville physician, for *The Shelby Sentinel*. He told me, "Bill, Medicare will fundamentally change the practice of medicine as we know it, and two things are going to happen: first, some doctors will get rich, and all will do a lot better financially than ever before; and, second, the doctor-patient relationship will be damaged forever as the government and insurance industry take over the profession."

Dr. Klein, of course, was prophetic. It's the insurance company, not the doctor, who generally decides now how long a person stays in the hospital. I had a friend in Louisville years ago who was booted out of a hospital on Thursday following serious surgery and died on Monday. There is a young man whose heart is only pumping at 30 percent, but the insurance company only authorizes a heart pump if the function is down to 25 percent. In all reality, it's the insurance company, not the doctor, who either approves or disapproves the medical therapy that the doctor has ordered or knows is needed. You certainly get the idea of the changes that cause me concern.

One thing I have learned over the years is never, ever have surgery unless it's absolutely necessary. There are far too many accidents in hospitals, far too many diseases transferred, or far too many surgeries botched. I can think of two people who went in for "routine" surgeries and didn't come out. One had bought a car on Tuesday and died in the hospital on Sunday following complications from a "routine" cleaning out of his carotid artery.

Nursing homes

Assisted living facilities and nursing homes have become such an integral part of today's living that one assumes they've been around forever. Not true. While we have had nursing homes (sometimes they were called "retirement homes") around in one form or another for a long time, assisted living facilities are relatively new.

Back in the old days, common practice was for a family to take in a relative who had become physically disabled or mentally challenged due to strokes or dementia. That rarely happens anymore as more and more facilities become available that have the resources and staff to accommodate the physically or mentally handicapped.

Unfortunately my wife, Else, has been exposed to both types of facilities (assisted living and nursing), and, for the most part, the experience has been better than I expected. What has impressed me most has been the extraordinary care she received at both Amber

Oaks, an assisted living facility, and presently at Crestview, a rehabilitation and nursing center. I'm not going to list all the names of nurses and caregivers at Crestview who have been so caring and attentive, but Toyya Tipton is among the best.

Advances in medicine have enabled many Americans to live longer, some longer than others. However, for every one of those who is 90 years of age or older and "fit as a fiddle," there is a dozen or more simply existing or wasting away in a nursing home. However sad or tragic this might be, no solution exists…at this time – other than the concept of the Living Will document in which you can specify ahead of time your wishes "when the time comes" that a decision needs to be made and you are not capable.

One cannot help but be saddened at the sight of so many individuals whose lives are, practically speaking, over or about over. I cannot understand why Americans insist on keeping "Aunt Matilda" or "Uncle Charlie" alive when they have become incontinent, mentally incompetent, and helpless. One resident has been totally paralyzed (she can move her eyes) for more than 20 years. Could this possibly be humane?

But not to be too negative, many individuals have lived relatively happy, useful lives in nursing homes. They are there simply because there is inadequate help at home to tend to their needs. Right offhand, I can think of at least three individuals, one of whom lived to be 108, who were mentally alert and physically able up to their last few weeks or months of life. So simply taking up fulltime residence in a nursing home doesn't have to mean unproductive living.

When the Affordable American Health Care Act, referred to as Obamacare, was first introduced, there were cries that "death squads" would be introduced to determine who would live and who would die. This, naturally, turned out to be a false concern.

One of my grandmothers, whom I loved very much, was institutionalized for the last 13 years of her life. Her life as I considered it ended in 1947; she died in 1960 at the age of 88.

Nursing homes make big profits because they charge big bucks and the need for them increases as more and more Americans seek their services. The result is that a higher and higher percentage of Americans will need to be covered by Medicaid because they will be unable to pay $80,000 to $100,000 per year for care.

Consequently one of the biggest, if not the biggest, problem we face as a nation is how do we care for literally millions of nursing home patients without going bankrupt. This is not a pleasant thought, but it's a very sad truth.

Meet the family

My parents, Robert F. Matthews and Zerelda Tribble Baxter, were united in marriage on May 8, 1922, in the parlor at the old Lafayette Hotel in Lexington. They eloped, in part, because my father's mother and my grandmother, Margaret Killgore Matthews, refused to sanction their wedding. In fact, she "took to her bed" for several months to protest her beloved son's nuptials. My grandmother did the same thing, retiring to her bedroom, when her other son, Charles T. (Ted) Matthews, announced his intention to marry a registered nurse, Mildred Sandbach, a few years later.

My mother, Zerelda, daughter of Junius and Harriett Baxter of Richmond, Kentucky, graduated from Model High in Richmond in May 1920 and got her teaching certificate on the same day (a rather unique trick back in those days). She came to Shelby County in September of that year to teach school, specifically music and home economics, at Finchville. There she lived with Dr. and Mrs. Evart Hankins.

Finchville was the only highly structured social community in Shelby County. One of the first expressions she heard was "The Doolans speak to the Duvalls, the Duvalls to the Veeches, and the Veeches to God."

Robert Foster Matthews

My father was the son of Benjamin Franklin Matthews, a farmer and Greek scholar, and Margaret Killgore Matthews. Further back, he was the great-great-great grandson of noted Indian fighter Bland Williams Ballard and his first wife, Elizabeth Williamson Ballard. Bland Williams Ballard's portrait hangs in both the Filson Historical Society in Louisville and the Kentucky Historical Society Museum in Frankfort.

Dad was the first university-trained lawyer to take up that profession in Shelbyville. All of his predecessors had "read" the law as apprentices to the other older lawyers in town.

Robert Foster Matthews

Dad, valedictorian at Male High School in Louisville in 1915, had served as an officer in the U.S. Navy in World War I before obtaining his undergraduate and law school degrees from the University of Michigan. He was Shelbyville City Attorney for two years before serving two terms as county attorney. He became a law partner of five-term Congressman Ralph Gilbert in 1925. The partnership ended in 1930 when he went into practice for himself.

It was during his days as county attorney that Dad, in 1927, handed over the indictment of Otho Vardaman, assistant cashier at the People's Deposit Bank, who was later convicted of embezzling more than $61,000 from the bank. The bank closed the same day and the shareholders had to make up the deficit.

Dad became the first popularly-elected mayor in 1934. Up to that time his predecessors had been chosen by the City Council. He served as mayor longer than any man or woman up to this time. His terms ran from January 1934 to January 1946 and again from April 1946 to January 1954. The second period was occasioned by the resignation in April 1946 of popularly-elected Lewis S. Frederick for "reasons of health." Dad was opposed twice, by Warren Briggs and E.A. "Son" Howser, and unopposed on the other two occasions.

During 1937 he spearheaded the community's response to the record-setting Ohio River rains that flooded much of Louisville, and sent many of their citizens to Shelbyville where they were fed and housed. The *Louisville Courier-Journal* was printed through the cooperation of *The Shelby News* and *The Shelby Sentinel.*

During World War II as mayor, he headed up Shelby County's Civil Defense Program, which included air raid practices and the collection of paper, old tires, and metal to boost the war effort on the home front.

Dad caught a lot of flak, even from the *Louisville Courier-Journal* for his failure to order a fire engine to Waddy when a major fire erupted in 1951. The fire destroyed the Waddy Christian Church and the Smith & Garrett Store, and threatened to destroy several residences. Dad argued that he couldn't leave the City of Shelbyville unprotected, but that didn't sit well for the Waddy folks. It was shortly thereafter that the East Shelby County Volunteer Fire Department was established at the Peytona Garage. Today, Shelby County has perhaps the finest network of volunteer fire departments in Kentucky.

Dad had three loves: his family, the practice of law, and the Upper Room Bible Class (although I'm not sure that's the correct order).

He served for eight years in the 1950s as the Democratic Party's State Finance Chairman. Governor Bert Combs was among those in the capacity crowd that filled the sanctuary at the First Christian Church for his funeral on April 16, 1961.

Zerelda Baxter Matthews

For all of Dad's high profile as mayor, church elder, and bank president, it was my mother who served as the family catalyst and enjoyed an equally high profile because of her many community activities, in addition to raising three sons.

Zerelda Matthews

Mother was a working president of the King's Daughters Hospital Board for many years, taught speech classes at Shelbyville High in the 1940s, taught voice lessons to such outstanding vocalists as Louise and Phyllis Kesler of Bagdad and Edna Katherine Henninger of Simpsonville, and starred as Abby in the Shelby County Community Theatre production of *Arsenic and Old Lace.*

According to an article written by Alan Butler in *The Sentinel-News* in 1983, she directed plays for 63 years, including the final one, *The Glass Menagerie*, the year before her death in 1984.

She told Butler that music and the theatre had always been her true love outside of her family. She studied at the Louisville Conservatory of Music for three years and originally intended to pursue a career as a singer in New York.

Her first two plays were musicals at Finchville High School. Her most memorable play, she told Butler, was *Pride &*

Prejudice, a beautiful classic, in Zerelda's view, presented in 1966 at Shelbyville High School. Performers included Doug Potter, H.B. (Benton) Kinsolving IV, Don Chatham Jr., Hunter Moody, Thomas Lynn Richie, Charlene Chatham, Loretta Moore, Libby Schmidt, Alice Amyx, Sharon Kemper, and Bibby McKay. Her actors and actresses performed waltzes in the aisles during intermission as an added attraction.

She taught voice in her home all during the 1940s, and was the soloist at hundreds of funerals at Shannon Funeral Home, which was right next door for many years and only four doors away when the family moved from 1122 to 1108 West Main Street in 1942.

She quit singing in 1957 because she felt she couldn't maintain the high standard that she had set. In Butler's article, she said, "I can't stand for people to keep on singing past the time they can't sing well."

After she quit singing, Mother became very involved later in the community theatre and said, "I'm very dedicated to the theatre. It's a marvelous thing; it brings together the city and the county, and also the young and the old."

She concluded, "I don't think there's been a theatre anywhere as successful as this one in Shelbyville."

Zerelda was the unpaid director of music at the First Christian Church for 22 years. She was a wonderful bridge player, and as a bowler, she made up for any shortage of skill with an unmatched enthusiasm for the game. She also won the Shelbyville Country Club Ladies Golf Title in 1940.

Robert Foster Matthews Jr.

Robert F. Matthews Jr. was born on September 14, 1923, at the King's Daughters Hospital in Shelbyville and graduated from Shelbyville High School in 1940 well before his 17th birthday.

He attended William & Mary College in Williamsburg, Virginia, where he majored in economics and political science. By going to school after his junior and senior years, he was able to complete college in three years and graduated in the fall of 1943. He had enrolled in the U.S. Navy's Midshipman training program prior to graduation.

He was sent to Great Lakes Naval Training Center where, after four months' training, he was commissioned an ensign in the Naval Reserve.

After serving a few months aboard a Destroyer Escort in the Atlantic, basically escorting merchant ships between the United States and Europe, he became the communications officer for two and half years in the Pacific aboard a rescue-and-salvage ship, the USS *Preserver.*

On October 20, 1944, the *Preserver* was headed to Leyte Gulf to support the invasion of the Philippines.

Robert F. Matthews Jr.

During General Quarters (when all sailors and

officers are at their battle stations), the ship's power went out and Bob complained to the engine room for someone to get his electric fan going again.

The reply came back, "Sir, we have an unexploded bomb in the engine room. We can either try to defuse the bomb or get your fan running again." His response was, "Carry on, men."

While at William & Mary, he romanced Betty Jean Buntin of Atlanta. They were married on March 24, 1945, in the chapel of the First Presbyterian Church in Atlanta. Nick Riner, longtime friend of his from Shelbyville, was the best man. I was an usher as a 14-year-old.

Following his discharge as a lieutenant in the spring of 1946, Bob began law school at the University of Virginia.

Following graduation in 1948, Bob and Betty returned to Shelbyville. He obtained a job as attorney with the Department of Revenue under Commissioner Clyde Reeves.

Bob and Betty and their first child, Charles Killgore Matthews, who was born on March 6, 1950, moved to Texas in June 1950 where Bob became an understudy to his "Uncle Charlie" Killgore who owned a 20,000 acre ranch. It was Bob's understanding that the ranch would someday become his because "Uncle Charlie" and his wife, Florence, had no children of their own. It was during this period that Bob and Betty became parents for a second time. A son, Alan Robert Matthews, was born on December 19, 1952.

Unfortunately, Bob became disenchanted with Texas and "Uncle Charlie," and he and the family returned to Shelbyville in 1953.

He became State Finance Commissioner in Frankfort before becoming Governor Bert Combs' chief administrative officer in 1961. It was during this period that *Courier-Journal* Frankfort Bureau Chief Kyle Vance wrote about Bob: "This Shelby Countian, who almost made a career as a Texas rancher, has a knack for organization, an ability to soothe short tempers, and shrewdness in law and politics which make him a perfect fit for the rough job of top administrative assistant to the Governor."

Bob was elected Attorney General in 1963 and sponsored legislation that strengthened the enforcement arm of the Attorney General's office.

Bob ran for the office of Lieutenant Governor in 1967 and lost by fewer than a thousand votes to Wendell Ford. Four years later he agreed, ill-advisedly, to run Bert Combs' campaign against Ford to regain the governor's chair.

Following his retirement in 1992 from a Louisville law firm where he was a senior partner, he volunteered as the Chief Administrative Hearing Officer for the City of Louisville. He also served on the Murray State University Board of Regents.

A superb tennis player, Bob retired the Byrd Cup after winning the city title three straight years. He and Shelby County High School basketball coach Bill Harrell were strong adversaries on the court and great friends off the court.

Bob's health began failing in 2008, and, after a prolonged stay at Crestview Health Care Center, he died on October 30, 2010.

Ben Gaines Matthews

Ben G. Matthews was born on October 19, 1926, at the King's Daughters Hospital and graduated from Shelbyville High School in May 1944. He won the Rotary Cup in his senior year as his class' most outstanding student. He and classmate Paul Swanson teamed to win the Kentucky High School Debate Championship in 1943, defeating Male High School in the semi-finals and Beattyville in the finals. The debate coach was longtime math teacher Sarah Lewis.

Ben originally studied at the University of Virginia where he made the Dean's List the first two semesters. He played varsity basketball at UVA, being coached by his longtime and well thought of mentor, Gus Tebell.

He joined the V-12 Program in 1945 and started his U.S. Navy career at Great Lakes Training Center. He finished his education at the University of Louisville. He had a close association with UL coaches Peck Hickman and Denny Crum.

Ben Gaines Matthews

He graduated from the University of Louisville Law School in 1949 and began the practice of law with his father the same year. He basically practiced criminal law from 1951 to 1961, when he inherited the civil practice upon his father's passing.

He served as City Judge from 1955 to 1960. His legal career had lasted 51 years when he retired in 2000. Among his partners along the way were Vic Brizendine, Gregg Neal, Judge William Stewart, and Cliff Walters.

Following the death of Lloyd Pollard in 1970, he was elected president of the Shelby County Trust & Banking Company the same year.

He retired from banking shortly after the directors voted to sell the institution to a Louisvillian, Darrel Wells, in 1980. The bank's name was later changed to Commonwealth Bank & Trust Co.

On the lighter side, in 1944 he scored what was then a school record 25 points against Bridgeport in the Shelbyville High School Gym (now Settle Gym). The record was broken several times after that and is now (and always will be) held by his nephew, Charlie Matthews, who scored 46 points at Owen County in 1968.

Ben was the second baseman on the Climax Roller Mills Team in the city softball league, which was a popular community attraction in the late 1940s-early '50s. "Chipmunk" Yount was the catcher, Johnny Kays the shortstop, Earl "Junie" Sorrells the third baseman and I was the first baseman. The Ashby twins, Bobby and Kenneth, of Bagdad, Joe Shuck, and Martin Deim comprised our outfield. Climax won the title in both 1948 and 1949. June Davis was the league commissioner.

Ben also bowled a perfect 300 game at Shelby Lanes on May 23, 1963. Also on that *Shelby Sentinel* team were W.M. (Dub) Curtis and Glenn ("Simp") Greenwell. Ben was also the Shelby County Duckpin Champion of 1950, defeating Mrs. Ruth Lipman for the title.

He is a renowned Life Master Duplicate Bridge Player, amassing well over the 300 points needed to qualify for that honor. He is the only Kentuckian to win all four events at the Lexington Sectional Bridge Tournament in May 1984.

Ben has been an enthusiastic railroad modeler for many years. One of the ultimate pleasures for all his nephews and grandchildren has been the opportunity to operate the trains in the basement of his home.

Else Vivian Jorgensen Matthews

My wife, Else, was born on September 23, 1930, in Detroit, Michigan, the daughter of Ellen and Adolph Jorgensen. Her parents had emigrated from Denmark in the 1920s. He was a mechanical engineer who retired after 36 years with General Motors. A housewife, Ellen, died in 1973, and he in 1978.

Else

Else was educated in the Detroit Public Schools. Her most famous classmate at Redford High School in Detroit was the actor and Oscar winner (for "Patton") George C. Scott. Her school annual lists no achievements or activities for Scott, saying simply that he wanted to be a "forester."

In 1952, she received her B.A. Degree in Education from the University of Michigan where we met. Instead of attending our graduation, we were married in the Martha Mary Chapel in Greenfield Village (Henry Ford Museum), Dearborn, Michigan, on Friday, June 13, 1952.

Else as the Queen of Transylvania in the Shelby County Community Theatre production of *My Fair Lady*.

After many years in this country and abroad, we moved to Shelbyville in 1962 when I bought *The Shelby Sentinel.* Moving with us were our daughter, Lisa, born in 1954, and our son, Beau, born in 1957. Ellen Baxter was born on November 29, 1962, and Bland Ballard on November 15, 1967.

Else has been a community leader from the outset of her time in Shelbyville. She was the co-founder of the Four Seasons Garden Club, which held its first meeting in our home in 1965. She is also a Master Gardener.

It was Else and Jean Logan who came up with the idea of a Fantasy Ball as the principal fund-raiser for the Shelby County Community Theatre. She was the general chairman for the theater's millennium celebration on the night of December 31, 1999-2000. More than $50,000 was raised that night to support the theatre.

She played the title role in two theatre productions, *The Matchmaker* and *Mame* and a cameo role in the production of *My Fair Lady*.

She received the Neil Hackworth Award for Volunteer Community Service in 2005.

She, along with Jane Purnell, Carolyn Walters, and Jean Matthews opened The Image Tree in 1974. She bought out her partners in 1979 and operated the business by herself until its sale in 1996.

Marriages, Grandchildren, and Great-Grandchildren

Else and I have four children: Lisa Gaines (deceased), William E. (Beau), Ellen Baxter, and Bland Ballard; six grandchildren, Dr. Laura Ellen Reynolds, Bradley William Matthews,

Philip and Henrik Oetinger, and Nolan and Ian Matthews; and three great-grandchildren: Archer, Palmer and Alice Reynolds.

Bob and Betty have two children: Charles Killgore, who is married to Melissa Moffett, and Alan Robert, married to Rosetta Catlett, and four grandchildren: Kate, Rob, Alex, and Baxter.

Ben and Jean have two children: Blair Lee, who is married to Hunter Louis, and Ben Gaines Jr., who is married to Sally Green, and two grandchildren: Sarah Blair and Ben Gaines III.

Else and I have been beautifully blessed with four great children, including, left to right, Ellen Oetinger, the late Lisa Gaines Matthews, William E. (Beau), and Bland Ballard Matthews.

Bland W. Ballard: "Indian fighter"

While this memoir is basically limited to the facts and recollections surrounding my life, it is important, I think, to mention my most illustrious ancestor, the man whose picture hangs in both The Filson Club in Louisville and the Kentucky Historical Society Museum in Frankfort. He is one of the original settlers who helped make Shelby County and Kentucky safe for future generations.

I am referring to my great-great-great-grandfather and Revolutionary War hero Bland Williams Ballard (1761-1853). When he died in 1853 he was buried close to family members on his farm near Simpsonville. A year later, in response to a resolution in the Kentucky State Legislature, his remains, along with those of his first wife Elizabeth, were re-interred in the Kentucky heroes section of the cemetery in Frankfort in a ceremony attended by many notables from around the state.

In 1842, while he was still living, Ballard County in far western Kentucky was named in his honor.

The story of Bland Williams Ballard is more than exciting. What made him such a colorful personality was his penchant for storytelling and killing Indians. No one on the frontier had his reputation for tangling with Indians. There is little doubt, according to several historians of the time, that Ballard was far more proficient in fighting Indians than either of the Boones, Simon Kenton, George Rogers Clark or some other notable frontier figures. And while today's public knows very little about him, his name and reputation were well known in his day.

Z.F. Smith's 1889 *History of Kentucky*, which devoted four pages to Ballard, identifies him as a premier soldier, scout and spy, especially in the Wabash expeditions of George Rogers Clark, Col. Charles Scott, and Gen. James Wilkinson. He also fought alongside "Mad Anthony" Wayne at the Battle of Fallen Timbers. Wilkinson described him as "a fearless, prudent, sagacious and reliable spy." He was described as six feet tall, "a strong, raw, bony man who weighed up to 200 pounds, passionate and quick."

Ballard also was at the settlers' disastrous run-in with the Indians at Long Run, and was captured at the Battle of the River Raisin during the War of 1812.

Going back to the beginning, Bland Williams Ballard was born on October 16, 1761, to Bland Ballard and a woman whose name has been lost to history. The future hero came to Kentucky in March 1779 which was about the time that Daniel Boone was first glimpsing Kentucky and future "Remember the Alamo" hero Davey Crockett was being born.

Besides his father and brother, the party also included James and Proctor Ballard whose progeny would include the numerous Ballards of Kentucky, including one-time U.S. Senator Thruston Morton.

In 1780 the two Bland Ballards, along with others of George Rogers Clark's men, built several log houses at an advanced base on the very spot where John Filson, eight years later, named Losantiville, now Cincinnati.

When not engaged in fighting Indians, Bland W. Ballard served as a hunter, scout and spy for Gen. Clark.

It was on March 31, 1788, that Bland W. Ballard was involved in the "Tick Creek Massacre" which, forever after, made him hate Indians. On this day about 15 to 20 Delaware Indians attacked the senior Ballard's cabin on Tick Creek, located about six miles east of Shelbyville.

Bland Williams Ballard was not in the cabin, but at the nearby Tyler Fort. But when he heard shouts and shots in the neighborhood of his home, he came running.

The first to die was his brother Benjamin, who was killed as he was returning to the cabin with some wood. The elder Ballard, his second wife Diane, and the children barricaded the doors and windows. But the Indians soon broke open the doors and murdered the senior Ballard and Diane, a daughter, and the daughter's half-sister, and scalped the youngest sister, Thursia, who recovered and lived to old age.

As the Indians were fleeing the scene, the younger Ballard went to work with his rifle and killed at least three of the Delawares.

In later life, Bland W. Ballard told historian Lyman C. Draper that he figured his guns and knives had extracted a toll of somewhere between "30 and 40 Indians, maybe more." Bland's recollections, as well as those who knew him, are in the Draper Manuscripts at the Wisconsin State Historical Society. He is remembered for his "fearlessness" and "daring."

Bland W. Ballad answered Kentucky Governor Isaac Shelby's call for volunteers at the outset of the War of 1812. He was badly wounded and taken prisoner at the Battle of the River Raisin. Fortunately he escaped just prior to the massacre of American prisoners at Frenchtown.

At the close of the War of 1812 he returned to Shelby County where he took up residence on the family farm. His home was a log cabin which he later weather boarded. Over his fireplace hung a buckskin string containing six or seven Indian scalps and over his front door hung his favorite gun. In the stone doorstep were carved the initials B. W. B.

Not only was he the era's leading Indian fighter, but he also served in other ways.

In 1792 he was a leading force in making the road which is now U.S. 60 the primary road from Shelbyville to the Falls of the Ohio. In 1798 he was appointed a trustee for the Shelbyville Academy. Ballard was not an educated man since there is no record of his school days, but he was remarkably persuasive as an orator and legislator. He was elected to the Kentucky State Legislature in 1800, 1803, and 1805.

Bland Williams Ballard and his first wife had seven children – James, Mary, Dorothy (Dolly), Susan, Sally, Martha, and Nancy. He had no children by either his second wife, Diane (died 1839), or third wife, Elizabeth Weaver Garrett Matthews (died 1841).

The top document on the opposite page is an original land-grant issued to Bland Williams Ballard by then Governor of Virginia and famed Revolutionary War hero Patrick Henry whose signature is very legible on the document; The bottom two original documents are muster rolls from the War of 1812 and confirm Ballard's status as a Captain in John Allen's regiment.

TO ALL TO WHOM these Presents shall come, Greeting: KNOW YE, that
Governor of the Commonwealth of VIRGINIA,
there is granted by the said Commonwealth unto Bland Williams Ballard
a certain Tract or Parcel of Land, containing
with its Appurtenances; TO HAVE AND TO HOLD the said Tract or Parcel of Land with its Appurtenances to the said
IN WITNESS whereof, the said Patrick Henry Esq. Governor of the Commonwealth of VIRGINIA, hath hereunto set his Hand and caused the lesser Seal of the said Commonwealth to be affixed at Richmond, on the Twelfth Day of July in the Year of our Lord, One Thousand Seven Hundred and Eighty-Six and of the Commonwealth the Eleventh.
P. Henry

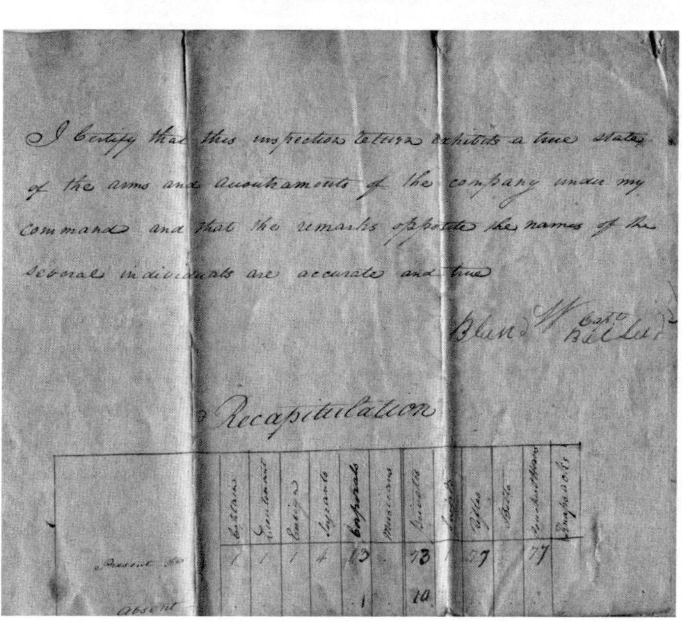
I Certify that this inspection return exhibits a true state of the arms and accoutrements of the company under my command and that the remarks opposite the names of the several individuals are accurate and true
Bland W. Ballard Captn
Recapitulation
Captains
Lieutenants
Ensigns
Sergeants
Corporals
Musicians
Privates
Rifles
Belts
Present
Absent

Inspection Return of Captain Bland W.
Colonel Commandant John Allen Regiment
pursuant to an Act of Congress passed the 10th day
Names and Rank of Officers and Men
Arms & Accoutrements
No
Remarks
Bland W. Ballard Captn
John Williamson Lieut
John W. Hall Ensign
Sergeants
Martin Jacobs
William Cooper
Corporals
Bland Ballard
Thomas Garnett
Present
Do

Murder of Gen. H.H. Denhardt

I was only seven years old when the Garr brothers, Jack and Roy, and their father, Dr. E.S. Garr, ambushed Brigadier General H.H. Denhardt at the intersection of 6th and Main Streets on September 20, 1937, and shot him to death. Of the conspirators only Roy was indicted for the murder because Jack wasn't armed, and E.S. had been committed to a sanitarium for treatment of mental illness.

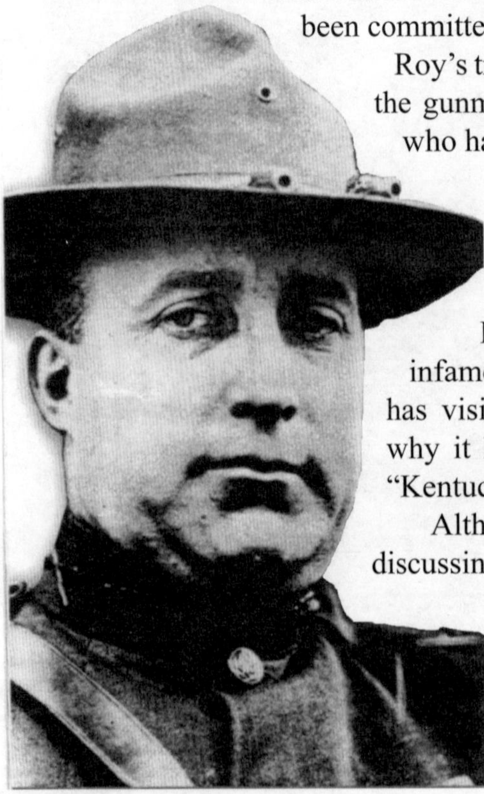

Gen. H.H. Denhardt

Roy's trial lasted a few days before the jury's vote to acquit the gunman brought forth many shouts for joy from those who had watched the proceedings.

I have included the Denhardt case in this book because its sensational nature brought news people to Shelbyville from many points in the globe, including Chicago, New York and even London, England. It is easily Shelby County's most infamous criminal case ever, and even today Shelbyville has visitors who are anxious to learn more of how and why it happened. At the time it happened, it was called "Kentucky's Crime of the Century."

Although I was only seven, I can remember Dad discussing the case with my mother because, as mayor, he was frequently asked to welcome news people as they came to town.

So let's go back to mid-November 1936 when Elizabeth Ann Barrickman of Oldham County, a 17-year-old freshman at Bowling Green Business College, took a dare and telephoned an accused murderer.

Miss Barrickman, now Ann Smiser (the widow of Jack Smiser), still remembers vividly the night when, acting on a dare from her roommates at 1328 College Street in Bowling Green, called Denhardt and asked him a simple question: "Why did you kill that beautiful woman from Oldham County?"

Elizabeth Ann Smiser

The general lived in an apartment just two blocks down the street from Elizabeth Ann's boarding house, so she was necessarily apprehensive when she asked the operator to ring him up. She remembers being actually surprised when he himself answered the phone.

"Who is this?" he demanded. Not wanting to give her name, Elizabeth asked no more questions and quickly hung up.

Now 95 years of age, Ann is the only person still living who not only remembers talking with Gen. Denhardt, but personally knew all of the principals in one of Kentucky's most celebrated criminal cases of the 20th or any other century.

Famed British novelist Agatha Christie couldn't have written a better "whodunit." The cast of characters included a 60-year-old U.S. Army officer, a one-time Warren County, Kentucky judge and former lieutenant governor of Kentucky from 1923 to 1927; a 40-year-old beautiful widow from Oldham County; well-known "loving brothers" and their mentally-challenged father; and some of the state's finest legal minds of the time, representing both the prosecution and defense.

For 12 months the case made for titillating reading in the press, worldwide. The *Chicago Daily News* and *The New York Times* dispatched reporters and photographers to cover the happenings. Even the *London Times* jumped on the case.

While the jury is still out 77 years after the saga began to unfold, on whether Gen. Denhardt did indeed murder Verna Garr Taylor on Nov. 6, 1936, there is no doubt that the Garr brothers and their father executed a murderous revenge on the General.

What became a tragedy began as a love story in the summer of 1936 when Gen. Denhardt began wooing the brunette beauty from LaGrange with all the fervor of a teenager enjoying his very first taste of true love. It wasn't long thereafter that he proposed matrimony and the beautiful widow accepted, despite the strong objections of her two daughters from a previous marriage, her two brothers, Roy and Jack, and her father, Dr. E.S. Garr.

One of the daughters, Frannie, was a friend and had gone to school with Elizabeth Ann Barrickman. Verna Taylor operated a successful laundry in LaGrange, and was a popular figure in both Oldham and Henry counties.

Denhardt, who had recently bought a farm in Oldham County, had been in the headines during much of the 1920s and even before. He had been decorated twice for bravery while serving in three wars, and had been in charge of the failed effort to save Floyd Collins from

Denhardt began running the short distance to the hotel entrance, zigzagging in an attempt to evade a hail of bullets. At least three bullets struck him, two in the back and one in the head. He died instantly. His body can be seen in the doorway.

a cave-in in 1925 that had made national and international headlines. For many years he had longed to be governor. But by 1936 his military and political careers were behind him.

November 6 started innocently enough with the couple enjoying a trip to Louisville in the General's car. They spent some time at the Pendennis Club where the social elite gathered, and had enjoyed something to eat at a restaurant in St. Matthews. Just before midnight they returned to LaGrange and continued toward New Castle on Highway 22. The temperature had dropped to freezing and there was still snow on the ground from an earlier snowfall.

Around 9 p.m., the car slowed to a halt, apparently caused by a bad battery. From then until Mrs. Taylor's body was discovered some 640 feet from the car an hour or so later, accounts vary as to who did what and in what sequence. What we do know is that a passing motorist, J.B. Hundley, stopped to render assistance and left for LaGrange to get a new battery.

Verna Garr Taylor

George Baker, near whose driveway the car had been pushed to get it out of the roadway, asked Mrs. Taylor if she would like to wait in his home with Mrs. Baker. She declined, saying that she preferred to stay with the General "who is indisposed."

Minutes later the Bakers heard a car approaching and assumed it was Mr. Hundley returning with the battery. It is not. Later it was determined that the car was that of Mr. and Mrs. Bernard Shepherd on their way to LaGrange.

The Bakers then heard at least one gunshot, possibly two, they later told investigating officers. Mr. Baker walked back toward the disabled car and found a distraught Denhardt, who said Mrs. Taylor had walked up the road "to look for a lost glove."

Denhardt suggested that he and Baker start looking for Mrs. Taylor. Baker and a neighbor, C.E. Shaver, joined them. Baker later testified that as they approached the car, Denhardt looked into the glove compartment and cried out, "My God! My revolver's gone. She must have taken it! What a pity. She was the finest lady I ever knew." The group was struck by the fact that the General was already speaking of Mrs. Taylor in the past tense.

Just as the group set out to find Mrs. Taylor, Mr. Hundley returned with the battery, and the search was momentarily halted while the battery was installed. The group found no trace of Mrs. Taylor in the immediate area, but as they expanded the search a still figure was spotted on a small hill next to the road about 640 feet from the vehicle. Mrs. Taylor was clutching a glove in her gloved left hand.

Closer inspection revealed a single bullet hole just above the left breast. Near the body lay a .45 caliber U.S. Army model 1917 pistol, which the general acknowledged was his. Soon Henry County Sheriff Evan Harrod appeared, accompanied by two deputies and coroner D.L. Ricketts. A quick examination of the revolver revealed two empty shell casings and four bullets still in the cylinder.

Denhardt and another man found the General's keys about150 feet from where Mrs. Taylor's body had been discovered. The men were struck by the General's lack of tears, or even a show of remorse for his loved one's demise. In fact, he hung back while the body was retrieved, only asking the coroner to remove Mrs. Taylor's engagement ring and put it in a safe place.

Among the unfavorable testimony directed toward Denhardt at the examining trial was that of Mrs. Baker, who quoted Denhardt as saying, even before they found Mrs. Taylor's body, that, "My, my she was the finest woman I ever saw." On the other hand, Denhardt acted like Mrs. Taylor was still alive, declaring, "I am not a killer. The engagement is still on."

Henry County Judge A.S. Morgan ordered Denhardt held to the Jan. 18 grand jury and directed that he be held in the Jefferson County jail because he feared possible violence.

Circuit Judge Clarence C. Marshall, a longtime jurist, subsequently granted bail to Denhardt and Dr. A. McCormack, who headed the Kentucky Department of Health, pledged the necessary $25,000 to get Denhardt out of jail.

While a Henry County jury on January 19, 1937, was indicting him for "willful murder," the accused was found enjoying a bottle of beer in an Eminence restaurant. He showed little, if any, alarm.

The trial began on April 20 with Commonwealth's Attorney H.B. Kinsolving Jr. of Shelbyville representing the state, aided by J. Ballard Clark, a friend of the Garrs. Denhardt was defended by Myers, John M. Berry Sr. of New Castle, and W. Clarke Otte of Louisville.

Jack Garr, left, smiled occasionally for photos with his father, Dr. E.S. Garr, center, and brother Roy Garr. The brothers were charged in the vengeance slaying of Brig. Gen. H.H. Denhardt.

The trial produced the largest number of people and the biggest traffic jams ever seen in New Castle. The one hotel in the town had long since been totally booked, and out-of-state media were accommodated in homes in Henry and Shelby Counties. Refreshments stands were set up, and all sorts of goods were peddled around the courthouse on the main street as the community enjoyed the state and national spotlight.

While Denhardt claimed he had a clear conscience and said he was sleeping well, tempers on both sides flared during the testimony, and even Judge Marshall threw a punch at a *Chicago Daily News* photographer who had bumped him. He threatened to throw the photographer in jail, but later apologized. The all-male jury (no women were even called) consisted of 11 tobacco farmers and a filling station operator. Both sides produced what they thought was compelling evidence

The defense team tried to discredit the testimony of the Bakers and Detective Messmer, and the General repeatedly told the jury during his more than three hours of testimony that "I loved her too much to hurt her." He claimed that Taylor talked of suicide several times during that fateful day, and urged the General to marry her as soon as possible. He even claimed that on one occasion she had grabbed the revolver from the glove box and seemed ready to kill herself before he wrestled the gun away from her.

The summation of both sides ran several hours. Defense counsel John M. Berry Sr. stressed the inconsistent testimony of the commonwealth's witnesses, saying that the state "invites you to come here and guess away the life, liberty and reputation of Gen. Denhardt."

Ballard Clark, summing up for the prosecution, said, "It's either murder or suicide, and we know Verna didn't kill herself ... If he killed her, then he killed her in cold blood."

Kinsolving punctuated the attack on Denhardt by declaring, "If you give him the death sentence, you won't give him any more than he deserves."

Finally, after 14 days of testimony and tension, Judge Marshall instructed the jury to find the General guilty, not guilty, or that he acted in self-defense. But after only a few hours of deliberation, the jury foreman told the judge that it was "Hopelessly deadlocked." An informal press poll after the result was announced revealed that the vote was 7-5 for acquittal.

Although Denhardt believed that there would be no second trial in the Taylor case "because I didn't do it," Commonwealth's Attorney Kinsolving had secured a docket date of September 21 for the retrial.

On the evening of September 20, Denhardt met with Attorney Myers who had rented rooms at the Armstrong Hotel at the corner of 6th and Main Streets in Shelbyville. After enjoying dinner at the hotel, they strolled along Main Street, and stopped at a restaurant where Denhardt enjoyed a bottle of beer. Upon returning to the hotel, they started across the street when Myers spotted the three Garrs situated at different points on the street. Myers cried out, "There are the Garrs!" Quickly Denhardt headed for the hotel, zig-zagging diagonally, with his attackers in hot pursuit. Bullets rang out from the guns of E.S. and Roy Garr and Denhardt collapsed on the front porch of the hotel. As the Garrs approached Myers to presumably kill him too, Myers cried out, "Don't shoot me, I'm just a lawyer." He would have been executed by E.S. Garr, but Roy intervened to save his life.

City Patrolmen Jeptha Tracy (grandfather to Mike Tracy) and Claude Hammond immediately arrested the Garrs who offered no resistance. They gave up their weapons, a .45 caliber Colt, which had been fired twice, and a.38 Smith & Wesson, which had been fired five times. Of the three bullets that ended Denhardt's life, only one was ever recovered.

The Garr brothers were treated like royalty in the Shelbyville jail. Visitors included friends and relatives who brought plenty of food and other necessities. E.S. Garr had been associated with M.A. Purdy in veterinary practice in Shelbyville many years before, and was still practicing in LaGrange. Roy was a nationally recognized dog breeder. Jack, also a dog breeder, was living in Washington, Ohio.

Denhardt received full military honors at his funeral in Bowling Green, attended by former Governors Ruby Laffoon and William J. Fields. He was not eulogized at the funeral, with Rev. Dr. George W. Cheek declaring, "We are not here to speculate as to where the soul of this man is today. That is between God and the deceased."

The tables were now turned insofar as prosecutors and defense lawyers were concerned. Ballard Clark, who had helped prosecute Denhardt on behalf of the Garrs, now became their chief defense counsel. He was joined by well-known local lawyers George L. Willis Jr. and former U.S. Congressman and County Judge Ralph Gilbert.

The slaying of Henry H. Denhardt played to an even greater national and international press than his trial for the death of Mrs. Taylor. In addition to the *New York Times, Newsweek, Life*, and even *The London Times*, played the story with much fanfare. The image they projected of the commonwealth was far from flattering. The press said quite openly that the Garrs had carried out a Kentucky-style form of vigilante justice.

Local reaction was far more restrained, with the editor of *The Shelby News* lamenting only that the shooting had brought the town some "bad publicity." Only the *Times-Journal* in Bowling Green, edited by J.G. Denhardt, the General's brother, seemed outraged by his execution.

The trial of the Garr brothers and their father began on October 1, 1937 minus E.S. Garr who had been placed in a sanitarium in Pewee Valley. He had suffered from a nervous disorder for years. He died in 1939.

On the witness stand, Roy Garr stuck with the story he had told earlier, mainly that he began firing only after he thought he saw Denhardt reach for a gun. The jury also heard numerous witnesses describe Denhardt in harsh terms, including such quotes as he was "power drunk," and "one of the most unscrupulous men I ever knew." Attorney Gilbert called Denhardt a "mad dog," and insisted that Roy had a "right to shoot a mad dog." It was as if it was Denhardt, rather than the Garrs, who was on trial.

Attorney General Hubert Meredith, prosecuting for the state, responded with the obvious: "Two men had shot down another unarmed man in cold blood."

The trial lasted just a few days, with the jury taking less than an hour to acquit Roy Garr of murder. Judge Marshall had already released Jack in response to a defense motion pointing out that Jack was unarmed. It was E.S. and Roy who had done the killing.

All of the principals in this case died many years ago, and the death of Verna Garr Taylor remains an unsolved mystery.

(Note: Sources for this story include Dr. William E. Ellis, The *Louisville Courier-Journal*, the *Shelby News*, court transcripts, *New York Times*, Mrs. Jack Smiser, and Mrs. Jean Logan. Photographs courtesy of the *Louisville Courier-Journal* and *The Shelby Sentinel*.)

Shelby County Communty Theatre

Before Christmas 2011, the Shelby County Community Theatre presented *The Homecoming*, a play based on the TV show *The Waltons*. In the cast were, front, from left: Jake Waford, Myria Grantham, Mackenzie Wise and Ryan Waford; second row: Phil Hogland, Maria Newill, Kenny Harris, Justin Moore, Erin Block, Trey Paris, Kaycie Gentry and Dr. Jack Wann (director); third row: Sue Snider, Jane Martin, Faith Hoover, Sarah Spurlak, Josh St. Esprit, Betty Zielinski, Cheryl Van Stockum, Bob Zielinski and Bill Stover; back: Lance Minnis, James Ray Morgan, Jerry Deaton, Richard Dotson III, Richard Dotson, Myra Dotson, Cook Farmer, Landen Bates and Reggie Van Stockum.

SHELBY COUNTY COMMUNITY THEATRE

(Note: Frances Smith and Bill Matthews collaborated on this article which appeared, in part, in *The New History of Shelby County, Kentucky*, 2003)

The idea of a community theater germinated in the mind and heart of Robert C. Shy who returned to Shelby County High School after serving five years as director of education and programming for Kentucky Educational Television. He brought with him the belief that

***Nunsense* in 2014**

a community theatre has the potential to bring people together from all walks of life in a way that enriched lives.

He believed that amateur musicians, actors, dancers, set designers and writers who opted for traditional careers could now express their artistic leanings, and, in so doing, create something very special for their friends and neighbors.

The creation of the Community Theatre came less than two months after the organization formally chartered on June 30, 1977. When the curtain went up for *The Music Man* on a very steamy night in August, nearly 200 volunteers had been involved in the staging of that popular musical. At the same time that the hammering and scene blocking was going on for that show, the board of directors was busy launching a membership and raising funds to support this substantial undertaking.

Then, in 1978, the production of *Reynaud the Fox* revealed the theater's potential for enticing youngsters to show their budding talents.

It was an easy decision to move the theater from its temporary status to a formal organization with new directors, each serving staggered terms. The original incorporators were William R. Hickman, president; Bruce Sweeney, Ryburn Weakley, Annabel Lewis, June G. Davis, and Carolyn Giltner.

The original board faced the risks of uncharted waters, and the ongoing board had to deal with how to keep a good thing going.

Under the leadership of Presidents June Davis, Quintin Biagi, John Sanderlin, Calvin Schmidt, Mary Helen Miller, S.K. Zimmerman, Jim Smith, Jon Jacoby, Bill Giltner, Carolyn Peterson, Gary Steinhilber, Mark Burks and Pat Wetherton, the next generation of board members proved equal to the task.

As the reality of the undertaking set in, the board was confronted with the departure of the founder of the theatre when Bob Shy moved out of the area. Then there was the need to build a solid financial foundation for the organization, and the troupe of actors bumped up against increasing logistical problems with the staging of productions in facilities where the theatre was a "guest."

Producing *Anatomy of a Murder* in the Shelby County Courthouse, *The Odd Couple*, in the Floral Hall at the Fairgrounds, and *Fiddler on the Roof* at East Middle School meant carting construction materials from place to place and tying up space that belonged to someone else for several weeks.

True to its heritage of a community effort, solutions to these problems came from many corners. The director's void was filled by several volunteers who graciously stepped forward.

Later, Zerelda Matthews expressed concerns regarding the demands on a director's time during productions, and urged the board to consider paying directors who had the training and experience in the theater.

She contended that amateur actors needed a professional director if they were to do their best.

Enter Eugene Stickler, a drama teacher and stage master with the Jefferson County Public School System. During his 19-year association with the system, he was not only a stage director, but a set designer, confidante to the board, and utilized his many skills in every way imaginable to benefit the theater.

Ongoing financial security for the theater got its first and continuing major boost from an idea advanced by Else Matthews. She believed community supporters would respond well to an annual ball and suggested that it could be held in Floral Hall at the fairgrounds.

With the help of dozens of volunteers, Floral Hall was transformed into a virtual spring flower garden and the first Fantasy Ball, named by Ann Porter, became a huge success. With many individuals and local and regional businesses donating items and services of great value, the silent and live auctions raised over $10,000 annually. Over the next 20 years it was to raise more than a quarter million dollars. Jean Logan was highly instrumental in the Fantasy Ball and of the theater itself. Else Matthews served as general chairman of the Millennium Ball which was held on the night of Dec. 31, 1999. It raised more than $50,000.

The Fantasy Ball was important in helping end the vagabond existence of the theater. But there are many other people who deserve to be mentioned in helping to put the theater on a permanent financial footing.

In the fall of 1979, June Davis, Nancy Crabtree, and Frances Smith traveled together to Morehead, Kentucky for a meeting of statewide community theater board members. On the drive back, Davis expressed his overriding thought, "If the theater is to survive, it must have its own home." Obsessed by this conviction and with the backing of highly regarded architect and board member Quintin Biagi, Davis called an emergency meeting. There was a building at the corner of 8th and Main Streets available for purchase. Acting with board approval and a line of credit from local financial institutions, the building was secured for $30,500, on October 17, 1979, as the theater's permanent home. Mrs. Helen Schmidt, widow of Paul Schmidt, contributed $30,000 toward the building's purchase.

When the lights went up for *Oklahoma* in August 1981, filled-to-capacity crowds electrified the air. After eight sold-out performances and two holdover shows, director Gene Stickler proved that, "Yes, a big musical can be successfully staged in an area smaller than an auditorium." Musical performances moved directly into the spotlight in 1982 when the artistic committee initialed the Command Performance.

Envisioned by Frances Smith and developed by producer-director pianist Betty Jean Chatham, the Command Performance showcased local vocalists and musicians whose talents had not previously been extended to countywide audiences.

Betty Jean Chatham

A major theatrical offering to the children's theater was the creation of the Pop Corn Theater. The key person in developing this newest offering by the local theater was Harolyn Sharpe, wife of Presbyterian Minister Roy Sharpe. She recognized the interest of children in acting lessons and began Saturday morning seminars followed by productions where their new found skills could be shown off.

Sharpe's other, most important contribution was moving production into state and regional contests. She directed *The Dining Room* locally, and, after a successful run, took the performers to competitions where they won the Kentucky Theater Association Award and advanced to regional competition. Later, in 1993 the production of *And the Tide Shall Cover the Earth* won awards in both state and regional competition.

In 1987 the theater was able to purchase the adjoining property on Main Street. The goal to create local opportunities for involvement in the arts was realized when the theater backed the work of local director turned playwright, Eugene Stickler who collaborated with local composer and pianist Betty Chatham to create a musical around the local historical landmark Science Hill School. Entitled *Science Hill 1919*, it got rave reviews and a waiting list for all nine performances.

In the intervening years the Shelby County Community Theatre has gained increasing prominence in the area, and the performances of most shows are sold out.

Hansel and Gretel

Significant dates in Shelby County history

There are many dates in Shelby County history that are significant, some more than others. The following represent those dates that stand out as especially meaningful and that show the remarkable progress we have made since the Tick Creek Massacre in 1788. The following represents our progress (and lack of progress) -- educationally, racially, politically and spiritually -- since those early days when Bland Williams Ballard and his brave band of settlers decided to stake their lives in what was to become Shelby County.

1788 – Tick Creek Massacre occurred about six miles east of Shelbyville. Bland Ballard, his wife and two children are killed. His son, Bland Williams Ballard, kills a number of Delaware Indians during the attack. This is the last documented Indian attack in the area known today as Shelby County.

1790 – Painted Stone settlement was established by Squire Boone (brother to Daniel Boone) and others. Fort lasts only a few years and is abandoned several years later following multiple Indian attacks.

1792 – Shelby County was formally established; Shelbyville incorporated.

1794 – First church was constituted at Brackett Owen's house in the southeast area.

1844 – President William Henry Harrison visited what is known as Stockdale, home to the home of Charles Stewart and Letitia Shelby Todd, daughter of Kentucky's First Governor Isaac Shelby … today it's the home of Sherry and Dr. Lawrence Jelsma.

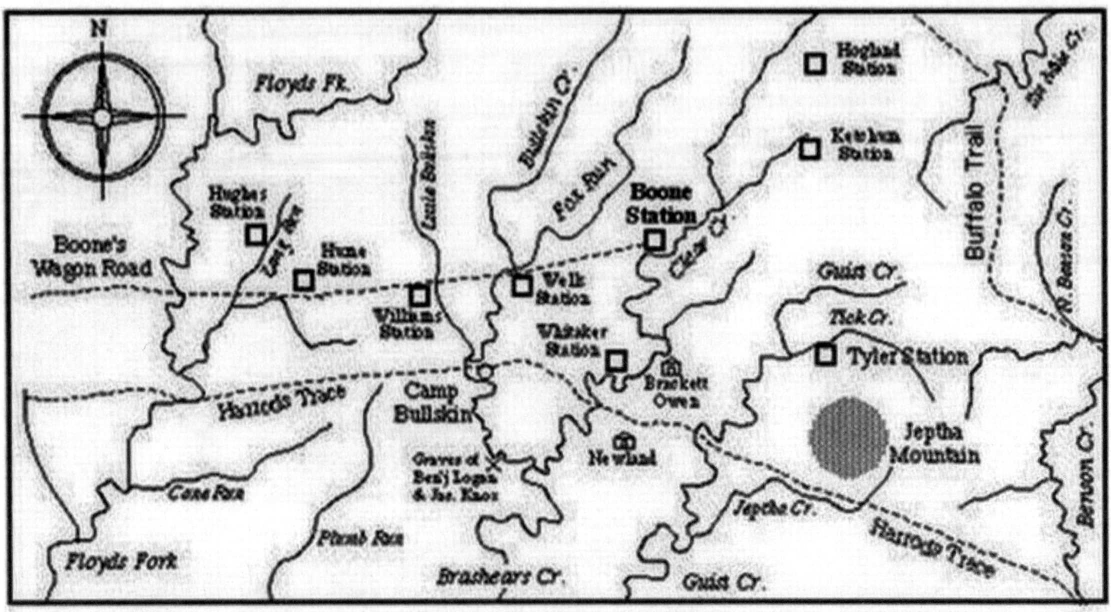

SHELBY COUNTY ~ 1785

0 10

Scale in Miles

1869 – Scholars from around the country, including professors from Harvard University, gathered at Shelby College (site of the old Northside School on College Street) to study an eclipse of the sun through a super powerful telescope.

1880 – The Louisville, Cincinnati, and Lexington Railroad Company established a line that ran from Shelbyville through Finchville to Bloomfield.

1880 – The official census for Shelby County was 16,603. (In 2014, 44,000).

1881 – John Vonderheide, a white man, was last man legally hanged (for raping a white girl). The gallows from which he was hung were erected in the middle of the street at Fifth & Main.

1899 – Fire destroyed block of downtown buildings between Fifth and Sixth streets.

1891 – The American Saddlebred Horse Association registered the first horse farm in Shelby County.

1900 – Electric lights were turned on in downtown Shelbyville; Luther Willis, mayor, ordered the lights be kept on for 24 hours. School was dismissed so youngsters could enjoy the festival atmosphere.

1903 – A Carnegie grant of $10,000 helped establish the Shelby County Public Library.

1905 – The only Shelby Countian to ever play in the World Series, Dan McGann, captained the New York Giants. He set record for stealing bases in 1904 that was not equaled until 1974 and not surpassed until 1991.

Taft

1906 – William Howard Taft campaigned here for U.S. Presidency. He was elected and eventually became chief justice of the U.S. Supreme Court.

1908 – Shelbyville City Council directed that every adult be vaccinated against smallpox. All school children were similarly vaccinated.

1910 – Famed astronomer Edwin Hubble lived with his parents during the summer on Bland Avenue in Shelbyville. A telescope named for him was placed in orbit in 1990 and continues to provide images from space.

1911 – Interurban began service between Louisville and Shelbyville. It became a major means of transportation not only for passengers but also for farmers who shipped milk and other goods to Louisville daily.

1918 – The worst blizzard in recorded county history dropped 16 inches of snow in 24 hours, with the temperature dipping to 16 below zero.

1920 – First motion "picture show" opened to sellout crowds. The "silents" were a popular draw until the first "talkies" arrived in 1928.

1927 – Leading citizen and Deposit Bank of Shelbyville cashier Otho Vardaman convicted of embezzling $61,000. The embezzlement led to the bank's closing the same day that the thefts were discovered. He was sentenced to 16 years in prison.

1934 – Interurban car 107 made its final run from Shelbyville to Louisville. The tracks remained until 1943 when they were taken up to benefit the war effort.

1937 – General H.H. Denhardt killed by the Garr brothers and their father as he tried to reach the Armstrong Hotel at Sixth & Main Streets. He was to have been tried the following day for the murder of the brothers' sister, Verna Garr Taylor. Roy and Jack Garr were acquitted of Denhardt's murder.

1946 – Margaret Truman, daughter of President Harry S. Truman, visited Shelbyville and is taken on a tour of her great-grandparents' homes (both on the Truman side) in the Christiansburg area. One of the homes is still being used as a residence.

1948 – President Truman stopped in Shelbyville during his whistlestop tour across America on behalf of his re-election bid. He won an upset victory over Republican Thomas E. Dewey in the November election.

President Truman

1948 – Shelbyville High School became the first school in the county to play in the Kentucky State High

School Basketball Tournament, at the old Armory in Louisville.

Overall, from 1948 to 1967, Coach Evan Settle had seven teams play in the event.

1951 – Main Street became one-way east, Washington Street one-way west. Legend has it that Kentucky Governor Lawrence Wetherby's vehicle was stalled in Main Street traffic on Derby Day in 1949 and was so upset that he initiated state help to finance the project.

1953 – First Ruritan Club organized at Bagdad.

1954 – Shelbyville native Willie Fleming became one of the first two blacks to graduate from the University of Louisville law school.

1957 – Charles and Helen Crabtree and their son Redd launched their Saddlebred horse stables known as Crabtree Farms near Simpsonville.

1960 – Col. Harland D. Sanders of Kentucky Fried Chicken fame became a Shelby County resident and subsequently opened a restaurant adjoining his home on U.S. 60 West. The restaurant was called "The Colonel's Lady," later changed to Claudia Sanders Dinner House.

Col. Sanders

1963 – The Shelbyville city swimming pool was integrated without incident. The previous year, whites swam on certain days of the week and blacks on the others.

1964 – I-64 opened to traffic between Shelbyville and Louisville.

1966 – The Shelby County Rockets, behind All-Stater Mike Casey (named "Mr. Basketball"), won the Kentucky state basketball title. The Rockets win their second title in 1978, led by Charles Hurt and Norris Beckley.

1972 – *The Shelby Sentinel* and *The Shelby News* merged to form *The Sentinel-News.*

1975 – Consolidation of the city and county school systems was finalized.

1977 – The Shelby County Community Theatre gave its first performance, with Bob Shy directing more than 100 locals in *The Music Man.*

1979 – Shelby County Rockets won the Kentucky High School Baseball Championship with Tracy Driver winning the tournament's Most Valuable Player title.

1981 – Jack Green passed away, one of 10 children born to D.L. and May Green. He captained Army's undefeated national championship football teams in 1944 and 1945 and is in National College Football Hall of Fame.

Gov. Collins

1983 – Bagdad native Martha Layne Hall Collins became the first and only woman governor of Kentucky. A second county high school built in 2010 was named in her honor.

1987 – Reggie Hicks led the Shelby County Rockets to the State High School 4A football title, scoring the winning touchdown to upset the heavily favored and unbeaten Boone County.

1998 – The chapel at Grove Hill Cemetery was refurbished and rededicated after being closed for almost 35 years. The renovation costs were 10 times the original and were raised by Betty Matthews, who was later named Shelbyville Citizen of the Year.

2000 – A new West Middle School opened off KY 53 South, vacating the building it used since 1975 following consolidation – ending a tradition of 1155 Main Street serving as a school for students since 1918.

2004 – Elaine Farris of Clark County became Kentucky's first black school superintendent, taking over the leadership of the Shelby County Public Schools.

2010 – A 4.5-mile stretch of roadway officially opened as a bypass project from east to west that had first been discussed about 15 years prior.

2011 – Ann-Blair Thornton, granddaughter of Bill and Ann Borders of Shelbyville, became the first with Shelby County ties to be named "Miss Kentucky." She lives in Bowling Green.

2013 – Fire destroyed and/or damaged five buildings in the 600 block of Main Street. The Collins High School Titans defeated Highlands High School to win Kentucky's 4-A state football title.

Several downtown buildings were consumed by flames on a March morning in 2013.

Events in my lifetime

It is unlikely that there has ever been another era in world history in which so much has happened since I was born in 1930. Wars have killed more people than ever before. Medical advances have made living healthier and longer a reality… for most. The development of atomic energy has been both blessing and curse (see Hiroshima and Nagasaki). The Oklahoma City bombing and the 9/11 destruction of the Twin Towers in New York and the other plane attacks elsewhere have given the word "terrorism" a more menacing meaning. The computer age has changed the dynamics of communicating and problem-solving.

And, most regrettably, two separate studies – one at the University of the Netherlands and the other at Stanford University – indicate that the Intelligence Quotient (IQ) of the Western World has declined 11 to 14 percent in the last 50 years. So, it does not appear that we have grown smarter over the past 85 years in spite of all the technological and medical advances that have been made. Technology, in fact, may have caused a "dumbing down" of our society.

So, look back and marvel at what we have done to and for each other. Have we progressed or regressed?

1930 – The planet Pluto was discovered; The U.S. population reached 122 million (it is over 400 million in 2014).

1931 – Al Capone was jailed for income tax evasion; Oswald Mosely organized the Fascist Party in Great Britain.

1932 – The radio played "Brother, can you spare a dime?" as the Great Depression worsened; Mahatma Gandhi was arrested in India.

1933 – Newly-elected President Franklin Delano Roosevelt declared, "The only thing we have to fear is fear itself;" The first baseball All-Star Game was held.

1934 – In Canada, a farm wife gave birth to the Dionne quintuplets; Driving tests were introduced in Britain.

1935 – Alcoholics Anonymous was founded in New York City; In Baton Rouge, La., "Dictator" Huey Long was assassinated.

1936 – Adolf Hitler got "99 percent" of the German vote, as the Nazis gained control; Margaret Mitchell won the Pulitzer Prize for *Gone with the Wind.*

1937 – The Hindenburg dirigible exploded while landing at Lakehurst, New Jersey; DuPont introduced a new fabric called nylon.

1938 – A 40-hour work week was established; Howard Hughes flew around the world in 3 days and 19 hours;

1939 – Judy Garland starred in *The Wizard of Oz*; Hitler's German troops attacked Poland.

1940 – FDR re-elected for an unprecedented third term; 7-time World Heavyweight Champion Boxer Jack Dempsey retired from the ring;

1941 – Japanese bombers caused thousands of casualties in a surprise attack on Pearl Harbor; Greta Garbo made her last movie.

1942 – Major General Doolittle's Raiders bombed Tokyo; Enrico Fermi succeeded in splitting the atom.

1943 – "Hepcats" wore zoot suits and danced the Jitterbug; Food rationing was started in the U.S.

1944 – The Germans launched their final offensive called "The Battle of the Bulge;" The development of penicillin promised a medical revolution.

1945 – War in Europe officially ended May 9; FDR died and was succeeded by Harry S. Truman.

1946 – The U.N. General Assembly held its first meeting; President Truman created the Atomic Energy Commission.

1947 – The Dead Sea Scrolls were discovered; *The Diary of Anne Frank* was published.

In December of 1941, the Japanese launched a surprise attack on Pearl Harbor.

1948 – The Kinsey Report on Sexual Behavior was published; The World Council of Churches was founded in Amsterdam.

1949 – Ireland was proclaimed a Republic; Ballroom dancers discovered the Samba.

1950 – North Korea invaded South Korea; Alger Hiss was sentenced for perjury;

1951 – Truman relieved General Douglas MacArthur of his Far East Command; Nuclear-generated power lit up Arco, Idaho.

1952 – George VI died in England and was succeeded by Queen Elizabeth II; Richard Nixon spoke to the nation about his cocker spaniel named "Checkers."

1953 – Josef Stalin died in Russia; Julius and Ethel Rosenberg were executed as Soviet spies.

1954 – The McCarthy hearings led to the censure of the Wisconsin senator; Film fans enjoyed Alfred Hitchcock's *Rear Window*.

1955 – Blacks in Montgomery, Alabama staged a successful bus boycott; The Salk Vaccine offered hope for the end of polio;

1956 – Eisenhower re-elected president over Democrat Adlai Stevenson; Hungarian "Freedom Fighters" rebelled against their Soviet oppressors.

1957 – The National Guard marched into Little Rock, Arkansas to enforce school desegregation; The Suez Canal reopened after Egypt's Nasser seized it.

1958 – Alaska added a 49th star to the U.S. flag; Cardinal Roncalli was elected Pope John XXIII.

1959 – Hawaii was admitted to the Union as our 50th state; Anne Bancroft was the star in *Miracle Worker* (the story of Helen Keller).

1960 – The word "laser" entered our vocabulary; America pilot Gary Powers was tried in the USSR for espionage.

1961 – Alan Shepard became the first American in space; Bobby Fischer, 17, won the U.S. chess championship for the fourth time; The Bay of Pigs was a CIA-directed disaster.

1962 – President John F. Kennedy stood up to the Russians in Cuba; Widespread birth defects in Europe were blamed on the drug thalidomide; astronaut John Glenn became the first American to orbit the earth.

1963 – Dr. Martin Luther King Jr. declared: "I have a dream;" Winston Churchill was granted honorary U.S. citizenship; President Kennedy was assassinated.

President and Mrs. John F. Kennedy in Dallas

1964 – The Warren Commission returned its findings on the Kennedy assassination; An earthquake left 114 dead in Alaska.

1965 – Malcolm X was assassinated in New York; A Soviet cosmonaut floated in space for 10 minutes; Ralph Nader published *Unsafe at Any Speed*.

1966 – Charles de Gaulle requested the removal of NATO troops from France.

1967 – Dr. Christian Barnard performed the first heart transplant; New York Yankees' Mickey Mantle hit his 500th home run.

Dr. Martin Luther King Jr.

1968 – Three astronauts orbited the moon in Apollo 8; Dr. Martin Luther King Jr. was assassinated in Memphis.

1969 – Sirhan Sirhan was convicted of murdering Robert Kennedy; From the moon came the immortal words, "The Eagle has Landed" on July 20.

1970 – Pope Paul VI reaffirmed "Priestly Celibacy;" Khrushchev's memoirs were published in the West.

1971 – Cigarette commercials were banned from U.S. television; Amtrak began passenger rail traffic; A five-day uprising at Attica Prison in New York left 42 dead.

1972 – Gov. George Wallace, a candidate for U.S. President, was shot and partially paralyzed; Mark Spitz won eight medals for swimming at the Olympics.

1973 – Vice-President Spiro Agnew resigned; Americans faced gas shortages as the "Oil Crisis" began.

1974 – India exploded a nuclear device; The Watergate investigation came to a close with President Richard Nixon's resignation.

1975 – Margaret Thatcher became the leader of Britain's Conservative Party; Heiress Patty Hearst became a fugitive from justice.

1976 – The Concorde began supersonic air service between Europe and the U.S.; Saigon in Vietnam was renamed Ho Chi Minh city.

1977 – Alex Haley's *Roots* was a television sensation; President Jimmy Carter pardoned nearly all draft evaders; The disco craze hit, with millions caught up in *Saturday Night Fever*; "Seattle Slew" won racing's Triple Crown.

1978 – The first non-Italian in five centuries was elected Pope; "Proposition 13" led to an unprecedented "tax revolt."

1979 – Soviet troops invaded Afghanistan; Margaret Thatcher became the first woman to lead the British government.

The Iranian hostage crisis

1980 – One of the Beatles, John Lennon, was killed on a New York street corner; Television audiences wondered "Who Killed J.R.?" in the show *Dallas*.

1981 – The Iranian hostage crisis ended with the inauguration of President Ronald Reagan; The space shuttle Columbia made its first flight; Prince Charles and Lady Diana Spencer were married.

1982 – The personal computer revolution was in full swing; Great Britain and Argentina went to war over the Falkland Islands; Millions of moviegoers befriended *E.T.*

1983 – 212 U.S. Marines died during a suicide attack on our barracks in Beirut; Sally Ride became the first American woman to travel in space; Video and Rock joined forces on MTV.

1984 – Democrats nominated Geraldine Ferraro for the vice-presidency, representing the first woman named to a spot on a national ticket; Los Angeles hosted the Olympic Games, boycotted by the Soviet Union.

1985 – A killer earthquake reduced much of Mexico City to rubble; President Reagan and Soviet Premier Gorbachev met face-to-face for the first time.

1986 – Americans were shocked and saddened as they witnessed on television the explosion of the space shuttle Challenger, which carried the first teacher to space; The Chernobyl meltdown gave the world its worst nuclear disaster.

1987 – Gary Hart gave up his presidential bid when his extramarital episode hit the headlines; American televangelism was exposed.

1988 – Vice President George H. W. Bush swept to presidential victory over Massachusetts Governor Michael Dukakis; Soviet troops abandoned Afghanistan; Broadway was under the spell of *The Phantom of the Opera.*

1989 – U.S. troops invaded Panama; The Berlin Wall came tumbling down.

1990 – East and West Germany were reunited; Nelson Mandela was released from a South African prison after 27 years; The "Greed Decade" was officially over.

1991 – Yellow Ribbons appeared everywhere in support of the Desert Storm troops; *Silence of the Lambs* won four major Oscars at the Academy Awards.

1992 – Bill Clinton won the presidential race over incumbent George Bush; Hotel Queen Leona Helmsley started serving time in prison for income tax evasion.

1993 – U.S. and allies launched bombing raids on Iraq; Japan's once thriving auto industry suffered sagging sales and stagnant markets.

1994 – Former professional football player O.J. Simpson was charged with murdering his wife and friend; A major earthquake rocked Los Angeles; Former President Nixon died at 81.

1995 – Brash New House Speaker Newt Gingrich was TIME's Man of the Year; O.J. Simpson was found Not Guilty of murder; Rose Kennedy, matriarch of the famous clan, died at 104.

1996 – Clinton defeated Bob Dole handily to win a second term; TWA flight 800 exploded over the Atlantic, killing 230; The FBI caught a man called the "Unabomber."

1997 – Scientists in Scotland successfully cloned a sheep; India and the world mourned the passing of Mother Theresa; Princess Diana was laid to rest following a tragic car wreck.

1998 – George W. Bush, son of former president, becomes the 43rd president; Terrorists bombed two U.S. embassies in Africa; John Glenn returned to space, three decades after his historic first orbital flight.

1999 – Two teenagers opened fire at Columbine High School in Colorado, killing 12 of their classmates and a teacher, and injuring 21 more, before turning their firearms on themselves; Euro currency is launched in Western Europe; President Clinton is not impeached following U.S. Senate trial; Stock market reaches 10,000 for the first time.

2000 – Last "Peanuts" comic strip is published; Vermont becomes first state to allow civil unions; Confederate submarine Hunley raised after 136 years on the ocean bottom.

2001 – Apple announces iTunes device at Macword Expo; Same sex marriage ruled legal in Netherlands, first country to allow it; Timothy McVeigh executed for his role in Oklahoma City bombing; Terrorist-operated planes destroy New York's Twin Towers.

2002 – President Bush signs "No Child Left Behind" law; U.S. invades Afghanistan; Netherlands legalizes euthanasia.

2003 – Space shuttle Columbia disintegrates upon re-entry after 16 days, all astronauts killed; Department of Homeland Security begins operations; British and U.S. troops invade Iraq.

2004 – City of San Francisco issues marriage licenses to couples of the same sex; Ireland becomes first country to ban smoking in all public places; Oldsmobile quits building cars after 107 years.

2005 – Cardinal Ratzinger elected Pope Benedict XVI; New Zealand's first civil union takes place; U.S. bans medical marijuana.

2006 – Western Union discontinues its historical telegram service; Comair Flight 5191 crashed at Bluegrass Field in Lexington, Kentucky, killing 49 of 50 on board.

2007 – Apple announces new iPhone; Nancy Pelosi becomes first woman speaker in the U.S. House of Representatives; Gunman kills 32 people, wounds 23 at Virginia Tech University; Former Soviet Premier Boris Yeltsin dies.

2008 – New Hampshire legalizes civil unions; "Black Monday" for U.S. stock market; Tornadoes leave 58 dead, many injured in several southern states.

2009 – U.S. Airways Flight 1549 makes a "miraculous" landing on the Hudson River with everyone on board saved; Barack Obama is sworn in as nation's first African-American president; Chrysler files for bankruptcy.

2010 – 54-year-old soap opera *As the World Turns* makes its final telecast; Obama signs law banning "Don't Ask, Don't Tell" practice in the U.S. military; Horizon drilling oil rig explodes, killing 11 and causing environmental disaster.

2011 – Gunman kills six, wounds U.S. Congresswoman Gabrielle Giffords; Thousands revolt against Egyptian strongman Mubarak; Protests begin against Libyan strongman al-Gaddafi; Final launch of space shuttle Discovery.

2012 – Queen Elizabeth marks her 60th anniversary as British Monarch; U.S. soldier kills 16 civilians in Afghanistan; 11 Secret Service individuals are involved in South American scandal.

2013 – John Kerry succeeds Hillary Clinton as Secretary of State; Massive blizzard kills 15, causes millions of dollars of damage in the northeast; Pope Benedict XVI "retires" and is succeeded by Argentinian Pope Francis I.

Reflections

As I look back over 84 years of living, it's difficult to comprehend how life has changed so dramatically for everyone … except, perhaps, for a few tribes in the Amazon Rain Forest or some Aborigines in Australia. For the rest of us, upwards of 99.9 percent, the changes have been far too many to recite or remember, but I'm still going to list what I consider my Top 15. Readers may agree or disagree or, more importantly, you may be challenged to make your own list.

Globally

1. The advance in all forms of science, with particular reference to space exploration and technology;
2. The advances in medical discoveries, surgical methods and techniques, and prescription drugs;
3. The development of nuclear power for both the benefit and destruction of mankind;
4. The scary phenomenon known as "global terrorism" that has put 9/11 on a par with 12/25 in our memory banks;
5. The first moon landing (1969);
6. The United States election of its first African-American president (2008);
7. The Great Depression that started in 1929 and lasted until World War II;
8. The decline of marriage in the Western World;
9. The United States' trend toward secularism and away from a religious-based culture;
10. The increased disparity between the "haves" and the "have-nots;"
11. The decline of the English language, both written and spoken, as our ability to communicate with each other becomes increasingly difficult without the aid of technology;
12. The relaxation, if not outright trashing, of what were once known as "standards of conduct," "standards of dress," "standards of speech;"
13. The Supreme Court decision approving abortion and, to counter that decision, the accompanying rise of the right-to-life movement;
14. The sharp increase in racial diversity and the widespread acceptance of inter-racial marriage; and
15. The Supreme Court decision striking the ban on gay marriage.

Shelby County

Locally, here are my selections for the 15 most important changes:

1. The consolidation of the city and county school systems, finalized in 1975;
2. The building of I-64 through Shelby County in the late 1950s;
3. The virtual collapse of the retail business sector, as family-owned stores … such as Lawson's, Smith-McKenney, Van's, Brazin's, Wadlington's, Rothchild's (later Briggs-Hower), Maidie's, The Prescription Shop, Hall & Davis, and Western Auto … gave way to "Big Box" stores such as Walmart, CVS, Lowe's, Tractor Supply and Rural King;
4. The staggering increase in the use of illicit drugs in 2014 from virtually zero in the 1930s;

No. 11: The decline of tobacco as Shelby County's No. 1 cash crop.

5. The creation in 1977 and continuing importance of the Shelby County Community Theatre for the young and old;
6. The establishment of Wakefield-Scearce Galleries in 1947 as a local, state, and national attraction;
7. The creation of Guist Creek Lake (formerly Chandler Lake) in 1956;
8. The locating of more than 85 saddlebred horse farms, making Shelby County the Saddlebred Capital of the World;
9. The creation in 1974 of one of the finest park and recreation systems in Kentucky, if not the United States;
10. The election in 1983 of Shelby County native Martha Layne Collins, Kentucky's first and only female governor;
11. The decline of tobacco as Shelby County's No. 1 cash crop, the reduction of pork producers and the virtual elimination of dairy farms;
12. The sharp increase in field crops and cattle farms following tobacco's demise, as well as the influx of a strong industrial/manufacturing segment;
13. The sharp increase in felony crimes, from under 100 in 1930 to an average of 558 annually from 2008 to 2012;
14. The prospective opening in 2014 of the first outlet center, called "Outlet Shoppes of the Bluegrass;"
15. Shelby County's change from a strongly Democratic- to Republican-leaning county — especially in national elections.

Big City Life

Having lived in some major cities in my life, it is fairly easy to compare big city and small-town living. Big cities have one big advantage, their accessibility to big-time sports, the theatre, museums, fine and fancy restaurants, and what I call anonymity of lifestyle. Living anonymously means not knowing your neighbors and what they're doing. In return, they don't know what you're up to. In short, there's little to gossip about because one's circle of friends is small.

We left Washington, D.C., for Shelbyville in 1962, but both Blacks and Whites were beginning to feel "edgy" about living or shopping in the District. Riots came later in the same decade, and now, almost 50 years later, the District offers all the signs of an "armed camp." There are armed guards about every 50 yards on the Washington Mall.

This 2011 photo captured one of the coffee groups that gathers at McDonalds almost daily. From left to right are John Byrd, Al Brown, Duvall Burk, Ken Graham, Bill Wilder, Jerry Nichols, Dr. Edward Hayes and Dru Terhune.

Small Town Life

In most small towns, one certainly knows his or her neighbors, good or bad.

There are several downsides to small-town life and I can think of two in particular.

The first revolves around the expression "We've never done it that way." My late daughter, Lisa, used to get very frustrated when she would suggest a new approach to an old problem and the answer would come back invariably, "We've never done it that way."

The second involves the expression, "Go along to get along." Years ago I was concerned about the nepotism attached to the possible appointment of a quasi-public official. Even as I was being assured that the appointment would never be made, I had that sinking feeling that indeed it would be. The normal procedure would have been to "post" the job in appropriate offices around the state. When it did come to pass and I mentioned it to the official, he remarked, "Bill, you must remember that in small towns, 'You have to go along to get along'." So much for getting the best person for the job!

For many years Shelbyville has had a number of coffee clubs, where men (and occasionally a female) gather to talk about basketball (generally the University of Kentucky Wildcats) discuss their health, and, also, to just plain gossip.

When I first came back to Shelbyville from my time in the nation's capital, former extension agent Maurice Cole came to the *Sentinel* office one day and asked me to join his group at the old Jennings Restaurant on Main Street. When I explained that I had my own coffee pot, and really didn't have time to "drink and chat," he responded, "If you would sit down with us just one day a week, we wouldn't have to talk about you, what you're doing and where you're going all the time." I think Maurice's observation sums up what "coffee cups" are all about.

However, there is a wonderful sense of comradeship and a "do unto others as you would have others do unto you" philosophy in a small town.

I can think of any number of instances in which our neighbors were helpful or interested in our welfare. Way back in the 1930s, Mr. and Mrs. John Davis lived next door on Main Street in the home now occupied by Shannon Funeral Service. I remember vividly how she let me run her vacuum cleaner as a 6-year-old.

Unlike today, personal safety was never an issue as friends and neighbors looked after us as we grew up and played various games on Magnolia, Brown, and Plainview. Later, living on Main Street in the '60s, our kids rode their bikes and skated all over town without drawing any concern on our part.

The same has been true after moving in to a home on Sequoyah Drive. Neighbors consistently have been helpful and/or generous. Whether it is a sharing of tomatoes, looking after the other person's house while he or she is gone, picking up the mail, calling for Dan the locksmith to help open a car, or contacting AAA for automobile help, there are many other ways that we are and can be neighborly.

Late in 2013, through poor driving on my part, I put the left rear wheel of my car in a six-foot ravine at the convergence of the Old Zaring Mill Road and Kentucky Street. I was giving grandson Henrik an abbreviated driving tour of the county. During the time that it took AAA to get a wrecker to the scene, no less than eight different people stopped to volunteer their services. One man even went home, got chains, and returned. Henrik was amazed, remarking, "No one would have stopped where I live" (outside of Philadelphia).

Made a difference

Sam Chandler

Mark Scearce

Deborah Magan

Kerry Magan

Wm. Shannon

Jim Cleveland

Betty Matthews

Don Baker

Each year, beginning in 1983, the Shelbyville City Council has selected a **Citizen of the Year**. The award, initiated by former Mayor Neil Hackworth soon after his election in 1982, recognizes city residents for their distinguished contributions to the community. Those who have been recognized include ministers, volunteers, teachers, business people, coaches, physicians, journalists, and farm leaders. They include:

1983 – Charles Hurt
1984 – Sam Chandler
1985 – Jane Bailey
1986 – Mark J. Scearce
1987 – Briggs Lawson
1988 – William Lee Shannon
1989 – Emma Ellis
1990 – Bennett Roach
1991 – Deborah F. Magan
1992 – Randy Brown
1993 – Sam Beckley
1994 – Jean Logan
1995 – Marnell Moorman
1996 – Marvin Byrdwell
1997 – Dr. Donald Chatham
1998 – Mary Helen Miller
1999 – Betty B. Matthews
2000 – Hubert Pollett
2001 – Joan Goodwin
2002 – Mary Simmons
2003 – Marshall Long
2004 – Pat Roberts
2005 – Gary Walls
2006 – Bobby Hudson
2007 – Charles and Lucy Long
2008 – Don T. Baker
2009 – Jim Cleveland
2010 – Christy Meredith
2011 – Donald Cubert Sr.
2012 – Torrey Smith
2013 – Kerry Magan

The Neil Hackworth Volunteer of the Year Award is determined by a committee of the board of directors of the Shelby Development Corporation, and is based on the contributions which the recipient has made to the downtown area. Recipients include:

1994 – Bill Matz
1995 – Bill Bryant and Neil Hackworth
1996 – Rita Hall
1997 – Charles T. Long
1998 – Billie Wade
1999 – Mary Mayrose
2000 – Belinda Nichols
2001 – Charles T. Long
2002 – Else J. Matthews
2003 – Hubert Pollett
2004 – Walt Reichert
2005 – Sherry Jelsma
2006 – Wanda Hawkins
2007 – Sharon Nichols
2008 – Linda Casey
2009 – K.C. Crahan
2010 – Linda Allewalt
2011 – S.K. Zimmerman
2012 – Leslie McCarthy
2013 – Elizabeth Pulliam

Neil Hackworth

Elizabeth Pulliam

Sherry Jelsma

Epilogue

To paraphrase Charles Dickens: The time period, through which I have lived, represents "the best of times, and the worst of times."

The "worst" has had to do with the number of wars and the millions of dead and wounded, the increased worldwide poverty, the diminished amount of goodwill among men, the rise of the "me too" generation, and the general decline in peoples' conduct, dress, and speech.

As for the "best," we must give thanks for the medical advances that have saved millions of lives and extended the lives of more millions. We must be thankful for the development of a multi-faceted technology that apparently knows no bounds and has led to the development of new products and services that have made our lives easier and simpler. The new social media has given the ordinary citizen a "voice" in government, business, and everyday affairs. Ground-breaking agricultural practices have enabled us to not only feed Americans more fully and nutritionally, but also to save millions of others in Africa and Asia from starving to death.

To quote someone more recent and positive, a TV broadcaster named Tom Brokaw, I am privileged to be a part of what he labeled "The Greatest Generation." He said that those who grew up during the Depression and went on to fight and win World War II and do their part on the Home Front represented "the greatest generation any society has ever produced." This generation did not fight for "fame and recognition," but because "it was the right thing to do."

More than anything else, I am fortunate to be born an American in a democratic country committed to doing "what's right" at home and abroad. We have fared poorly when it comes to exporting democracy. In fact, why we keep trying is a mystery to some and annoying to others. However, still, we try.

Most importantly, I was born to loving parents and caring brothers, married a wonderful girl, and was given the educational opportunities that permitted me to earn a living, enjoy the companionship of friends and relatives, and give thanks to God for life itself.

Special Thanks for Photos

Historic Kentucky is indebted to the following individuals for providing many of the photographs used in this book: Greg Biagi, Katherine and the late Henry Cleveland, Jim Cleveland, James Mulcahy, Cheryl Van Stockum, Kevin Swank, Linda Mahone, and Jerlene Rose.

Special Thanks for Wikipedia

Many of the dates, casualty figures and other historical facts about the Hungarian Revolution, Bay of Pigs, and the Cuban Missile Crisis were taken from the special sections on those events provided by Wikipedia, the free Encyclopedia. We are greatly appreciative of those individuals who provide the research and contribute their expertise on people, places, and world events from which we and millions of others benefit daily.

Index